**Institute for
Research on
Public Policy**

**Institut de
recherche
en politiques
publiques**

F ounded in 1972, the Institute for Research on
Public Policy is an independent, national,
nonprofit organization.

IRPP seeks to improve public policy in Canada
by generating research, providing insight and sparking
debate that will contribute to the public policy
decision-making process and strengthen the quality of
the public policy decisions made by Canadian
governments, citizens, institutions and organizations.

IRPP's independence is assured by an endowment
fund, to which federal and provincial governments and
the private sector have contributed.

F ondé en 1972, l'Institut de recherche en politiques publiques (IRPP) est un organisme canadien, indépendant et sans but lucratif.

L'IRPP cherche à améliorer les politiques publiques canadiennes en encourageant la recherche, en mettant de l'avant de nouvelles perspectives et en suscitant des débats qui contribueront au processus décisionnel en matière de politiques publiques et qui rehausseront la qualité des décisions que prennent les gouvernements, les citoyens, les institutions et les organismes canadiens.

L'indépendance de l'IRPP est assurée par un fonds de dotation, auquel ont souscrit le gouvernement fédéral, les gouvernements provinciaux et le secteur privé.

Institute for Research on Public Policy

Institut de recherche en politiques publiques

Forging the Canadian Social Union: SUFA and Beyond

edited by

Sarah Fortin,

Alain Noël and

France St-Hilaire

b 2485 1279

Printed in Canada
Dépôt légal 2003

National Library of Canada
Bibliothèque nationale du Québec

CATALOGUING IN PUBLICATION

Forging the Canadian social union: SUFA and beyond /
Sarah Fortin, Alain Noël, France St-Hilaire, editors.

Includes bibliographical references.
ISBN 0-88645-194-9

1. Framework Agreement on Canada's Social Union.
2. Federal-provincial relations—Canada. 3. Canada—
Social policy. I. Noël, Alain II. St-Hilaire, France
III. Fortin, Sarah, 1966- IV. Institute for Research on
Public Policy.

JL27.F67 2003   320.471   C2003-905443-8

Suzanne Ostiguy McIntyre
VICE-PRESIDENT, OPERATIONS

Sarah Fortin
PROJECT DIRECTOR

TRANSLATION
Magee & Nguyen Associées

COPY EDITING AND PROOFREADING
Jane Broderick

COVER DESIGN
Schumacher Design

COVER ILLUSTRATION
Marie Lafrance

INTERIOR BOOK DESIGN
Schumacher Design

PRODUCTION
Chantal Létourneau

PUBLISHED BY
Institute for Research on Public Policy (IRPP)
Institut de recherche en politiques publiques
1470 Peel Street, Suite 200
Montreal, Quebec H3A 1T1

I N THE SPRING OF 2000, THE INSTITUTE FOR RESEARCH ON PUBLIC POLICY (IRPP) launched a research initiative to provide an independent evaluation of the Social Union Framework Agreement (SUFA), which all Canadian governments, except Quebec, had signed in February 1999.

The project rested on the conviction that SUFA represented a significant development in the evolution of the Canadian social union, as the first nonconstitutional but formal agreement framing the respective social policy roles of the two orders of government. This appreciation of the importance of the negotiations and resulting agreement/disagreement on the social union had been present at the IRPP early on in the process. In November 1998, concerned by the lack of public debate about and awareness of the negotiation process on the social union, IRPP held a policy conference in Ottawa and published a special issue of *Policy Options*. These two initiatives provided an opportunity for major stakeholders to present their positions to the public and to benefit from the expertise of well-known scholars, who produced background analysis on some of the key issues.

A little over a year later, in February 2000, the IRPP joined the Saskatchewan Institute for Public Policy (SIPP) in hosting a conference to assess the state of SUFA's implementation on its first anniversary. As these early discussions revealed, SUFA was not very satisfactory at the outset. At the time, however, observers could only speculate on how it would unfold as it was implemented. This was precisely the focus of the present project — to examine the implementation of SUFA and its impact on intergovernmental relations and social policy in order to determine whether and under what terms it should be renewed.

In the fall of 2000, the IRPP commissioned seven leading scholars with recognized expertise in social policy and intergovernmental relations to examine various dimensions of the agreement. Their research papers were first presented at a workshop of experts and practitioners organized by the Institute in March 2001 in Montreal. Over the following months, all but one of the papers were published as *Policy Matters* or *Enjeux Publics*.

We are now very pleased to bring the English versions of all these papers together into this edited volume, which provides thoughtful analysis on the challenges that lie ahead as the process of forging the Canadian social union continues. The studies tell us a great deal about SUFA and its implementation, but in so doing they also address the larger issues underlying the social union in Canada — managing intergovernmental relations, resolving democratic shortcomings and improving social policy. In that sense, even though the essays were written in a specific context and time frame — to coincide with the review process of the agreement — they remain very relevant in light of current political events.

The introductory chapter provides an update on recent developments in the intergovernmental arena and an original analysis of the prospects with respect to intergovernmental relations and the social union beyond SUFA. As elaborated on in this chapter, readers will find in this volume important insights and arguments that are instructive in the context of current negotiations on the proposed health council and the upcoming provincial and territorial leaders' discussions about the new Council of the Federation. Except for Yves Vaillancourt and Bruno Théret's chapters, which were initially published in French, all the chapters are reproduced here as written at the time when they first appeared.

Even though SUFA has not left a strong, lasting heritage, the issues and challenges associated with the Canadian social union will continue to dominate the policy agenda in the foreseeable future. For this reason, this volume can be read as a guide to issues that will be central to Canadian political life and of interest to policy makers and to students of Canadian federalism and social policy for some time to come.

This book would not have been possible without the collaboration, participation and support of many people. First and foremost, we thank all of our contributors, who agreed to share their knowledge, expertise and insights with us. We also want to thank the commentators on the first drafts for their useful and constructive comments: David R. Cameron, Harvey Lazar, Tom McIntosh, Matthew

Mendelsohn, Michael Mendelson, Pierre Paquette, Johanne Poirier, John Richards, François Rocher, Claude Ryan, Richard Simeon, Norman Spector, Denis Saint-Martin, F. Leslie Seidle and Carol S. Weissert. All the participants in the March 2001workshop helped us gain a better grasp of the issues; in particular, we are grateful to Daniel Béland, Andéas Brandl, Clément Bourque, Tom Courchene, Aaron Dobbin, Alain-G. Gagnon, Diane Gray, Paul Howe, Jane Jenson, Junichiro Koji, Diane Morissette, Daniel Schwanen, Julie Simmons and Ron Watts. Finally, we thank the IRPP staff, whose unfailing professionalism and enthusiasm, as always, helped make this endeavour so much easier and more enjoyable: Suzanne Lambert, Chantal Létourneau, Suzanne Ostiguy McIntyre and Francesca Worrall. We wish to extend our warmest thanks to all of them, and in particular, to Hugh Segal, president of the Institute, for his continued support.

Sarah Fortin, Alain Noël and France St-Hilaire
Montreal, October 2003

L e a r n i n g   f r o m
t h e   S U F A
E x p e r i e n c e

A T THE CLOSE OF THEIR 44TH ANNUAL CONFERENCE IN JULY 2003, THE CANADIAN premiers unveiled a five-point plan "to build a new era of constructive and cooperative federalism."[1] While news coverage of the conference focused primarily on the proposed new Council of the Federation and on Quebec Premier Charest's role in promoting the idea, the plan also calls for annual first ministers' meetings co-chaired by the prime minister and the chair of the new council, consultations on federal appointments (to the Senate in particular), and the establishment of federal/provincial/territorial protocols of conduct to prevent unilateral actions in intergovernmental relations.

The premiers' ambitious proposals, and their assertion that "the current dynamic of Canadian federalism is not working well enough for Canadians, as demonstrated by recent experiences in areas such as health care issues, public health emergencies...and the fiscal imbalance," may have come as a surprise to casual observers of the federal-provincial scene.[2] After all, in the past four years the first ministers have announced a number of "landmark" agreements — starting with the Social Union Framework Agreement (SUFA) in 1999 and leading to the much touted "health accords" of 2000 and 2003 — which were meant to establish more constructive and cooperative relationships in these specific policy areas. In all cases, however, the reality has fallen well short of the rhetoric found in official documents.

The 2000 health accord, for instance, described by some provincial officials as a mere communiqué, was widely interpreted as a pre-election stop-gap measure on the part of the federal government to defuse the health care issue. While the transfer payment increases announced at the time were quite substantial ($21.1 billion over five years), they have not had a transformative impact on health services. Less than three years later, the first ministers went back to the drawing board to reach a new "health accord." This latest agreement came on the heels of two major reports on the future of health care in Canada, the report of the Standing Senate Committee on Social Affairs, Science and Technology chaired by Michael Kirby, and that of the Commission on the Future of Health Care in Canada chaired by Roy Romanow.[3] It provides for still more federal funding, but this time most of the money is to be directed into a separate Health Reform Fund earmarked for primary health care, home care and catastrophic drug coverage. Also, in response to one of the main recommendations of the Romanow report, the agreement calls for the establishment, within three months, of a new Health Council composed of experts and representatives from both orders of government and the public to monitor progress and prepare annual reports.

While it is too soon to assess whether the 2003 first ministers' "Accord on Health Care Renewal" will bring about the desired changes, there is little evidence thus far of a more "constructive and cooperative federalism." The very first day after the accord was put in place, the premiers expressed their disappointment regarding what they considered less than adequate levels of federal funding and their frustration at a process that was driven by hard bargaining and left little illusion regarding a possible new era of collaboration. The discussion ended with a "take it or leave it" threat from the prime minister.[4] The federal government boasted of a joint commitment on the future direction of the health care system, but the provincial premiers were quick to dismiss the outcome as simply an "arrangement" that they had not signed, indicating furthermore that they would soon be back with new financial demands.[5]

Five months later, at their 2003 annual conference, the premiers were calling on the federal government to address the "Romanow gap" in its 2004 budget. They argued that Ottawa pays only 16 percent of the costs of health care in the country and that this share should rise over time to 25 percent of provincial expenditures, as suggested by the Romanow Commission. Citing concerns over the mandate and the potential costs of the new Health Council, they also indicated that they might postpone discussions on these issues until after the arrival of the next prime minister.[6] The federal government's unofficial response has been that, given the significant transfer increases recently announced as part of the health accord, the provinces should not expect any new money in the near future. There were also indications that Ottawa was prepared to move ahead with the new council, even without unanimous provincial support.[7] The September 2003 meeting of health ministers made some headway toward the creation of the new body. The ministers agreed to step up work on the nomination of representatives, mandate definition and financial issues; however, their recommendations were subject to approval by their respective first minister. The real breakthrough, therefore, has yet to materialize.[8]

This sort of intergovernmental wrangling and jostling has been occurring since the mid-1990s. This is, in fact, why social union negotiations were initiated in 1995, to come to terms with the somewhat dysfunctional state of federal-provincial relations on social policy and fiscal issues. Health care funding was then, as it is now, the most contentious area of dispute. The 1999 Social Union Framework Agreement was meant to provide common guiding principles and a "code of conduct" to manage the interaction between the two orders of government in health care, post-secondary education, training, social assistance and social services.[9] The stated objectives were to help governments work jointly to address the needs of Canadians; ensure adequate, stable and sustainable funding for social programs; prevent overlap and duplication; avoid and resolve intergovernmental disputes; and enhance public accountability and transparency. Yet more than four years after the adoption of this framework agreement the same old disputes continue, based on the same core issues and conducted in more or less the same manner.

From this perspective, SUFA seems to have failed. Neither the 2000 nor the 2003 health accords, for instance, even refer to this agreement.[10] Both documents reiterate the same commitments to the principles of public accountability (reporting to Canadians), transparency and joint planning put forward in SUFA, but the evident lack of agreement on such fundamental issues as the current level of Ottawa's new financial contribution to health care[11] and the ideal level to ensure sustainable funding,[12] how exactly the provinces are expected to report on how they spend this contribution, and the mandate and scope of the new Health Council[13] suggest that "accord" may indeed be a misnomer.

The lack of public interest and debate at the time of SUFA's renewal in 2002 and during the review process that took place between 2001 and 2003 also suggests that the agreement has become marginal, if it was ever important, to the actual workings of Canadian intergovernmental relations. After all, SUFA was meant to demonstrate to Canadians their governments' willingness and ability to co-operate, to be held accountable and to involve citizens in both setting social priorities and reviewing outcomes. However, one of the principal conclusions that can be drawn from the consultation and review process that the Federal/Provincial/Territorial Ministerial Council on Social Policy Renewal undertook to fulfill SUFA's three-year review requirement is that there is a profound lack of public awareness of and interest in the agreement.[14]

Still, SUFA remains the only nonconstitutional framework addressing the respective roles of the two orders of government in social policy, and it has been influential in some less politicized areas of social policy — family policy, for instance.[15] More fundamentally, the agreement points to the broader issues underlying Canada's social union. Indeed, it is not possible to have an overall perspective on the country's social policy architecture without taking into consideration the ways in which the division of powers and financial resources — and the intergovernmental arrangements that have emerged as a consequence — have shaped the country's social programs.

This book assesses the influence and contribution of the Social Union Framework Agreement from this perspective. Our purpose is not so much to dissect the text of an agreement that ended up having relatively little significance as to use SUFA as a starting point to discuss the relationship between intergovernmental relations, democracy and social policy in Canada.

In Europe, governments and scholars have started to think about redefining and redesigning the welfare state for the new century, and as they do so, they have to consider seriously the respective roles of social actors, subnational and national governments and the European Union, as well as the mechanisms through which these different actors can coordinate their actions.[16] This discussion has already had some echoes in Canada, but much remains to be done, particularly with respect to intergovernmental arrangements. Ken Battle and Sherri Torjman, for instance, advocate going beyond incremental changes and piecemeal innovations and propose "a new architecture of social policy for the new century," but they give little thought to the difficulty of implementing ambitious designs in a context of divided or shared sovereignty. They simply acknowledge that "virtually all problems are complex and do not respect the neat jurisdictional borders of government organization charts," and assert that "Ottawa must rise out of its torpor and reassert its crucial role in helping the provinces and territories reform and finance social, employment and health programs that fall under their jurisdiction."[17]

Canada is a relatively decentralized federation, and its economic and social union can never be taken for granted. Only governments can construct a workable economic and social union for the federation, and this can only be done jointly, in a more or less effective and more or less collaborative fashion. The purpose of this book is to explore the difficulties and possibilities of such joint efforts, through an analysis of the most ambitious attempt yet to design an explicit framework for the social union.

As a way of introducing the following chapters, which were written in the months leading to the 2002 deadline for the renewal of SUFA, three questions that cut across all of them are addressed. First, in what ways is Canada a social union, and what does this reality entail for the federation? As we will see, the concept of a social union is a recent political creation, but the reality it describes is much older and is deeply anchored in our institutions. Second, is there anything left of the Social Union Framework Agreement? From the outset, SUFA was a low-profile enterprise, and it has become even less visible over the years. Yet, the agreement remains in force and it has altered the political and institutional landscape of the country. Third, beyond SUFA, what are the prospects for intergovernmental relations and for the social union? Is the changing of the guard in Ottawa, Quebec and Ontario likely to facilitate collaboration, or are current relations defined by structural rather than contextual factors? On this last question, we can only speculate. Nevertheless, we can certainly identify the main challenges that will need to be addressed in the coming years.

Canada's Social Union

UNTIL THE 1980s CANADA WAS RARELY, IF EVER, CHARACTERIZED AS AN ECONOMIC and social union. A relatively long-standing federation with a fairly integrated internal market and significant pan-Canadian social programs, the country was more often compared with unitary states than with new intergovernmental arrangements such as those emerging in Europe. Still, between 1927 and the end of the 1960s the foundations of a *social* union were laid through a series of reforms that introduced old age pensions (1927), unemployment insurance (1940), family allowances (1944), old age security (1951), unemployment assistance (1956), hospital insurance (1957), Canada and Quebec pension plans (1965) and medicare (1966). Looking back on this incremental building process, some observers have described it as the product of a postwar "mission statement" or as the expression of a social compact.[18] Indeed, a number of eloquent and forward-looking reports were tabled in the mid-1940s stating the case for a comprehensive, nationwide social security system. Though the federal government's commitment at that time to a "grand design" for a "charter of social security for the whole of Canada" is a matter of debate,[19] the fact remains that by the late 1960s these programs helped define the country's social and economic union.

What is significant for contemporary dynamics is that the debate around the adoption of many of these social programs was as much a matter of defining the role of the state and the rights of Canadian citizens as it was a question of delineating constitutional responsibilities. Then, as now, social policy outcomes were intrinsically linked to federal-provincial negotiations over jurisdictions and funding. This period saw the emergence of an original Canadian compromise whereby the federal government would share equally with provinces the cost of social programs falling under their jurisdiction. In some cases, Quebec was able to proceed on its own (in pensions and post-secondary education, for instance).

The notion of Canada as an economic union that needs to be strengthened was first expressed in 1985, with the publication of the Report of the Royal Commission on the Economic Union and Development Prospects for Canada (Macdonald Commission Report). Driven by a strong preference for market solutions, the Macdonald Commission presented the country's economic union as highly imperfect and marred in particular by the institutions and practices of federalism. The report recommended a strong role for the federal government as the only body able to provide a "unified political framework for private economic activity" and to act as an "advocate and catalyst for the effective functioning of the economic union." This concept of economic union also encompassed social policies, and the federal government was again seen as "primarily responsible for redistribution between regions and provinces, between social and economic interests, and among individual citizens."[20] This particular standpoint was reflected in subsequent major federal policy decisions, and it was raised as a constitutional issue during the "Canada Round" that led to the drafting of the Charlottetown Accord in 1992. In response to the federal government's demand for a commitment in favour of measures to formalize the economic union, the Ontario government, then led by NDP Premier Bob Rae, juxtaposed the idea of a social charter that would contribute to entrenching social rights in a context of market integration and liberalization. The two ideas were eventually merged in the accord as a nonbinding clause on "the social and economic union."[21]

Following the rejection of the Charlottetown Accord in the 1992 referendum and the election in 1993 of a new Liberal government committed not to talk about the constitution, discussion of a social and economic union was set aside. The ambitious and ill-fated social security review undertaken by Lloyd Axworthy in 1994, for instance, did not refer to the social union, and nor did the 1995 federal budget speech, in which the new Canada Health and Social Transfer (CHST) and the government's drastic plan to tackle mounting deficits were announced. This speech only mentioned the need to develop "through mutual consent, a set of shared principles and objectives that could underlie the transfer."[22] The social union idea soon resurfaced, however, because it still had currency and could serve many purposes.

The near loss of the 1995 Quebec referendum by the federalist side sparked efforts by the Chrétien government to demonstrate that a nonconstitutional renewal of the federation could be achieved. As part of this initiative, the federal government reintroduced the idea of a social union and reiterated its commitment to "work with the provinces and Canadians to develop by mutual consent the values, principles and objectives that should underlie, first, the Canada Health and Social Transfer and, building on this, the social union more generally."[23] In this context, the social union referred to a set of common social values and objectives that tie Canadians together, and it was evoked to counterbalance the implications of decentralization entailed by the federal government's deficit-cutting measures and other nonconstitutional reforms. The term, however, could also take on a different meaning.

A few months earlier, the provinces had created their own Ministerial Council on Social Policy Renewal to define a common response to the major cutbacks in federal transfers announced in the recent budget with the creation of the CHST. Soon the provinces would also use the term social union, less to emphasize common values, however, than to stress the federal nature of the country and the intergovernmental collaboration and respect it should entail. When the Quebec government joined this alliance to form an interprovincial consensus in Saskatoon in 1998, this understanding of the social union as a decentralized model of intergovernmental relations was reinforced.

The Social Union Framework Agreement, which was eventually signed in February 1999, left unresolved the exact meaning of the term "social union," because it referred both to common values and objectives and to the importance of the division of powers and of collaboration in the federation. Both sides, argues Harvey Lazar, found elements reflecting their views of the social union in the agreement. The provinces obtained some procedural guidelines to help govern an intergovernmental social union, and the federal government saw the idea of a pan-Canadian citizenship — with mobility rights and equal opportunities — acknowledged.[24] The reconciliation of views, however, was only superficial.

First, of course, Quebec was not a party to the final agreement, and as Christian Dufour argues in his chapter, there was no serious attempt to reach an understanding with the Quebec government, even though it was able to find common ground with the other provinces in Saskatoon in 1998.[25] When Quebec joined the other provinces, Dufour writes, it "implicitly accepted the implications of a Canadian social union." Reaching an agreement would have taken more time and effort, but it could have brought about "a new beginning in Canada-Quebec relations."

Second, as Dufour also notes, numerous contradictions and ambiguities can be found in the agreement, "well beyond the normal tensions and contradictions inherent in any political agreement." Whether they relate to the principles and objectives, the binding character of commitments or citizen engagement, most clauses appear difficult to interpret, let alone operationalize. "In fact, the contradictions," concludes Dufour, "are so deep and fundamental that one might legitimately ask what the agreement is or whether an agreement even exists."

Third, as Alain Noël explains in his chapter, the principles and guidelines introduced with the framework agreement must be read within the broader context of Canadian intergovernmental relations. SUFA, writes Noël, "merely consolidated an evolution that was already under way, as a result of federal fiscal and social policies." Transfers to the provinces were reduced drastically and integrated into one major block transfer (the CHST), universal transfers to individuals were gradually converted into more selective and targeted transfers, and new direct spending programs were introduced to define a new, more visible and distinct social policy role for the federal government. These different trends all have one thing in common: they maintain or enhance "Ottawa's flexibility and control." Increasingly, the federal government "targets and spends, for one purpose and one budget at a time," in a mostly unilateral fashion that "appears basically at odds with the idea of a social union."

The other contributors to this volume, and most observers, tend to concur with these severe assessments of an agreement that could have been a more meaningful and more satisfactory compromise, a more transparent and effective framework, and an opportunity to break from a pattern of intergovernmental relations characterized primarily by unilateralism and distrust. Even those who remain optimistic about SUFA acknowledge these difficulties and deplore the lack of trust in the federation.[26]

Beyond SUFA, however, the question of the social union remains. In a federation, the term social *union* can be somewhat misleading because it tends to portray the country as in some ways less and in other ways more integrated than it really is. If one carries the analogy with the European Union too far, for instance, one could overlook the importance of transfers and equalization in the Canadian federation. In 2001, the European Union's entire own-resources budget was equivalent to 1.11 percent of the combined gross national product (GNP) of the 15 member states, whereas in Canada equalization payments alone accounted for nearly as much, at 1.0 percent of the country's gross domestic product (GDP).[27] Canada's commitment to equalizing fiscal capacity among provinces is simply out of reach for the European Union, at least in its current form.[28] There are also important direct transfers to persons — retirees, families and the unemployed, for instance — that are administered by Ottawa and for which there is no equivalent in Europe.

On the other hand, the social union image may also lead one to overemphasize the existence of unity and uniformity in a federation like Canada, where social and economic diversity remains a key characteristic and where the constitutional division of powers between the two orders of government constitutes a perennial issue.[29] By contrast, there is no formal division of powers in the European Union, and community law is understood as having a direct effect on and supremacy over national laws. In this respect, deplores Francis Delpérée, the European Union professes to be international and pre-federal but thinks of itself in a unitary fashion.[30]

If it is to be helpful in the Canadian context, the concept of social union must therefore be considered carefully with respect to both its social mission and its political imperatives. It should not be associated simply with an intergovernmental arrangement as in Europe, where the centre has few social policy instruments of its own and limited redistributive capabilities. Nor should it be seen merely as the reflection of a unity of purpose, objectives and values, which in effect would negate the federal principle.[31] A social union is more fruitfully understood as a challenge, one of many policy objectives that can never be fully achieved precisely because it conflicts with other important objectives.

In a recent analysis, Mark MacDonald describes the economic union in a federation as a fundamental trade-off between the search for economic integration and the need to preserve and enhance social and political diversity. In recent years, concludes MacDonald, Canadian politicians have increasingly agreed on the benefits of liberalization, and they have favoured integration over diversity, at least with respect to trade.[32] Hence, in 1994 they all signed the Agreement on Internal Trade (AIT). Negative integration, however — that is, the prohibition of barriers to trade — has been easier to pursue than positive integration — that is, the harmonization of policies.[33] The latter is more demanding and requires more elaborate collaborative efforts.[34] This is what is at stake with the social union.

To sum up this first section, the Social Union Framework Agreement may not have succeeded as an enduring and meaningful compromise, but it did bring to a close, for a moment, a five-year debate over the social union in Canada. SUFA also remains the only attempt to formalize the intergovernmental workings of the social union in Canada. With the social union, as with the economic union, trade-offs continually have to be worked out between the benefits of integration and harmonization and the advantages of maintaining a strong federal principle. Such trade-offs are an integral part of the Canadian federation, and they will continue to define our political debates in the coming years. Whether or not SUFA will be an important milestone in this respect, however, remains uncertain.

Is There Anything Left of SUFA?

THE POSTELECTION MAIL-BACK SURVEY THAT THE 2000 CANADIAN ELECTION STUDY team conducted in November 2000 included a few questions about the Social Union Framework Agreement.[35] The main conclusion that can be drawn from this survey is that Canadian citizens were not very informed about or even very aware of the agreement signed 21 months earlier. Indeed, more than 85 percent knew little or nothing of the agreement's existence: only 2.1 percent of the respondents claimed they had heard "a great deal" about it, while 12.4 percent said they had heard "some"; 27.6 percent responded "not much," 46.8 percent responded "nothing at all" and 11.1 percent were "not sure."[36] Given these results and the small size of the sample claiming to be informed, it would not be judicious to go too far into the specifics and probe, for instance, the correlates of support for the agreement. Some results, however, are worth noting.

First, the proportion of respondents that had heard "a great deal" or "some" about the agreement did not vary all that much from one region of the country to another. Compared with 14.5 percent across Canada, it was 9.5 percent in the Atlantic provinces, 15.9 percent in Quebec, 14 percent in Ontario, 14.8 percent in the Prairies and 18.4 percent in British Columbia. Contrary to what one would expect given the Quebec government's opposition to the agreement, awareness of SUFA was not much higher in Quebec than elsewhere in the country.

Second, a majority, 53.5 percent, thought that the agreement had not done much, if anything, to improve social programs. One should note here that many respondents simply did not answer the question, or stated that they were not sure, which is consequent with the low awareness revealed by the first question.[37] In this case, evaluations proved more negative in Quebec, where 63.2 percent thought the agreement was not very helpful, compared with 45.4 percent in the Atlantic provinces, 41.8 percent in Ontario, 58.4 percent in the Prairies and 59 percent in British Columbia.

Finally, a fair majority stated that it was a serious or very serious problem that Quebec did not sign the agreement (59.9 percent).[38] Interestingly, this preoccupation was least present in Quebec, where only 52.5 percent saw the province's exclusion as a problem, compared with 60.8 percent in the Atlantic provinces, 65.3 percent in Ontario, 62.4 percent in the Prairies and 63.9 percent in British Columbia. This result is explained by the relative indifference of those Quebec respondents who were in favour of sovereignty. Among those opposed to Quebec sovereignty, 66.4 percent saw the fact that Quebec did not sign SUFA as a problem, a result very similar to that found elsewhere in Canada, whereas only 34.6 percent of Quebecers in favour of sovereignty thought the same. In this latter group, half the respondents (49.4 percent) thought that Quebec's exclusion was not a very serious problem or not a problem at all. These citizens had already made up their mind about Quebec's place within Canada, and in this light SUFA did not appear all that important.

Overall, then, the Social Union Framework Agreement does not seem to be perceived very positively by the public. In fact, most Canadians appear not to even know about it. These survey findings concur with Roger Gibbins' assessment in his chapter on the political foundations of SUFA. "If SUFA were to die," writes Gibbins, "few Canadians would notice the obituary, much less mourn its passing." The agreement, he argues, "rested on a broad intergovernmental coalition glued together by financial self-interest," and it "is only shallowly implanted in the soil of Canadian federalism." This is so because SUFA has "almost no public visibility and therefore no public constituency that would come to its defense should the support by political actors wane." Whether in Ottawa or in the provinces, there does not seem to be much enthusiasm or incentive for going forward to improve or extend an agreement born in the "shifting sands" of intergovernmental relations. Governments will probably preserve SUFA, if only by the sheer force of inertia, but are not likely to enhance it.

These observations are certainly borne out by the recently completed three-year review of the agreement. The review process was a very low-key affair that generated little public interest and a rather lukewarm report on progress made to date.[39] We would also argue that, relative to the remaining challenges identified in this report, the recommendations for improvements are quite modest and limited in scope.[40] Ironically, those who did participate in the process were especially critical of governments' efforts to inform Canadians and put in place mechanisms for citizen participation.

In her chapter on this question, Susan Phillips points in the same direction. The Social Union Framework Agreement, she observes, "marks the first time that the federal and provincial governments have made a joint commitment to engage citizens in the governing process." Both orders of government, however, "have failed miserably in keeping their promises." Like Matthew Mendelsohn and John McLean, Phillips considers that citizen engagement is compatible with, and indeed beneficial to, intergovernmental relations.[41] The understanding of citizen engagement written in the agreement, however, was quite vague and relatively narrow. Citizens were primarily expected to play the role of watchdogs in intergovernmental conflicts. In any case, almost nothing was done to make this new role operational and effective. Even the formal commitment to a three-year review that would engage citizens Phillips sees as unlikely to be seriously implemented: "A few regional meetings, a toll-free phone line and some workbooks do not constitute meaningful engagement," she writes. The actual review process turned out to be even more modest than she expected. Basically, a Web site was opened where documents and comments could be posted.[42] The idea, explained a federal civil servant in a personal interview, was to respect the commitment made in SUFA while keeping the whole process as low key and low profile as possible. As Phillips notes, the limited impact of the framework agreement made this feasible: citizens simply did not "have much to say, since so little has happened."

Change, concludes Phillips, will come from the bottom up, as the organization and mobilization of civil society makes it increasingly difficult for governments to ignore the views and demands of citizens. The problem, she acknowledges in her chapter, is that such mobilization rarely pertains to intergovernmental affairs per se. It occurs primarily in the provinces — Phillips mentions Newfoundland and Labrador and Quebec — in the context of specific programs or policy issues. In Quebec, Yves Vaillancourt notes in his chapter, social movements have played a critical role in building and promoting the new social economy.[43] Similar developments are taking place elsewhere in Canada.[44] As Vaillancourt points out, in the social union there are not only the *union* aspects to consider, but also the *social* ones. Change, therefore, may come as much, and perhaps more, from the gradual transformation of social policy as from the evolution of intergovernmental relations.

In his chapter on the relationship between the Social Union Framework Agreement and Canadian social policy, Michael Prince does take social policy as a starting point, and he is moderately optimistic. Acknowledging that SUFA's impact on social policy has been modest — "more akin to a ripple than a sea change" — Prince nevertheless notes a number of trends that are consistent with the agreement and contribute to social policy renewal. First, new understandings around shared principles are emerging (although often without Quebec), especially in sectors that, unlike health care, are not too visible and contentious. This is the case, for instance, with the disability and children's policy agendas. Second, collaboration among governments and between governments and social actors is improving, at least at the level of specific programs.[45] Again, Prince refers to disability policy, but also to relations with Aboriginal organizations. Third, federal funding is being restored, sometimes directly, sometimes in new ways, through the tax system, for instance.[46] Fourth, Ottawa is increasingly, although grudgingly, acknowledging that for the most part social policy jurisdiction belongs to the provinces, and that federal interventions require intergovernmental agreements. Fifth, there is a growing emphasis on sharing information and knowledge, and governments are beginning to design policy instruments to make policy learning easier. Working against these five trends, Prince also sees, as do most other contributors to this book, an "enduring custom in Canada of executive dominance over the governmental process" and an ongoing "concentration of power within Canadian executive federalism."

The positive trends Prince identifies are supported by empirical evidence. As he recognizes, however, they are still at an "early stage" and are certainly counter-balanced by powerful forces pulling in opposite directions. In health care, for instance, "hard bargaining, late-night negotiations and last-minute compromises" still seem to prevail. Moreover, these positive trends predate SUFA. They owe as much to the rise of ideas associated with the new public management, to shifts in public opinion and to the new fiscal context defined by the federal government's growing budgetary surplus. Still, when one looks at social policy, program by program, it is possible to identify patterns that are consistent with the principles set forth in the Social Union Framework Agreement.

In a similar vein, but from a different perspective, Yves Vaillancourt suggests in his chapter that while SUFA as it was signed, without Quebec, proved to be a stillborn initiative — the agreement did not help much, but it did not really hurt either — a better union could be designed if social preoccupations prevailed over intergovernmental relations. Without denying the importance of constitutional issues, to which he paid much attention in his earlier work, Vaillancourt proposes that much could be gained, for Quebec and for the other provinces, if more effort were devoted to exchanging information and learning from each other's social policy innovations. In recent years, argues Vaillancourt, the Quebec government, in collaboration with civil society actors, has developed a new social model that, in many ways, is more distinctive than the previous model that emerged out of the Quiet Revolution in the 1960s and 1970s. This model is based in particular on the state's recognition and support for the social economy, which makes possible a number of new initiatives and approaches in social housing, early childhood development, home care, and programs for people with disabilities. According to Vaillancourt, these approaches are well established and progressive, and they make it advantageous for the Quebec government to partake in the exchange of information and ideas proposed in

SUFA. If these exchanges lead to a diffusion of Quebec's approaches, all the better; the more these initiatives are known, appreciated and possibly emulated, the more embedded they will be.

Prince's and Vaillancourt's guarded optimism, based on their assessment of the evolution of social policy in Canada and in the provinces, is confronted with their own recognition, and the observations of the other contributors to this book, that the intergovernmental context overall remains unfavourable, defined as it is more by unilateralism and distrust than by genuine collaboration. A number of studies suggest that the evolution of intergovernmental relations does not facilitate social policy renewal. At best, Vaillancourt suggests, these trends could prove inconsequential, leaving the picture largely unchanged. At worst, Noël argues, they could be detrimental, making policy choices less than optimal. With respect to post-secondary education, Herman Bakvis and David Cameron see SUFA as basically "irrelevant" and conclude that "the ineluctable thrust established by Ottawa in the early postwar period, to set the tone and direction of university life, appears to be alive and well."[47] Similarly, in health care, SUFA hardly altered the pattern defined by a federal role that, according to Antonia Maioni, "has become at once more unilateral in process and less effective in practice."[48] Labour market policies also have evolved basically outside the realm of the Social Union Framework Agreement.[49] Even the National Child Benefit, viewed by many as the early prototype that inspired SUFA, can be seen as a less than ideal outcome of a collaborative process that placed more stress on the need to reach an agreement than on social policy objectives. There "is no guarantee," argues Gerard Boychuk, "that collaboration will necessarily produce stronger, more effective social policy than an approach predicated on a greater respect for the existing federal division of powers."[50]

These limited direct policy impacts may explain why the Social Union Framework Agreement does not seem all that important to a good number of civil servants involved in intergovernmental affairs in Ottawa and the provinces, even though genuine efforts have been made to make the agreement operational.[51] Most federal and provincial policy initiatives simply do not require intergovernmental collaboration, at least not under the terms specified in SUFA. A superficial and ill-defined agreement was not sufficient to modify the ways of a federation that remains largely disentangled.

In Canada's institutional and political context, it was probably a mistake to build an agreement on "fundamental values," "principles" and the "needs of

Canadians." In this respect, the pragmatism and openness to diversity of the European Union member states is worthy of consideration. In the last chapter of the book, Bruno Théret compares Canada's federal experience with the recent evolution of the European Union. From the outset, Théret stresses the differences between these two situations, which, he says, are actually "reverse images" of one another. What makes the comparison possible and fruitful, according to Théret, is a similarity in the dynamics involved, which make the two cases converge from opposite directions: the European Union is slowly becoming federalized, whereas Canada is, gradually and with much difficulty, becoming more explicitly multinational. Observers from Canada may be less optimistic than Théret about the capacity of their country to come to terms with its multinational character.[52] But Europeans would probably also be more critical of their own situation than Canadian observers, who tend to be fascinated by the European experience.

The most important thing here is to consider what we can learn from the European experience in governance, which is relatively successful in a context where diversity simply cannot be overlooked. Viewed from Canada, the level of trust in Europe appears quite remarkable. "Member states of the European Union," notes Joseph Weiler in this respect, "accept their constitutional discipline with far more equanimity than, say, Quebec."[53] They do so, he adds, because they commit themselves voluntarily and autonomously, and on a continuously renewed basis, to shared norms. Says Weiler, "the Quebecois are told: in the name of the people of Canada, you are obliged to obey. The French or the Italians or the Germans are told: in the name of the peoples of Europe, you are invited to obey."[54]

In social policy, as Bruno Théret explains, these joint commitments are now increasingly defined through the Open Method of Coordination (OMC), an approach that was first developed with the European Employment Strategy and then generalized to other policy areas at the European Council of Lisbon in March 2000. Very much in the spirit of shared norms and voluntary convergence evoked by Weiler, the OMC brings member states to define common objectives, which they then implement on a national level through their own National Action Plans.[55] It is still too early to assess the European experience with the OMC, but however difficult and fragile it is, the process appears better engaged than that of SUFA, if only because all member states accept the principle and play by the rules. If the process works, concludes Anton Hemerijck in terms that echo Canadian debates, "successes achieved through OMC are likely to enhance the legitimacy of the EU as a social union."[56]

Prospects for the
Social Union

THE THIRD QUESTION RAISED IN THE BEGINNING OF THIS CHAPTER CONCERNED THE prospects for intergovernmental relations and for the social union in the coming years. As we completed this volume, a change of the political guard had taken place in Quebec and Ontario, and was underway in Ottawa. In Quebec, a federalist and more conservative government led by Jean Charest was elected in the spring of 2003, while in Ontario the provincial Liberals took power in the fall. In Ottawa, Paul Martin was rapidly working his way toward the leadership of the Liberal Party and the position of prime minister.

The new Quebec government, notably, came out of the April 2003 election committed to redefining Quebec's role in the federation, and to do so it proposed a renewed discussion on fiscal imbalance, a thorough revision of the Social Union Framework Agreement and a new Council of the Federation to better institutionalize intergovernmental relations.[57] In Ottawa, however, there was little openness to such proposals. After the Quebec elections, Paul Martin reiterated that there simply was no fiscal imbalance in the federation and therefore not much to negotiate.[58] Initially, Quebec's proposals for change in intergovernmental relations were received with almost as little enthusiasm in many provinces as they were in Ottawa. Still, the outcome of the annual premiers' conference in July 2003 suggests that change is indeed possible. The premiers announced that they would meet shortly to finalize the mandate and structure of the newly created Council of the Federation (without the federal government, for the time being), and they have agreed to establish a Secretariat for Information and Cooperation on Fiscal Imbalance, which will operate under the mandate of the council, as will the existing Premiers' Council on Canadian Health Awareness and similar provincial/territorial coordinating bodies.

The contributors to this volume focused more on the structural than on the contextual issues, and overall they were not optimistic about a major or even significant renewal of the Social Union Framework Agreement. Roger Gibbins' prediction that the agreement would remain in place, if only because of institutional inertia, turned out to be correct. The third anniversary of the agreement came and went without fanfare or amendments. The results of the review process came more than a year late, but few noticed. More fundamentally, as indicated at the beginning of this introduction, the nature and tone of intergovernmental relations have changed very little as a result of SUFA. While mobility provisions and accountability requirements have become *de rigueur* in ad hoc social policy agreements, Yves Vaillancourt's characterization of SUFA as basically an "empty shell" still appears appropriate.

What about the social union itself? A specific agreement may fail to meet expectations or not take hold, but the issues raised by the need to harmonize and coordinate social policies remain. In a federation, collaboration is not always necessary and in some cases may even be detrimental, as Boychuk notes in his study of social assistance and the social union.[59] Governments may well coordinate their actions informally, move forward by emulating each other, or even decide to pursue a separate course of action in line with their electorate's preferences. However, since social policy responsibilities and resources are divided between the two orders of government, some collaboration is probably useful. More importantly, misunderstandings about the social union very much reflect broader misunderstandings about the nature of the country. Improving the functioning of the social union could therefore be an avenue to renew the federation through nonconstitutional means. This was, indeed, one of the original purposes of the social union discussions. From this perspective, and beyond the Social Union Framework Agreement itself, four major challenges can be identified that cut across the studies presented in this book.

First, of course, as Christian Dufour, Yves Vaillancourt and Bruno Théret underline, no meaningful social union can be constructed without the inclusion of one of its constituent parts, namely Quebec. This first challenge is not an easy one, because previous decisions, on the constitution as well as on the social union, have strong implications for future discussions. For this reason, one should not count excessively on the presence in Quebec of a federalist government, even one that has promised a new emphasis on collaboration. For Quebec governments, intergovernmental relations are something akin to foreign policy. A clear and consistent line runs from one government to the next, which defines the broad outlines of what can and cannot be done or accepted. Radical turnarounds are generally not possible. If anything, a federalist government led by someone suspected of not having a strong anchoring in Quebec politics may be even more constrained by the official line than a government committed to Quebec sovereignty and therefore seen as less likely to yield on important principles.[60] Quebec governments will change, but Quebec society, with its demands and expectations, will remain, to a large extent, the same. For instance, Quebec has already indicated that it is putting in place its own system to monitor its health care system and report to citizens, and that while it is willing to collaborate with the proposed Canadian Health Council, it will not be part of it, even if all provinces participate.[61] Truly including Quebec in a social union process remains an important challenge, and it cannot be met with superficial accommodations. That being said, there are clear indications that the new Quebec government seeks to redefine the province's role and to re-establish for Quebec a leadership position within the federation. Whether SUFA becomes part of that agenda remains to be seen.

Second, the broader issue of power relations in the federation also has to be addressed. As Alain Noël and Roger Gibbins explain in their chapters, the provinces initiated the social union process precisely to deal with the federal government's excessive power and unilateralism. The Social Union Framework Agreement failed to deliver effective rules and constraints in this respect, or even to make progress in this direction. In recent years the dispute has in fact broadened and now encompasses the larger question of the fiscal imbalance in the federation.[62] What is at stake, then, is not only the sufficiency or adequacy of transfers for social programs, but, more fundamentally, the allocation of fiscal resources in the federation, as well as the use by the federal government of a "spending power" that in effect negates the established constitutional division of powers.[63] Once again, the challenge is a daunting one. In recent years, Canada has experienced more, not less, concentration of power at the centre, and the difference in the relative fiscal prospects of both orders of government for the coming years will not facilitate change or accommodation. If anything, the recent disagreements surrounding the 2003 health accord demonstrate that without some rebalancing of powers and resources the social union is unlikely to function effectively.

Third, it is not possible to consider the future of Canada's social union without taking into account the challenges raised by the current evolution of social policies, in Canada and abroad. As Alain Noël and Yves Vaillancourt explain in their chapters, Canadian social programs emerged gradually, in Ottawa and in the provinces, over several decades. The process was long and to a large extent incremental, but overall it was coherent because it largely built on ideas about the state and society that were developed in the 1940s.[64] In recent years many of these ideas and policies have been challenged by the emergence of new social risks and new expectations associated with the postindustrial economy and societal changes, including more diverse family forms, a more advanced capacity to heal and care, an aging population, and a more educated and engaged citizenry. Governments tend to respond to these changes incrementally by adjusting policies within established parameters. Increasingly, however, they will have to rethink the parameters themselves, to rebuild a welfare state architecture that is better suited to the needs and demands of a postindustrial, more pluralistic society.[65] In the Canadian context, a new social policy architecture necessarily involves intergovernmental relations. But, as both Michael Prince and Yves Vaillancourt argue, the challenge in this case is also very much a social policy challenge. Ottawa and the provinces will have to find new ways to address issues of income security, family policy, health care and social services, ways that are appropriate for an increasingly diverse, postindustrial society with more demanding citizens.

This last point leads to the fourth challenge, the need to democratize governance in Canada. Susan Phillips, Michael Prince and Yves Vaillancourt see modest but difficult and halting progress on this front, with governments committed in principle to citizen engagement but reluctant to go too far in this direction. There is no going back, however. Contemporary citizens are at once more cynical about the political process and more eager to be engaged in decision-making and policy implementation.[66] In Canada, intergovernmental relations have been shaped primarily by politicians, civil servants and experts, and they have not been very conducive to citizen engagement. If anything, public debates around the constitution have made governments and experts even more skeptical than before about the merits and potential of public deliberation.[67] Phillips and Prince, like Mendelsohn and McLean, insist that more can nevertheless be done to make intergovernmental relations more open and democratic.[68] This is probably true. But it may be wise to start first in the provinces and in specific policy sectors where democratization appears more advanced and more promising. As Vaillancourt suggests, with the emergence of new and more democratic social models in the provinces, it may become easier to achieve a social union that is amenable to citizen engagement.

As is the case with the economic union, forging a workable social union is a continual challenge for a decentralized and multinational federation like Canada. The 1999 Social Union Framework Agreement did not respond satisfactorily to this challenge. It failed to meet expectations on a number of counts: it did not take into account Quebec's view of the federation and, as result, left out one of the union's constituent parts; it did not help clarify the respective roles of each order of government in social policy; it did not produce effective rules to balance power in the federation; and, finally, it did not provide solid foundations for a new social policy architecture or mechanisms for citizens to engage meaningfully in setting social priorities. The agreement remains with us, but so do these unresolved issues. Whether it is in the context of the debate on fiscal imbalance, ongoing negotiations on health care financing or the introduction of new social programs, these social union challenges will re-emerge. It is therefore important to ponder carefully the Social Union Framework Agreement, which turned out to be a missed opportunity to improve intergovernmental relations in this country. There will, of course, be other opportunities. Recent developments indicate that the need for better instruments and new institutions to improve the workings of the federation is as great as ever. Governments, experts and citizens should therefore learn from the SUFA experience and start to consider better options for the future. This volume on Canada's social union is meant to be a contribution to this process.

1   Premiers of Canada (2003*b*).

2   The other issues raised as problematic concern international agreements and relations and internal trade.

3   Standing Senate Committee on Social Affairs, Science and Technology (2002); Romanow (2002).

4   Bueckert (2003).

5   "The one thing the Premiers didn't do is that they didn't sign the Accord," said Alberta Premier Ralph Klein. Ontario's Ernie Eves likewise concluded that the agreement "certainly doesn't resolve the issue," and he added, "we will be back." See Bueckert (2003); Harper and Whittington (2003). Territorial leaders were even more negative and rejected the outcome as "appalling." "There is nothing in this deal for us," concluded Northwest Territories Premier Stephen Kakfwi. In the following weeks, however, a new arrangement was reached with the Territories. Gray (2003); Walkom (2003).

6   Premiers of Canada (2003*a*).

7   Laghi and Clark (2003).

8   Laghi (2003).

9   These are the areas implicitly understood to be within SUFA's purview. The fact that the agreement does not specify the range of programs and services it covers and the lack of a definition of what is meant by a social union have been identified as a weakness, in the first instance, and a fundamental flaw, in the second, by participants in the three-year-review consultations. See Federal/Provincial/Territorial Council on Social Policy Renewal (2003, p. 5).

10 First Ministers of Canada (2000, 2003).

11 TD Economics (2003); Canadian Centre for Policy Alternatives (2003); Brimacombe (2001, p. 1).

12 This particular dispute, which dates back to the mid-1990s, has been described as the principal irritant in federal-provincial relations and a serious impediment to health care reform. It has also given rise to the broader, ongoing debate on vertical fiscal imbalance. See Lazar, St-Hilaire and Tremblay (2003*b*).

13 The premiers consider that the council should only be an advisory body to health ministers, with a limited budget. See Premiers of Canada (2003*a*).

14 See Federal/Provincial/Territorial Council on Social Policy Renewal (2003, pp. 2-3).

15 Family policy is often considered the most successful expression of SUFA's commitment to collaboration, with the first ministers' agreement on developing a National Children Agenda, which predates SUFA by a year, the Early Childhood Development Agreement (2000), and the Agreement on Early Learning and Childcare (2003). Critical assessments of developments in this area, however, also reveal how the process (i.e., consultation and collaboration) can appear to hinder progress. See White (2002) and Friendly (2001).

16 Hemerijck (2002).

17 They do acknowledge, however, that the nature of the federal role has changed, from "first among equals" to "an equal partner with the provinces and territories." See Battle and Torjman (2002, p. 2).

18 Lazar (2000*a*, p. 4).

19 See Guest (1985, chap. 8).

20 Report of the Royal Commission on the Economic Union and Development Prospects for Canada, quoted in Rocher (1998, p. 140).

21 Webber (1994, pp. 172-173); Russell (1993, pp. 170-186).

22 Human Resources Development Canada (1994); Greenspon and Wilson-Smith (1996, pp. 74-75, 138 and 143); Martin (1995, p. 18).

23 Government of Canada (1996).

24 Lazar (2000*b*, pp. 114-115).

25 See also Noël (2000*a*, pp. 9-35) and Noël (2000).

26 Lazar (2000*a*, pp. 32-34); Cameron and Simeon (2002, p. 68).

27 For the last 20 years Canadian equalization payments have declined as a percentage of the country's income. In 1982, they were at

1.3 percent of GDP. Under the current rules, the European Union's own resources cannot exceed 1.27 percent of Europe's GNP. European Commission (2000, p. 3, 2003); Commission on Fiscal Imbalance (2002, p. 92).

28 "Though creative accounting, economic growth, and enlargement may create temporary lack of interest to EU policy analysts, there is no medium-term prospect of significantly lifting the formal fiscal ceiling — the overall 1.27 per cent constraint. EU budgetary policy is subject to unanimity and thus remains tightly controlled domestically by finance ministers, foreign ministers, and heads of state and governments." Moravcsik (2001, p. 169).

29 See Watts (1999, pp. 48 and 65; and 2003, p. 143).

30 Delpérée (2000, pp. 81-83 and 103-104). So far, argues Joseph Weiler, the absence of boundaries to protect national competences and divide power has worked for Europe, but it is "a ticking constitutional time bomb which could one day threaten the evolution and the stability of Community." No federation, he notes, has ever developed without providing some legal protection to the different orders of government. Weiler (1997, pp. 123-124).

31 Margaret Biggs, for instance, associates the social union with "our shared sense of social purpose and common citizenship." She also approvingly quotes Ken Battle and Sherri Torjman, who write: "The problem is not diversity. The problem is diversity in the absence of national principles and basic standards." For these authors, the problem is indeed diversity, whenever it makes a difference. Much of this unitary vision found its way, albeit in a nonenforceable way, into the principles stated in SUFA. See Biggs (1996, pp. 1-2).

32 MacDonald (2002, pp. 138-139).

33 On this distinction, see MacDonald (2002, p. 139); Courchene (1995, p. 61); and Scharpf (1999, pp. 43-83).

34 This is not say that trade integration has proceeded steadfastly and steadily. In fact, despite progress, including four protocols of amendment, much remains to be done eight years after the ratification of AIT. See Appendix 1 in MacDonald (2002, pp. 149-155) and Internal Trade Secretariat (2001).

35 For the data, see Blais, Gidengil, Nadeau and Nevitt (2000). For more information about the survey and the context, see Blais, Gidengil, Nadeau and Nevitte (2002).

36 The question was: "The federal government and all the provinces except Quebec signed an agreement on social programmes in 1999, called the Social Union Framework. How much have you heard about this agreement?" Because this last part of the National Election Study was a mail-back questionnaire, it elicited a lower response rate, with probably a bias overrepresenting the respondents most interested by politics and thus most likely to be aware of SUFA.

37 While 1,495 respondents gave an answer to the awareness question, only 630 responded to the second question, with 136 (21.6 percent) saying that they were not sure. The exact question was: "How much do you think the social union agreement has done to improve social programmes?"

38 The exact question was: "How serious a problem do you think it is that Quebec did not sign the agreement?" A total of 629 people responded to this question, and 84 (13.4 percent) said they were not sure.

39 The public consultations component consisted of three regional roundtables (in Saskatoon, Ottawa and Moncton), with invited participants, plus submissions to a Web site — there were 49 submissions by individuals and 43 by national organizations.

40 See Federal/Provincial/Territorial Council on Social Policy Renewal (2003).

41 Mendelsohn and McLean (2002, pp. 33-34).

42 The address is www.sufa-review.ca

43 See also Noël and Martin (2002, pp. 5-15); Noël (2002).

44 Rice and Prince (2000, pp. 30-31 and 207-255).

45 On this issue, see also Prince (2001*a*).

46 See also Prince (2001*b*).

47 Bakvis and Cameron (2002, p. 97).

48 Maioni (2002, pp. 5-9).

49 McIntosh (2002, p. 71).

50 Boychuk (2002, p. 66).

51 On the views of civil servants, see Inwood, Johns and O'Reilly (2001, pp. 23-24). For examples of efforts to think about the implementation of SUFA, see McLean and Dinsdale (2000) and Provincial/Territorial Council on Social Policy Renewal (2001).

52 See, for example, McRoberts (1997) and Mendelsohn (2002).

53 Weiler (2001, p. 57).

54 Weiler (2001, p. 68).

55 Théret (2002, pp. 448-456); De La Porte and Pochet (2002, pp. 11-26).

56 Hemerijck (2002, p. 212).

57 Quebec Liberal Party (2001).

58 Cornellier (2003, p. A1).

59 Boychuk (2002, p. 66). In a similar fashion, Evert A. Lindquist points out that the problem of overlap may not be as dysfunctional as efforts at reducing it might lead us to think. See Lindquist (1999).

60 For instance, in 1992, Robert Bourassa's support for the Charlottetown Accord was dramatically undermined by civil servants who were heard saying in a cell-phone conversation that he had "caved in." See Noël (1994, p. 73).

61 Buzetti and Dutrisac (2003).

62 See St-Hilaire and Lazar (2003); Lazar, St-Hilaire and Tremblay (2003*a*).

63 See Noël (forthcoming).

64 Rice and Prince (2000, pp. 70 and 78).

65 Rice and Prince (2000, pp. 232-255); Esping-Andersen (2002, pp. 1-25); Jenson, (2003).

66 Warren (2002, pp. 677-701); Roese (2002, pp. 149-163).

67 Mendelsohn (2000, pp. 245-273).

68 Mendelsohn and McLean (2002).

Bakvis, Herman, and David M. Cameron. "Old Wine in New Bottles: Post-Secondary Education and the Social Union." In *Building the Social Union: Perspectives, Directions and Challenges*, ed. Tom McIntosh. Regina: Canadian Plains Research Center, University of Regina, 2002.

Battle, Ken, and Sherri Torjman. "The Architecture of Smart Social Policy." Paper presented at the TD Forum on Canada's Standard of Living, Ottawa, October 2002. Available at www.td.com/economics/standard/standard.html

Biggs, Margaret. "Building Blocks for Canada's New Social Union." Working paper no. F02, Family Network. Ottawa: Canadian Policy Research Networks, 1996. Available at www.cprn.org

Blais, André, Elisabeth Gidengil, Richard Nadeau and Neil Nevitte. *Anatomy of a Liberal Victory: Making Sense of the 2000 Canadian Election*. Peterborough: Broadview Press, 2002.

———. *2000 Canadian Election Study*. Montreal: Université de Montréal, 2000. Available at www.fas.umontreal.ca/POL/Ces-eec

Boychuk, Gerard W. "Social Union, Social Assistance: An Early Assessment." In *Building the Social Union: Perspectives, Directions and Challenges*, ed. Tom McIntosh. Regina: Canadian Plains Research Center, University of Regina, 2002.

Brimacombe, Glenn G. "The First Ministers' Accord on Health Care: Can the Discussion Move to Structure from Money?" *Members' Briefing*, 318-01. Ottawa: Conference Board of Canada, May 2001. Available at www.conferenceboard.ca

Bueckert, Dennis. "Klein Casts Doubt on Health Accord: Provinces Didn't Endorse Deal, Alberta Premier Maintains." *Halifax Herald*, February 7, 2003.

Buzetti, Hélène, and Robert Dutrisac. "L'unanimité...à neuf: toutes les provinces sauf le Québec acceptent de participer à la mise sur pied du Conseil national de la santé." *Le Devoir*, September 5, 2003.

Cameron, David, and Richard Simeon. "Intergovernmental Relations in Canada: The Emergence of Collaborative Federalism." *Publius: The Journal of Federalism*, Vol. 32, no. 2 (spring 2002): 49-74.

Canadian Centre for Policy Alternatives. "Alternative Federal Budget 2003: Technical Backgrounder on the Health Accord." Technical Paper #5. Ottawa: February 14, 2003. Available at www.policyalternatives.ca

Commission on Fiscal Imbalance. *A New Division of Financial Resources in Canada*. Quebec: Commission on Fiscal Imbalance, 2002. Available at www.desequilibrefiscal.gouv.qc.ca

Cornellier, Manon. "Paul Martin au *Devoir*: Détente en vue avec les provinces." *Le Devoir*, April 29, 2003.

Courchene, Thomas J. *Celebrating Flexibility: An Interpretive Essay on the Evolution of Canadian Federalism*. Toronto: C.D. Howe Institute, 1995.

De La Porte, Caroline, and Philippe Pochet. "Introduction." In *Building Social Europe through the Open Method of Co-ordination*, ed. Caroline De La Porte and Philippe Pochet. Brussels: P.I.E.-Peter Lang, 2002.

Delpérée, Francis. *Le fédéralisme en Europe*. Paris: PUF, 2000.

European Commission. *Budget, Public Finance Figures of the European Union*, consulted May 7, 2003. Available at http://europa.eu.int/comm/budget/pubfin/index_en.htm

———. *The Budget of the European Union: How Is Your Money Spent?* Europe on the Move Series. Brussels: European Commission, February 2000. Available at http://europa.eu.int/comm/publications/booklets/move/21/index_en.htm

Esping-Andersen, Gøsta. "Towards the Good Society Once Again?" In *Why We Need a New Welfare State*, ed. Gøsta Esping-Andersen. Oxford: Oxford University Press, 2002.

First Ministers of Canada. *2003 First Ministers' Accord on Health Care Renewal*. Ottawa: First Ministers' Meeting, February 5, 2003. Available at www.scics.gc.ca

———. *Communiqué on Health*. News release, ref: 800-038-004. Ottawa: First Ministers' Meeting, September 11, 2000. Available at www.scics.gc.ca

Federal/Provincial/Territorial Council of Social Policy Renewal. "Rapporteur's Report on the Social Union Framework Agreement Roundtables." In *Three Year Review Social Union Framework Agreement*, Appendix A, June 2003. Available at www.sufa-review.ca

———. "Web Site Submissions Summary." In *Three Year Review Social Union Framework Agreement*, Appendix A, June 2003. Available at www.sufa-review.ca

Friendly, Martha. "Is This as Good as It Gets? Child Care as a Test Case for Assessing the Social Union Framework Agreement." *Canadian Review of Social Policy*, Vol. 47 (2001): 77-82.

Government of Canada. "Speech from the Throne to Open the Second Session of the Thirty-fifth Parliament of Canada." Ottawa, February 27, 1996. Available at www.pco-bcp.gc.ca

Gray, Jeff. "Health Deal Ignores North, Territories Say." *The Globe and Mail*, February 6, 2003.

Greenspon, Edward, and Anthony Wilson-Smith. *Double Vision: The Inside Story of the Liberals in Power.* Toronto: Doubleday, 1996.

Guest, Dennis. *The Emergence of Social Security in Canada* (2nd edition). Vancouver: University of British Columbia Press, 1985.

Harper, Tim, and Les Whittington. "$35B for Medicare Not Enough: Premiers Complain Cash Doesn't Match Romanow Findings," *Toronto Star*, February 6, 2003.

Hemerijck, Anton. "The Self-Transformation of the European Social Model(s)." In *Why We Need a New Welfare State*, ed. Gøsta Esping-Andersen. Oxford: Oxford University Press, 2002.

Human Resources Development Canada. *Improving Social Security in Canada: A Discussion Paper.* Ottawa: Supply and Services Canada, 1994.

Internal Trade Secretariat. "Strengthening Canada: Challenges for Internal Trade and Mobility – Conference Proceedings." National Conference on Internal Trade and Mobility in Canada, Toronto, May 31-June 1, 2001. Available at www.intrasec.mb.ca under "public consultation."

Inwood, Gregory J., Carolyn M. Johns and Patricia L. O'Reilly. "Who Is Doing What, with Whom, and How? The Roles, Responsibilities and Functions of Intergovernmental Officials." Paper prepared for the State of the Federation Conference, Institute of Intergovernmental Relations, Kingston, November 2-3, 2001.

Jenson, Jane. "Redesigning the 'Welfare Mix' for Families: Policy Challenges." Discussion Paper — Family Network, no. F30. Ottawa: Canadian Policy Research Networks, February 2003. Available at www.cprn.org

Laghi, Brian. "Ministers Take Step Toward Health Council." *The Globe and Mail*, September 5, 2003.

Laghi, Brian, and Campbell Clark. "Health Council Finally Coming, PM Says." *The Globe and Mail*, August 20, 2003.

Lazar, Harvey. "In Search of a New Mission Statement for Canadian Fiscal Federalism." In *Canada: The State of the Federation 1999/2000: Toward a New Mission Statement for Canadian Fiscal Federalism*, ed. Harvey Lazar. Montreal and Kingston: McGill-Queen's University Press, 2000a.

———. "The Social Union Framework Agreement and the Future of Fiscal Federalism." In *Canada: The State of the Federation 1999/2000: Toward a New Mission Statement for Canadian Fiscal Federalism*, ed. Harvey Lazar. Montreal and Kingston: McGill-Queen's University Press, 2000b.

Lazar, Harvey, France St-Hilaire and Jean-François Tremblay. "Vertical Fiscal Imbalance: Myth or Reality?" In *Money, Politics and Health Care: Reconstructing the Federal-Provincial Partnership*, ed. Harvey Lazar and France St-Hilaire. Montreal: Institute for Research on Public Policy and Institute of Intergovernmental Relations, 2003a.

——. "Federal Health Care Funding: Toward a New Fiscal Pact." In *Money, Politics and Health Care: Reconstructing the Federal-Provincial Partnership*, ed. Harvey Lazar and France St-Hilaire. Montreal: Institute for Research on Public Policy and Institute of Intergovernmental Relations, 2003*b*.

Lindquist, Evert A. "Efficiency, Reliability, or Innovation? Managing Overlap and Interdependence in Canada's Federal System of Governance." In *Stretching the Federation: The Art of the State in Canada*, ed. Robert Young. Kingston: Institute of Intergovernmental Relations, 1999.

Macdonald, Mark R. "The Agreement on Internal Trade: Trade-offs for Economic Union and Federalism." In *Canadian Federalism: Performance, Effectiveness, and Legitimacy*, ed. Herman Bakvis and Grace Skogstad. Don Mills: Oxford University Press, 2002.

Maioni, Antonia. "Roles and Responsibilities in Health Care Policy." Discussion paper no. 34. Ottawa: Commission on the Future of Health Care in Canada, November 2002. Available at www.healthcarecommission.ca

Martin, Paul. *Budget Speech*. Ottawa: Finance Canada, February 27, 1995. Available at www.fin.gc.ca

McIntosh, Tom. "When Good Times Turn Bad: The Social Union and Labour Market Policy." In *Building the Social Union: Perspectives, Directions and Challenges*, ed. Tom McIntosh. Regina: Canadian Plains Research Center, University of Regina, 2002.

McLean, John, and Geoff Dinsdale. *Implementing the Social Union Framework Agreement: A Learning and Reference Tool*. Document prepared for the CCMD Roundtable on the Implementation of the Social Union Framework Agreement, Ottawa: Canadian Centre for Management Development, 2000. Available at www.ccmd-ccg.gc.ca

McRoberts, Kenneth. *Misconceiving Canada: The Struggle for National Unity*. Don Mills: Oxford University Press, 1997.

Mendelsohn, Matthew. "Four Dimensions of Political Culture in Canada Outside Quebec: The Changing Nature of Brokerage and the Definition of the Canadian Nation." In *Canada: The State of the Federation 2001: Canadian Political Culture(s) in Transition*, ed. Hamish Telford and Harvey Lazar. Kingston: Institute of Intergovernmental Relations, 2002.

——. "Public Brokerage: Constitutional Reform, Public Participation, and the Accommodation of Mass Publics." *Canadian Journal of Political Science*, Vol. 33, no. 2 (June 2000): 245-273.

Mendelsohn, Matthew, and John McLean. "Getting Engaged: Strengthening SUFA through Citizen Engagement." In *Building the Social Union: Perspectives, Directions and Challenges*, ed. Tom McIntosh. Regina: Canadian Plains Research Center, University of Regina, 2002.

Moravcsik, Andrew. "Federalism in the European Union: Rhetoric and Reality." In *The Federal Vision: Legitimacy and Levels of Governance in the United States and the European Union*, ed. Kalypso Nicolaidis and Robert Howse. Oxford: Oxford University Press, 2001.

Noël, Alain. "A Report That Almost No One Has Discussed: Responses to Quebec's Commission on Fiscal Imbalance." In *Canadian Fiscal Arrangements: What Works, What Might Work Better*, ed. Harvey Lazar. Montreal and Kingston: McGill-Queen's University Press, forthcoming.

——. *A Law Against Poverty: Quebec's New Approach to Combating Poverty and Social Exclusion*. Background Paper, Family Network. Ottawa: Canadian Policy Research Networks, December 2002. Available at www.cprn.org

——. "General Study of the Framework Agreement." In *The Canadian Social Union without Quebec: Eight Critical Analyses*, ed. Alain G. Gagnon and Hugh Segal. Montreal: Institute for Research on Public Policy, 2000*a*.

——. "Without Quebec: Collaborative Federalism with a Footnote?" *Policy Matters*, Vol. 1, no. 2 (March 2000*b*).

———. "Deliberating a Constitution: The Meaning of the Canadian Referendum of 1992." In *Constitutional Predicament: Canada After the Referendum of 1992*, ed. Curtis Cook. Montreal and Kingston: McGill-Queen's University Press, 1994.

Noël, Alain, and Claude Martin. "La démocratisation du social." In *Lien social et politiques*, no. 48 (autumn 2002): 5-15.

Premiers of Canada. *Health Care Remains Premiers' Number One Priority*. News release, ref: 850-092-016. Charlottetown: 44th Annual Premiers' Conference, 11 July 2003a. Available at www.scics.gc.ca

———. *Premiers Announce Plan to Build a New Era of Constructive and Cooperative Federalism*. News release, ref: 850-092-006. Charlottetown: 44th Annual Premiers' Conference, 10 July 2003b. Available at www.scics.gc.ca

Prince, Michael J. "Canadian Federalism and Disability Policy Making." *Canadian Journal of Political Science*, Vol. 34, no. 4 (December 2001a): 809-815.

———. "Citizenship by Instalments: Federal Policies for Canadians with Disabilities." In *How Ottawa Spends 2001-2002: Power in Transition*, ed. Leslie A. Pal. Don Mills: Oxford University Press, 2001b.

Provincial/Territorial Council on Social Policy Renewal. *Progress Report to Premiers*, No. 6, August 1-3, 2001. Available at www.scics.gc.ca

Quebec Liberal Party. *An Action Plan: Affirmation, Autonomy and Leadership*. Montreal: Quebec Liberal Party, October 2001. Available at www.plq.org

Rice, James J., and Michael J. Prince. *Changing Politics of Canadian Social Policy*. Toronto: University of Toronto Press, 2000.

Rocher, François. "Economic Partnership and Political Integration: Recasting Quebec-Canada's Economic Union." In *Beyond the Impasse: Toward Reconciliation*, ed. Roger Gibbins and Guy Laforest. Montreal: Institute for Research on Public Policy, 1998.

Roese, Neal J. "Canadians' Shrinking Trust in Government: Causes and Consequences."

In *Value Change and Governance in Canada*, ed. Neil Nevitte. Toronto: University of Toronto Press, 2002.

Romanow, Roy J. *Building on Values: The Future of Health Care in Canada. Final Report*. Ottawa: Commission on the Future of Health Care in Canada, 2002. Available at www.healthcarecommission.ca

Russell, Peter H. *Constitutional Odyssey: Can Canadians Become a Sovereign People?* 2nd ed. Toronto: University of Toronto Press, 1993.

Scharpf, Fritz W. *Governing in Europe: Effective and Democratic?* Oxford: Oxford University Press, 1999.

Standing Senate Committee on Social Affairs, Science and Technology. *The Health of Canadians — The Federal Role*. Final Report on the State of the Health Care System in Canada (committee chaired by the Honourable Michael J. L. Kirby). Ottawa: The Senate, October 2002. Available at www.parl.gc.ca

St-Hilaire, France, and Harvey Lazar. "He Said, She Said: The Debate on Vertical Fiscal Imbalance and Federal Health Care Funding." *Policy Options*, Vol. 24, no. 2 (February 2003).

TD Economics. "Canadian Government Finances; Appendix 1 — The February 2003 First Ministers Health Accord." Toronto, TD Bank Financial Group, February 11, 2003. Available at www.td.com/economics

Théret, Bruno. *Protection sociale et fédéralisme: L'Europe dans le miroir de l'Amérique du Nord*. Montreal and Brussels: Presses de l'Université de Montréal and P.I.E.-Peter Lang, 2002.

Walkom, Thomas, "Two Key Romanow Points Are Neglected," *Toronto Star*, February 6, 2003.

Warren, Mark E. "What Can Democratic Participation Mean Today?" *Political Theory*, Vol. 30, no. 5 (October 2002): 677-701.

Watts, Ronald L. "Managing Interdependence in a Federal Political System." In *The Art of the State: Governance in a World without Frontiers*, ed. Thomas J. Courchene and

Donald J. Savoie. Montreal: Institute for Research on Public Policy, 2003.

——. *The Spending Power in Federal Systems: A Comparative Study*. Kingston: Institute of Intergovernmental Relations, 1999.

Webber, Jeremy. *Reimagining Canada: Language, Culture, Community, and the Canadian Constitution*. Montreal and Kingston: McGill-Queen's University Press, 1994.

Weiler, Joseph H.H. "Federalism without Constitutionalism: Europe's *Sonderweg*." In *The Federal Vision: Legitimacy and Levels of Governance in the United States and the European Union*, ed. Kalypso Nicolaidis and Robert Howse. Oxford: Oxford University Press, 2001.

——. "The Reformation of European Constitutionalism." *Journal of Common Market Studies*, Vol. 35, no. 1 (March 1997): 123-124.

White, Linda A. "The Child Care Agenda and the Social Union." In *Canadian Federalism: Performance, Effectiveness and Legitimacy*, ed. Herman Bakvis and Grace Skogstad. Don Mills: Oxford University Press, 2002.

S h i f t i n g   S a n d s :
E x p l o r i n g   t h e
P o l i t i c a l   F o u n d a t i o n s
o f   S U F A

I n t r o d u c t i o n

T HE ESTABLISHMENT OF THE SOCIAL UNION FRAMEWORK AGREEMENT (SUFA) ON
February 4, 1999, was greeted by some as a potentially fundamental transformation of the Canadian federal system that would bring an unprecedented
level of cooperation, formality and civility to intergovernmental relations. SUFA
also promised a new era of citizen involvement in what had theretofore been the
shrouded world of intergovernmental relations. Others were less impressed or
optimistic, and pointed to Quebec's exclusion from SUFA as a major flaw that
would promote a new form of 9-1-1 federalism[1] and perhaps grease the skids for
Quebec sovereignty.[2] Then, the signing of the health accord in the early fall of
2000 brought Quebec into the SUFA framework, at least in the critically important area of health policy.[3] The health accord moderated concerns about Quebec's
exclusion and thus tipped the balance toward a more positive assessment of
SUFA. As a consequence, the mandated review of SUFA and its potential extension in 2002 takes on considerable significance.

This is therefore an appropriate time to ask whether SUFA represents a
watershed in the evolution of the Canadian federal state. The question is not only
of historical interest, for the answer will tell us how much importance we should
invest in the upcoming SUFA review. In short, does SUFA matter?

This question is, of course, too large for one author to address satisfactorily. My more limited goal is to assess the political foundations upon which SUFA
rests and how they may have shifted since February 1999. This assessment of
SUFA's political foundations speaks directly to the prospects for a positive review.
At the same time, it brings into play the larger issue of the importance of the

agreement. SUFA will be extended or re-energized only if it continues to meet the needs of those driving Canadian intergovernmental relations. It is by no means clear that this will be the case.

The Creation of SUFA

SUFA EMERGED OUT OF A PARTICULAR SET OF POLITICAL CIRCUMSTANCES. IN THE early stages of negotiations that began in December 1997, provincial and territorial governments sought some formal constraint on the federal government's spending power. This pursuit followed significant cuts in federal transfers that had compounded the fiscal crisis facing provincial and territorial governments in the late 1990s. The cuts fanned a chronic fear that Ottawa would use its spending power to establish new programs and then, in times of duress, reduce its funding and leave the provinces holding an empty financial envelope. It was hoped, therefore, that SUFA would provide a mechanism that would not preclude federal government involvement in provincial areas of jurisdiction, but would ensure that such involvement would take place within a mutually agreed upon and predictable federal-provincial framework. In short, the spending power would be transformed from a federal government regulatory device into a multi-lateral device designed to meet the contemporary federal realities of fiscal imbalance and policy interdependence.

More generally, and perhaps more importantly, SUFA was promoted as a way to demonstrate that Canadian governments could work together in a productive and civil fashion, and that intergovernmental friction need not impair social programs designed to meet citizens' needs and aspirations. SUFA was meant to convince Canadians that the positive renewal of the federation was possible outside the constitutional arena, a project that fell a bit flat when Quebec refused to play. Nonetheless, SUFA was thought to provide an attractive framework should a nonsovereignist government come to power in Quebec. If a suitable intergovernmental stadium could be built, it was hoped and even assumed that Quebec would eventually come to play.

When the initial discussions about SUFA began, all Canadian governments were facing acute financial constraints. However, as the signing date approached, the fiscal circumstances of the federal government improved dramatically, and

Ottawa was able to put cash on the table in exchange for looser constraints on its spending power.[4] Thus what had begun in large part as a provincial and territorial initiative to bell the federal spending power ended up as a framework to facilitate federal government involvement in provincial programs. Such involvement would no longer be unilateral, but neither would it be curtailed. As Robson and Schwanen conclude: "It is clear that the lure of money swayed the nine provinces that signed the deal away from their unanimous stance in favour of restraining the spending power."[5]

SUFA therefore rested on a broad intergovernmental coalition glued together by financial self-interest. Admittedly, the exclusion of Quebec was a concern, particularly for those who feared that SUFA-without-Quebec would morph into a de facto government for English Canada (or for the "Rest of Canada") and would thereby encourage Quebec independence. Nonetheless, Quebec's exclusion did not raise the alarm bells that would have sounded a decade earlier if the redesign of federal arrangements had been indifferent to Quebec's participation. There was a sense that SUFA constituted a turning point in the evolution of the Canadian federal state, or would if its underlying coalition could hold together long enough for new patterns of intergovernmental relations to be locked into place. It is to this "if" that the present discussion is directed.

Before assessing the durability of the SUFA coalition, I would like to address a potential misinterpretation of my position. I am not arguing that SUFA rests *only* upon a particular combination of political circumstances and interests. As I have argued elsewhere,[6] the logic of SUFA fits better with the emerging world of e-government and e-democracy than does a conventional understanding of Canadian federalism. In a world where silos of any description — territorial or jurisdictional — are under assault by information and communications technologies and where citizens will soon have single electronic portals to all branches and levels of government, SUFA is very much in step with the times. It fits into a world where boundaries are increasingly blurred, where jurisdictional lines on maps seem obsolete and where managing interdependence is the challenge for contemporary governments. SUFA also addresses the perennial problems with the federal spending power and the equally perennial desire on the part of citizens for greater civility in intergovernmental relations. It therefore connects to a political universe that is larger than that circumscribed by intergovernmental relations.

At the same time, SUFA is only shallowly implanted in the soil of Canadian federalism. It has almost no public visibility and therefore no public constituency that would come to its defence should the support by the political actors wane. SUFA lacks an audience, much less champions outside the intergovernmental arena. If SUFA were to die, few Canadians would notice the obituary, much less mourn its passing. Therefore, until it acquires deeper roots, the shifting intergovernmental sands upon which it rests are of great importance to the prospects for a successful review.

Shifting Political Dynamics

BOTH SUFA AND THE 2000 HEALTH ACCORD WERE PRODUCTS OF THEIR TIMES, THE results of a particular set of political circumstances confronting the federal and provincial/territorial governments. Many of those circumstances have now changed, in some cases quite dramatically. The question, then, is whether the SUFA edifice can remain standing on these shifting political sands. In asking this question, we are not assuming a negative answer, for we know that political institutions, once created, often demonstrate remarkable staying power even when faced with political circumstances that are very different from those that attended their birth. The Canadian Senate springs to mind. Institutional inertia is difficult to overcome. Nonetheless, it is important to explore how the incentives and disincentives have changed for the parties participating in SUFA. Given that its foundations have only had two years to set, the matter of stability is not a minor one.

The Government of Canada

ALTHOUGH SUFA DID NOT ORIGINATE WITH THE FEDERAL GOVERNMENT, IT WAS INItially attractive to Ottawa as a project to demonstrate the nonconstitutional renewal of federalism. In this respect, it has been a modest success, even though its public profile has been very low. It has brought governments together in a generally productive and civil environment, and it has provided a vehicle for federal involvement in provincial program areas without overly constraining the spending power. Although this pattern of intergovernmental relations is by no means new, it has been reinforced and, to a degree, institutionalized by SUFA. If it has fallen short as a transformative step, it must still be judged a success from the federal government's perspective. It has hinted at the potential for nonconstitutional renewal of federalism while at the same time keeping the federal government fully in play with respect to provincial social programs. The question now is whether there are incentives for the federal government to adopt an aggressive "go forward" strategy for the SUFA review. Should it seek to expand or consolidate the agreement?

The incentives for adopting a "go forward" strategy at first glance appear to be weak. SUFA originally arose from the desire of the provinces to bring the federal spending power under federal-provincial control, and thus prevent a repeat of the financial offloading that had slammed provincial budgets in the mid-1990s. There was never much enthusiasm for this on the federal side, and now there will be even less. The 2000 election can be interpreted as an endorsement of an activist stance by the federal government with respect to provincial areas of jurisdiction such as health care. The fragmentation of the opposition voice in Parliament and the collapse of the Canadian Alliance have also removed any immediate electoral threat to an entrenched Liberal hegemony. An assertive stance toward the use of the spending power therefore carries no electoral risk beyond that which provincial governments might be able to mobilize.

One of the problematic aspects of SUFA from the federal government's perspective was the promise of a dispute settlement mechanism that could be applied to the use of the federal spending power and the interpretation of national standards. The push for a dispute settlement mechanism came from the provinces. Its logic closely follows the argument that provincial governments have met with considerable success in international treaty negotiations and with no success in negotiating a role for themselves in the appointment of justices to the Supreme Court of Canada. There is something odd about referees in federal-provincial disputes being appointed unilaterally by one side, and it is hardly surprising the provinces sought a more balanced dispute settlement mechanism for SUFA.

To date, no progress has been made on this front.[7] It could be argued, of course, that progress is just a matter of time; after all, it has only been two years since SUFA was put into effect, and two years is but a blink of an eye in federal-provincial relations. However, there is unlikely to be progress in the future. The 2000 federal election demonstrated the appeal to the Government of Canada of a unilateral dispute settlement mechanism in which it, and it alone, would be the arbiter of how well provincial governments are adhering to national values and national standards.

The Liberal campaign attack on the Canadian Alliance in the 2000 election, expressed as overt criticism of the Alberta government over alleged transgressions of the *Canada Health Act,* would not have been possible had a federal-provincial dispute settlement mechanism been in place. The Alberta government could have deflected federal attacks over to the dispute settlement process, which would in turn have taken them off the table during the federal election campaign in much the same way that policy debate can be frozen when a matter is "before the courts." The federal government may well want to retain the option of picking and choosing when to challenge provincial governments: when to spring into action, as it did in the case of Alberta's Bill 11, and when to take no action, as it did when faced with the virtually identical response to health care waiting lists in other provinces, like Ontario.[8] Ottawa's post-election embrace of the national leadership provided by the Alberta government and its premier, and the prime minister's musings about health care options that were condemned by his party during the election campaign, further demonstrate the desire to be unconstrained by formal federal-provincial agreements.

As a consequence, it is difficult to see how a dispute settlement mechanism will ever appeal to the federal government, which, of all parties, has the most to lose. The capacity to be arbitrary, even capricious, in the enforcement of national standards, is too great a political asset to surrender. Even more important is the political capital that comes from being the sole arbiter of national values and standards; this is a torch that Ottawa will not pass to some low-profile federal-provincial adjudication process that might in any event come up with the "wrong" answer. Thus, in the case of a dispute settlement mechanism, the promise of SUFA has come up short with little prospect of future improvement.

There may be a more general reluctance on behalf of the federal government to formalize anything. With substantial financial capacity and an iron grip on national office, there is little interest in any agreement that might limit its scope of action. The current government has been well served by an institutional status quo that favours the concentration of political power in the hands of the prime minister,[9] precludes any effective check on executive power and provides solid majority governments with 40 percent (plus or minus 2 percent) of the national popular vote. A more robust SUFA, particularly one with an effective dispute settlement mechanism, would work against the logic and architecture of power in Ottawa unless, as Noël argues, SUFA is seen as a way to increase central control of Canadian social policy.[10] In this context it should also be noted that federal-provincial conflict has been an important electoral asset to the federal Liberals. Battles with provincial governments in Quebec shore up the Liberal Party's credentials as the country's best line of defence against the sovereignists, just as battles with Alberta shore up the party's credentials in Ontario as the country's best line of defence against the conservative "forces of darkness" oozing north from the United States and east from Alberta. A more institutionalized SUFA, complete with a dispute settlement mechanism, would tie the federal government's hands.

The review of SUFA will most likely be approached by the federal government with a single, dominant question in mind: will the agreement reinforce rather than threaten the status quo? All of the above suggests that the Government of Canada will display little enthusiasm for an aggressive "go forward" strategy in the review. SUFA is the proverbial sleeping dog that should be left to lie, particularly if an economic downturn temporarily blunts Ottawa's interest in an expanded social policy agenda. However, there is one consideration that may generate greater enthusiasm. The federal government's prosperity, innovation and children's agendas may be difficult to advance without the full involvement of provincial and territorial governments, given that education, training programs, investment incentives and the strengthening of the university research sector all bring provincial and territorial governments into play. For the federal government, the litmus test for SUFA may well be the degree to which it can help move forward these agendas. If it can, then its review may be addressed with greater enthusiasm than the above-mentioned caveats might suggest. Yet this is a big "if," as the federal government's capacity for unilateral action even in these policy fields has been demonstrated by initiatives such as the Millennium Scholarship Foundation and the Innovation Fund.

One final concern is how the SUFA review might fold into the federal government's national unity strategy should the national unity issue once more move to the top of the federal government's priorities. Will SUFA provide the high ground from which to fight new pressure from Quebec sovereignists or the embers of Western alienation? To address this issue, we must in turn look at how the provincial and territorial governments are likely to address the SUFA review.

The Provincial and Territorial Governments

SUFA EVOLVED FROM BEING A PROVINCIAL AND TERRITORIAL INITIATIVE TO BEING A federal/provincial/territorial agreement in part because it provided a postreferendum opportunity to demonstrate to federalists in Quebec that nonconstitutional renewal of the federal system was possible. (How this was to be done, given Quebec's exclusion, remains somewhat of a mystery to analysts outside Quebec.) It makes sense, then, to begin with Quebec. It is difficult and unwise for a Quebec outsider to attempt to assess what the replacement of Lucien Bouchard with Bernard Landry has meant for Quebec's attitude toward SUFA. Nonetheless, it is impossible to see a positive engagement with the SUFA review in Quebec as an integral part of Landry's campaign to be the "last premier of Quebec." Everything about Mr. Landry's style and beliefs to date underscores hostility to the spirit of SUFA. This would suggest that the 2000 health accord should not be seen as a lasting step toward Quebec's inclusion in SUFA; the accord looks more and more like a one-off agreement keyed to the 2000 federal election campaign.

Pending the next provincial election, the PQ government is unlikely to endorse the extension or expansion of SUFA to Quebec. Given that there are no financial consequences to being outside SUFA, it is more likely that Quebec will seize upon any move in that direction as yet another affront. At the same time, however, SUFA's very low public profile reduces the chances that an intergovernmental imbroglio over its renewal would have much electoral resonance. If Ottawa lets the sleeping dog of SUFA lie, it will be difficult for the Quebec government to awaken the beast.

Recent political developments in the West also do not augur well for the spirit of SUFA. There is likely to be a drift, although by no means a stampede, toward greater provincial autonomy and thus away from the logic of SUFA. This drift will stem in large part from the collapse of the "West wants in" strategy epitomized at one time by the then Reform Party of Canada. For several decades

Western Canadians have pushed this strategy on many fronts: Senate reform, support for the Mulroney Conservatives, the creation of Reform and then the morphing of Reform into the Canadian Alliance. However, the strategy died in the wake of the 2000 federal election. The prospects for a Western-based or even Western-led political party winning national office are remote, and there is little interest on the part of the larger political community in institutional reform. Greater provincial autonomy became the default option, although not one that was passionately embraced, once the "West wants in" strategy was abandoned.

The drift toward greater provincial autonomy will be reinforced in Alberta by the province's burgeoning prosperity. It is difficult to believe that Alberta's improved fiscal circumstances will do anything other than undercut its government's enthusiasm for SUFA. Alberta posted a provincial surplus of more than $7 billion for 2000, a good part of which is a structural surplus stemming from a rapidly diminishing provincial debt and thus shrinking debt-servicing costs. Within two years Alberta will be debt-free and will, quite literally, have more money than it knows what to do with. It is therefore unlikely that Premier Klein would agree again to "sign in blood" any document that would provide greater federal government contributions to health care in exchange for federal conditions. Given the provincial surplus and growing political pressure from the Alberta wing of the National Citizens Coalition and the "Firewall Six,"[11] Premier Klein is more likely to forego federal health care funding than he is to accept greater conditionality.[12]

Although Alberta's political and fiscal circumstances are not representative of those of all Western provinces, the differences between them should not be exaggerated. British Columbia's new Liberal government will have its hands full with a very ambitious and contentious provincial agenda that includes a referendum on the treaty process and a fundamental restructuring of labour relations in the province. As the government seeks to overcome a decade of poor economic performance and at best indifferent fiscal management, it is not clear that the BC Liberals will have the time or the energy to devote much attention to the SUFA review. Nor is it clear that SUFA in any form would give the government additional leverage on its own provincial agenda. In Saskatchewan both the NDP/Liberal coalition government and the government-in-waiting, the Saskatchewan Party, feel bruised by federal indifference to agricultural problems in the province. SUFA, or at least a more robust SUFA, does not appear to be an attractive model for the Saskatchewan

Party. In the West, only Manitoba offers a potentially receptive political climate and government audience for the SUFA review.

Faced with a manifest inability to increase their influence in national affairs and armed with economic prosperity, Western Canadians in general and Albertans in particular will likely turn to protecting and perhaps enhancing the powers of their provincial governments. This may not be an optimal strategy given the strong national identities of most Western Canadians, but it is the only game in town. Part of SUFA's appeal is that it recognizes the interdependence of contemporary governments and tries to structure that interdependence in a positive way. However, if the federal partner is seen as indifferent or even hostile to regional aspirations, interdependence might be a threat. What remains to be seen is whether the prime minister and his government can repair relationships with the West to the point where some degree of enthusiasm for the SUFA review can be generated. This is by no means impossible, but the odds remain long.

The provincial political environment outside the West is more difficult to assess. The logic of SUFA works for the Atlantic provinces, and the federal Liberals used the 2000 election effectively to rebuild their political base in the region. The SUFA review therefore begins there with a generally positive and receptive environment. The situation in Ontario is different, perhaps dramatically so. The intergovernmental battles between the federal government and the Ontario Conservatives are overlaid with intense partisan conflict in a province where the potential election spoils are huge. In no other region are federal and provincial partisan conflicts so conflated. As a consequence, it may be difficult to bring an enthusiastic Mike Harris to the SUFA review. In addition, the federal Liberal caucus from Ontario will not support any SUFA agreement that might reflect well on the Harris government. All in all, it is hard to imagine a more difficult political terrain: Western Canada looks like a cakewalk by comparison.

None of these situations either precludes or guarantees a successful SUFA review. Nonetheless, the provincial scene does suggest that enthusiasm for a "go forward" strategy is limited. None of the large provinces — Ontario, Quebec, British Columbia or Alberta — appears to be poised to lead the SUFA charge. While there may be support for a more positive response to the review from some of the smaller provinces, there is limited interest from the federal government upon which to build. It would appear unlikely, therefore, that the SUFA review will be seized by government players as an opportunity to move the agreement forward in new directions.

Aboriginal Peoples

THE FEDERAL, PROVINCIAL AND TERRITORIAL GOVERNMENTS MAY NOT BE THE ONLY players in the SUFA review. At some point, Aboriginal voices will also want to be heard. If they are not, then it would become difficult to argue that First Nations governments are governments like other orders of government in Canada; their exclusion from the SUFA process would suggest instead that they are analogous to municipal governments, which are also bystanders to the SUFA process. This could be seen as a further retreat from the 1992 high-water mark of Aboriginal influence, when the text of the Charlottetown Accord wove a significant Aboriginal presence into virtually every institutional warp and woof of the Canadian federal state. There is a legitimate concern, therefore, that the review and potential reinvigoration of SUFA could further marginalize Aboriginal peoples. Not only would this marginalization be symbolically important, but it could also have more immediate and practical effects if SUFA shapes the evolution of Canadian social policy.

While this is an important concern, it is also important to note that we are not even close to constructing an effective interface between Aboriginal peoples and federal institutions.[13] In the case of SUFA, the construction of such an interface is rendered exceedingly difficult by the complexities on both sides. The SUFA process includes dozens of working groups, tables and ministerial committees. It is even difficult for the smaller provinces to participate effectively across the whole range of SUFA, and for the much larger number of much smaller First Nations governments the task is all but impossible. For those segments of the Aboriginal population such as the Métis, who do not have functional governments, the intergovernmental maze of SUFA is impossible to navigate.

What is required as a minimal condition for effective Aboriginal participation in intergovernmental affairs is an Aboriginal peak organization, or perhaps a small handful of peak organizations representing the constitutionally recognized categories of Aboriginal peoples.[14] Ideally, these organizations would be able to speak with authority on behalf of their constituent governments and would ensure that bargains struck at the SUFA tables were kept. They would be able to provide an ongoing and effective intergovernmental presence, thereby ensuring an Aboriginal voice was heard. However, we are probably a generation or more away from the creation of such Aboriginal peak organizations. The primary focus of Aboriginal political activity at present is either at the band or First Nations level or in the courts. There is no interest in surrendering even a portion of hard-won community autonomy to a peak organization. Thus we confront a fundamental structural dilemma that will preclude effective Aboriginal participation in the SUFA process.

This is not a fatal flaw for SUFA, which could work quite well for the non-Aboriginal governments representing the vast bulk of the Canadian population and intergovernmental community. Nonetheless, it is a weakness that should be recognized even if it cannot be readily corrected. The symbolic aspects of Aboriginal exclusion could be reinforced by the federal government's decision to launch a legislative review of the *Indian Act* at the same time that the SUFA review will be moving forward. This decision, which is already attracting a great deal of critical commentary from First Nations, could inflict some collateral damage on the SUFA review process.

Canadian Citizens

A LONG WITH THE PROMISE OF A DISPUTE SETTLEMENT MECHANISM, SUFA HELD OUT the promise of greater citizen involvement in the construction and assessment of government programs.[15] While it is not clear that anyone had any idea how to square citizen involvement with the dense thicket of intergovernmental relations created by SUFA, there was at least the hope that program performance indicators would give citizens a better opportunity to hold governments accountable. SUFA, then, reflected a loosely defined populist impulse that spilled into Canadian politics from the Quebec referenda, the national plebiscite on the Charlottetown Accord and the Reform Party of Canada. The underlying question is whether the initial promise of citizen involvement will ensure that Canadian citizens are at the table, at least in spirit, as the SUFA review begins.

Has a new form of federalism — less intergovernmental, more citizen-oriented — been ushered in by SUFA? The short answer must be no. Indeed, I would argue that SUFA represents the decisive triumph of intergovernmentalism over populism. SUFA has not only constructed a more complex intergovernmental process, but it has effectively drawn a veil across its operations. If anything,

transparency has been reduced, as governments meet more often in settings that
are less open to public scrutiny or even knowledge. As Alain Noël explains:

> For an external observer, it is becoming increasingly difficult to keep track of
> an evolution that is rapid, multi-faceted and fine-grained. Progress reports
> list a variety of minute achievements that do not add up easily into a cohe-
> sive or meaningful whole. In many instances, the progress seems to lie more
> in the process than in tangible policy outcomes.[16]

Perhaps there are citizen involvement reforms to come, but there are few signs of
government leadership or enthusiasm in this respect. Nor, for that matter, does there
appear to be much public interest. The populist surge of the 1990s is in retreat. Voter
turnout is in decline, and citizens confront a 24/7 world that offers less time for political
involvement. Faced with political processes that are increasingly opaque and governments that seem immune to electoral challenge, citizens can be forgiven if they turn their
attention elsewhere. Thus while the verdict is still out on whether SUFA and the 2000
health accord constitute significant milestones in the evolution of the Canadian federal
state, a positive verdict is unlikely to stem from the promise of citizen involvement.

This conclusion is not intended to slight the progress that individual governments are making within their own domains to increase citizen participation and
government accountability. There has been a good deal of experimentation with performance measures and innovative forms of citizen participation in the policy
process. The new Liberal government in British Columbia has even begun to telecast
some cabinet meetings. Rather, the point is that SUFA has done nothing to open up
the intergovernmental process to public scrutiny, and at the same time it has made
this process more important than ever for governance in the Canadian federal state.[17]

Conclusions

IT WOULD BE AN EXAGGERATION TO CLAIM THAT A SEA CHANGE HAS OCCURRED IN
Canadian intergovernmental relations since SUFA was signed in 1999 or since
the health accord was reached in 2000. However, it would also be premature to
conclude that SUFA is in danger of dying, as its own performance review has yet
to begin. Indeed, given the force of institutional inertia, SUFA is likely to survive.
Killing SUFA is fraught with political risks, and so having it lumber along is an

attractive alternative. SUFA may have failed to meet some important expectations, but it is difficult to argue that it has inflicted any real damage on intergovernmental relations. Its demise is not in sight.

At the same time, enthusiasm for SUFA among Canadian governments is in decline. Provincial and territorial governments in general, and the Alberta government in particular, enjoy greater financial security and are therefore less attracted by the financial inducements that brokered SUFA. The federal government also enjoys much greater financial capacity, barring a major downturn in the Canadian economy, and therefore has the capacity for unilateral action. In addition, the role of an enforcer able at its own discretion to take provincial transgressors to task is too attractive for the federal government to abandon to a dispute settlement mechanism. On top of all this, Aboriginal organizations are unlikely to approach the SUFA review with anything other than extreme wariness.

Finally, what about Canadians at large? Will they help sustain and perhaps reinvigorate SUFA? This too looks unlikely. SUFA has a very low public profile, and little is being done to raise that profile and convince Canadians that SUFA matters to their lives and aspirations. The upside of this is that Canadian voters are unlikely to hold governments accountable for failing to meet expectations of which they are unaware. The downside is that the rhetoric of citizen involvement rings hollow. SUFA is a still somewhat shaky monument to intergovernmentalism, and intergovernmentalism has never been a favourite child of the Canadian public.

SUFA was meant to demonstrate that nonconstitutional reform of the Canadian federal state was possible. The danger with this strategy was that such reform might proceed without Quebec, and would therefore further isolate the province. That concern has been moderated, and the "exclusion" of Quebec has not significantly damaged the fabric of national unity. However, given the generally antagonistic stance of the Landry government to things federal, and given, therefore, that any progress over the next two years will necessarily be without Quebec, it may be that the best course is to let the SUFA review slide past with little serious attention being paid to it. Canadians at large will neither notice nor care, Aboriginal organizations will be relieved, provincial administrations will have more autonomy, the Quebec government will have a smaller target and the Government of Canada will not face the potential constraints of a dispute settlement mechanism. In short, let's recognize SUFA as a modest reshuffling of the intergovernmental deck in Canada and not a new game.

1   The term 9-1-1 federalism refers to a situation whereby the Government of Canada would meet with the 10 provincial governments minus Quebec (the "9"), and then bargain bilaterally with Quebec. The territorial governments should also be included, in which case the expression would be "12-1-1." See Gibbins (1999, pp. 216-217).

2   Noël (2000) provides one of the most comprehensive and damning critiques.

3   First Ministers of Canada (2000).

4   Alain Noël accepts the role played by financial inducements but correctly notes that increased federal health care spending was inevitable, with or without SUFA. The provincial concessions with respect to the spending power were not necessary. See Noël (2000, p. 9).

5   Robson and Schwanen (1999, p. 3).

6   Gibbins (2000, pp. 684-685).

7   Although provinces have undertaken discussions on this issue. See Provincial-Territorial Council on Social Policy Renewal (2000, Appendix A).

8   Ibbitson (2001, p. A4).

9   Savoie (1999).

10   Noël (2000).

11   The Firewall Six, consisting of Stephen Harper, Tom Flanagan, Ted Morton, Rainer Knopff, Andrew Crook and Ken Boessenkool, wrote an "Open Letter to Ralph Klein." It proposes that Alberta withdraw from the Canada Pension Plan, collect its own tax revenue, prepare for the creation of a provincial police force to replace the RCMP, resume provincial responsibility for health care policy and use Section 88 of the Supreme Court's reference case on the secession of Quebec to put Senate reform back on the national agenda.

12   Alberta's fiscal autonomy may increase Ottawa's interest in a dispute settlement mechanism that could be used to bring moral suasion into play when the threat of punitive cuts in federal transfers loses its power. Thanks to David Cameron for pointing this out to me.

13   The failure to design such an interface was one of the major shortcomings of the Royal Commission on Aboriginal Peoples.

14   The case for Aboriginal peak organizations is made at length in Roslinski (2001). Roslinski argues convincingly that such organizations are essential if Aboriginal governments are to be incorporated effectively into the intergovernmental framework of the Canadian federal state.

15   In his own comprehensive proposal published just before SUFA was signed, Daniel Schwanen linked citizen involvement and the dispute settlement mechanism by arguing that citizens should have access to this mechanism with respect to mobility rights and the portability of programs. See Schwanen (1999, pp. 27-28).

16   Noël (2000, p. 6).

17   Ottawa has opened a Website at http://www.unionsociale.gc.ca, as an attempt to expand citizen involvement. But this is not sufficient to alter the line of argument presented here.

First Ministers of Canada. *Communiqué on Health.*
    News release, ref: 800-038-004. Ottawa:
    First Ministers' Meeting, September 11,
    2000. Available at www.scics.gc.ca

Gibbins, Roger. "Federalism in a Digital World."
    Canadian Journal of Political Science, Vol. 33,
    no. 4 (December 2000): 684-685.

——. "Taking Stock: Canadian Federalism and
    its Constitutional Framework." In *How
    Ottawa Spends, 1999-2000*, ed. Leslie A.
    Pal. Toronto: Oxford University Press,
    1999.

Ibbitson, John. "Private Cancer Care Raises Few
    Objections." *The Globe and Mail*, February
    20, 2001, A4.

Noël, Alain. "Without Quebec: Collaborative
    Federalism with a Footnote?" *Policy Matters*,
    Vol. 1, no. 2 (March 2000).

Provincial/Territorial Council on Social Policy
    Renewal. *Interim Report to Premiers*, no. 5,
    August 10, 2000.

Robson, William B.P., and Daniel Schwanen.
    "The Social Union Agreement: Too Flawed
    to Last." *Backgrounder* (C.D. Howe
    Institute), February 8, 1999.

Roslinski, John J. "A Peak Aboriginal
    Organization: The Need to Integrate Self-
    Government within Canada." MA thesis,
    University of Calgary, January 2001.

Savoie, Donald. *Governing from the Centre: The
    Concentration of Power in Canadian Politics.*
    Toronto: University of Toronto Press, 1999.

Schwanen, Daniel. "More Than the Sum of Our
    Parts: Improving the Mechanisms of
    Canada's Social Union." C.D. Howe
    Institute, *Commentary* no. 120 (January
    1999), pp. 27-28.

Power   and
Purpose   in
Intergovernmental
Relations

Introduction

O N FEBRUARY 4, 1999, THE FEDERAL GOVERNMENT AND THE GOVERNMENTS OF ALL
the provinces and territories except Quebec agreed to a "Framework to
Improve the Social Union for Canadians." The Social Union Framework
Agreement (SUFA) acknowledged the legitimacy of the federal spending power in
areas of provincial jurisdiction and codified, more or less precisely, the rules that
would govern intergovernmental relations in social policy in the years to come.
As such, the agreement marked a turning point. Many observers also associated
SUFA with a broader trend toward growing intergovernmental collaboration in
the Canadian federation.

SUFA, however, remains a time-bound, administrative and to some extent
unfinished document. One of its clauses explicitly calls on governments to jointly
undertake a full review of the framework agreement and its implementation, and
to make appropriate adjustments by the end of the third year, in February 2002.
In the context of this review, it seems appropriate to reassess SUFA and its significance in the broader framework of intergovernmental relations. This is the purpose of this study, which considers the agreement and subsequent events in light
of longer historical trends in Canadian politics and argues that current changes are
not as collaborative as is suggested by the language of SUFA. To evaluate the
potential for renewal associated with the review process, we must go beyond the
text of the agreement and pay serious attention to the divergent interests of the
governments involved and to the conflicts left open by SUFA.

Consider, first, the standard view. Many observers are positive about the
recent evolution of intergovernmental relations in Canada. They deplore, however,

what they see as a lack of vision in Ottawa and in the provinces. From this point of view, Canadian federalism appears increasingly collaborative but somehow incoherent and disorganized. The collaborative process as such is seen as a success, but the policies it generates appear haphazard, poorly integrated and of uncertain value. A sense of purpose would therefore be needed, a "mission statement" that would set forth common values and objectives and help guide public debates and intergovernmental relations for the years to come.[1] SUFA did put forward common principles and a shared commitment "to work more closely together to meet the needs of Canadians," but these statements apparently did not constitute an effective mission statement. In this perspective, the renewal of the agreement, due in February 2002, could present an opportunity to define and institutionalize collaboratively a more significant mission statement.

There is much truth to this interpretation. Indeed, there is no master plan or explicit vision underlying the various arrangements that have defined Canadian intergovernmental relations and public policies in recent years. Problems appear to be solved one at a time, as they become pressing. Political improvisation, however, may well be the normal way to govern, in Canada and elsewhere. It may also produce coherent policies. As jazz musicians know, improvisation starts from established patterns. It requires ideas and a sense of direction, and generates a largely unplanned yet meaningful production. The patterns and the direction may not be explicit or visible, but they nevertheless structure and give sense to the performance.

This study proposes an interpretation along these lines. In contrast to those who see collaboration and incoherence in Canadian intergovernmental relations, I stress conflict and coherence. To some extent, this is a question of emphasis. Collaboration and conflict are the two ends of a single continuum, and the same is true, of course, of coherence and incoherence. The idea is not to deny the existence of collaboration or the presence of significant incongruities in public policy, but rather to underline the importance of power and purpose in this process. What I propose is not simply a different point of view. In my opinion, it is a more satisfactory representation, an interpretation that better accounts for the current situation and provides more helpful indications about the prospects for the coming years.

The discussion proceeds in three steps. First, after offering some background information, I will present what could be called the "mission statement interpretation" of collaborative federalism, to explain how it accounts for recent developments and what it may suggest for the review and renewal of SUFA. I will

argue that this diagnosis suffers from important anomalies and may not constitute the most useful guide for SUFA's review and adjustment process.

Second, I will offer my own interpretation of collaborative federalism, an
interpretation that emphasizes conflict, power and purpose. The argument is simple and fairly classical. It starts from the idea that, in intergovernmental relations,
governments defend their interests and policy orientations. Even when they remain
implicit, power and purpose matter, and they account for the recent evolution of
Canadian federalism. Without a mission statement, Canadian social policy has
changed significantly in the 1990s, and it has done so in a rather systematic way.
Over the years, intergovernmental arrangements have moved from cost-shared programs and conditional transfers with national standards to almost equal per capita
funding with an emphasis on outcome indicators, and pan-Canadian social programs have evolved from more or less universal entitlements to more or less targeted benefits. In the provinces, policies have changed as well, but not always in the
same direction. As a result, a new welfare state is emerging in Canada, and it cannot be attributed only to fiscal retrenchment or ad hoc responses to new problems.

The last section discusses the political foundations of collaborative federalism and suggests that provincial and territorial governments adjusted their
expectations and demands downward when they accepted the agreement.
Provinces diverge significantly in their orientations toward both federalism and
social policy, and they are not likely to act in a concerted and forceful fashion.
Still, they could alter the course set in 1999. The September 2000 Action Plan for
Health System Renewal (the 2000 health accord) may be instructive in this
respect, because it indicates the potential, as well as the limits, of a stronger
provincial stance on intergovernmental relations.[2]

The conclusion brings the different elements of the argument together
and evokes the broader question of democracy and democratic deliberation in
a federal society.

Collaboration without Purpose?

THE EVOLUTION OF CANADIAN FEDERALISM CAN BE CHARACTERIZED IN LIGHT OF
three interrelated dimensions: the structure of fiscal arrangements, the

nature of intergovernmental relations and the federal government's preferred types of social policy instruments. On this basis, most scholars agree on three distinct periods: the era of cooperative federalism in the 1950s and early 1960s; the era of executive federalism from the middle of the 1960s to the beginning of the 1990s; and the current period of collaborative federalism.[3] Exact time markers cannot be established because transitions are long between each period.

Between the Second World War and the beginning of the 1960s, the federal government was the dominant actor in intergovernmental relations and social policy. During the war the federal government had occupied most of the tax fields, and after 1945 it withdrew only partially.[4] By 1955, Ottawa collected more than two-thirds of all tax revenues (70 percent of the total, compared to 16 percent for the provinces), in a context of economic expansion and welfare state development.[5] Initially, the federal government acted alone, often with the approval of the provinces, and reached Canadians directly with more or less universal income security programs. Unemployment insurance was created in 1940, family allowances in 1945 and old age security in 1952.[6] In areas other than income security, however, such as health care, post-secondary education, social assistance and social services, direct federal expenditures were more difficult. The provinces had clear constitutional jurisdiction and an established capacity to administer these service-oriented programs. In many cases, in health care in particular, some provinces actually were at the forefront of policy innovation.[7] However, instead of leaving more tax room to provinces confronted with rising demands for social programs, the federal government preferred to establish open-ended but conditional cost-shared programs. These programs, along with equalization mechanisms that gave poorer provinces the means to offer comparable services, were used to promote more or less standard measures in areas of provincial jurisdiction. With these transfers and conditions, the central government confirmed its dominance in social policy, against financially dependent and often politically conservative provinces.[8] By 1961, federal transfers had become conditional for the most part, and they accounted for about 30 percent of provincial revenue.[9] The fiscal dominance of the federal government translated into rather low-key intergovernmental relations, where programs tended to be designed in a cooperative way by civil servants from line departments. Because cost-sharing was the privileged policy instrument, each side had to agree on the specific configuration and management of social programs. The "Ottawa Men" praised by historian Jack Granatstein were the emblematic figures of the period.[10]

In the 1960s, the capacity and ambitions of the provinces started to grow and the serene atmosphere of cooperative federalism gradually gave way to the more contentious climate of executive federalism. This new mode of operation gave a central role to first ministers and to high-profile political negotiations that Richard Simeon adequately described as "federal-provincial diplomacy."[11] The relative fiscal position of provincial governments improved. By 1975, they collected 34 percent of total tax revenues (compared to 16 percent in 1955) and the federal government 55 percent (compared to 70 percent 20 years earlier). As a percentage of gross domestic product, total tax collection had also increased, from 22 percent in 1955 to 29 percent in 1975, making all governments better able to design and implement new programs.[12]

Over time, the federal government became increasingly concerned with the growing costs, lack of control and poor visibility associated with conditional cost-shared programs. Provincial governments also worried about programs that were expensive and complex and that distorted their priorities. In 1965, following a suggestion from the Quebec government and lengthy negotiations, the federal government offered a "contracting out" arrangement that conceded an extra tax abatement on the federal personal income tax to any provincial government willing to design and run its own social programs. Only Quebec took advantage of this offer.[13]

The general move from cost-sharing programs to block grants came in 1977 with the adoption of Established Programs Financing (EPF). EPF solved many of the problems associated with cost-sharing while at the same time avoiding further moves in the direction of "contracting out."[14] Confronted with rising deficits and caught with social policy commitments over which it did not have much control, Ottawa conceded additional (equalized) tax points, pooled together health and post-secondary education transfers, and reduced its control, in exchange for an end to automatic cost-sharing. At the outset, many provinces welcomed the flexibility associated with tax points and block grants.[15] In time, however, they would realize that EPF left them without a federal commitment to contribute to costly and rapidly growing social programs. In health care, this approach did not even prevent the federal government from imposing conditions. In fact, with the *Canada Health Act*, adopted in 1984 to prevent user fees and extra-billing, federal rules became more specific and more strictly enforced than before.[16]

Overall, there was no clear winner or loser in this period's "tug of war."[17] The federation, however, changed. Provincial governments gained fiscal autonomy and became more assertive, the federal government grew wary of out-of-control financial commitments and replaced cost-sharing by block funding, and retrenchment, rather than expansion, came to define the social policy agenda. By the end of the period, in the early 1990s, expenditures had been curtailed in most areas, including the core income security programs managed directly by the federal government.[18] Beyond social policy, in the broader constitutional arena, executive federalism also reshaped the country, with a new constitution and a charter of rights, but also with political divisions more profound than ever before, in the aftermath of the failed Meech Lake and Charlottetown accords.

With the election of a Liberal government in 1993, a new period began. At the outset, there was no mention of collaborative federalism or of a social union.[19] Still, an end to the high-stakes politics of constitutional reform was announced, and a social policy renewal process was launched under the leadership of Human Resources Development Canada (HRDC) minister Lloyd Axworthy. More importantly, the fight against the deficit prevailed over every other objective. The fiscal agenda was the prime motive behind the introduction, in the 1995 budget, of the Canada Health and Social Transfer (CHST), which completed what EPF had started and combined federal transfers for health, post-secondary education, social assistance and social services into a single, smaller and less conditional block grant. Some have argued that practically all transfers to the provinces had become overwhelmingly unconditional.[20] One should keep in mind, however, that residency requirements in social assistance and the *Canada Health Act* remained in effect.[21] It would be more correct to characterize the introduction of the CHST as the definitive end of cost-sharing as a major policy instrument.[22] With the end of the Canada Assistance Plan (CAP), which financed social assistance and social services, the last major federal transfer program with national standards and shared costs was gone. By the end, the standards associated with the CAP had become minimal and not very constraining.[23] The key change was the termination of Ottawa's faltering commitment to share the costs of social assistance expenditures.[24] Remnants of EPF and CAP were definitely eliminated in the February 1999 budget, when the distribution of CHST entitlements was adjusted on an equal per capita basis, leaving behind the needs-based distribution implicit in earlier CAP payments. CHST cash transfers do involve some redistribution because they take into account the varying value of the tax points conceded to the provinces in 1977.[25] Still, social transfers to the provinces are now largely unrelated to their social needs, and much smaller.[26] Between 1992–93 and 1998-99, cash social transfers to the provinces decreased by 32 percent, while provincial expenditures for social services, education and health increased by 12 percent.[27] From 22 percent of provincial revenue in 1971, federal cash transfers had dropped to 13 percent by 1999.[28]

From the strict point of view of fiscal federalism, the current period may appear to be one of decentralization.[29] Provincial governments increasingly rely on their own revenues. Apparently, they can also allocate most of the federal transfers as they wish, and have fewer standards and conditions to respect. Federal-provincial negotiations no longer concern federal standards and audits; they are mostly about comparable performance indicators and accountability procedures. The logic at play, however, is not so simple. Indeed, the federal spending power is also a powerful instrument when it is used "in reverse."[30] The federal government's heavy reliance on its "de-spending" power was, in fact, what sparked interprovincial efforts to redesign the social union. It was to prevent unilateral and unpredictable changes in federal transfers and social programs that the provincial and territorial governments initiated the social union process in 1996. Along with others, I have argued that these governments did not obtain much on this count when they signed SUFA.[31] More positive assessments concede that the agreement's constraints on the federal spending power remain light, but note that previously there were simply no rules. From this perspective, SUFA may be part of a new way to manage intergovernmental relations, and only time will tell whether or not this new approach truly makes Canadian federalism more collaborative.[32]

Nevertheless, some time has passed since the February 1999 adoption of the framework agreement, and the first indications are not convincingly collaborative. Consider, first, the evolution of transfers. In the last two years, in a context defined by an important federal surplus and by anticipated elections, transfers to the provinces have increased significantly and some of the ground lost with the introduction of the CHST has been recovered. The manner in which this reversal has been conducted, however, is revealing. Indeed, an important part of the increase in social transfers has occurred through the allocation by the federal government of ad hoc funds that are conditional and earmarked for health care, early childhood development or post-secondary education.[33] These funds are neither related to actual provincial expenditures nor governed by a formal and agreed upon growth formula. Offered unilaterally and with little prior consultation, these extra funds are often tied to specified purposes and leave the provinces without much of a say and without predictability. In the first years of SUFA, with respect to transfers at least, control trumped collaboration.[34]

When we consider other areas of intergovernmental relations, the picture appears more complex. There are instances where collaboration seems possible, as with policies for children or for persons with disabilities, but there are also important areas where federal unilateralism prevails. Significant federal initiatives were announced through federal budget speeches. This was the case in health care (various investments in health-service delivery reforms, health information, health-related research and innovation, and targeted services such as prenatal nutrition), in post-secondary education (Canadian Foundation for Innovation, Canada Research Chairs) and in family policy (enhanced employment insurance provisions for parental benefits), as well as with the federal homelessness initiative.[35] Direct spending in areas of provincial jurisdiction certainly remains an appealing option for the federal government. When this approach is possible, and when the political and financial stakes are high, it tends to prevail over collaboration.[36] As Geoffrey Hale observes in an article about recent budgets, "the majority of new spending commitments are in areas directly under federal and Finance Department control."[37] Hale is referring primarily to new direct instruments such as the Canada Child Tax Benefit and employment insurance parental benefits. The same could be said of social transfers that remain ad hoc and earmarked, and which are in effect new fiscal federalism policy instruments.

To sum up, collaborative federalism and SUFA in particular have not produced a more institutionalized and stable fiscal federalism, have not eliminated unilateral federal initiatives in core areas of provincial jurisdiction and have given prominence to new policy instruments that increase control or freedom for the central government. This is where the "mission statement" argument comes into play. Acknowledging much that is presented in this balance sheet, those who wish to remain optimistic about collaborative federalism are tempted to associate these features with a lack of vision. This interpretation, of course, is consonant with the popular representation of the Chrétien government as driven by pragmatic and short-term considerations.[38] More interestingly, it allows one to explain away most of the difficulties that mar collaborative federalism, and to attribute them to a lack of perspective or of good will. What if these difficulties made sense? What if they were not anomalies, but rather the product of coherent decisions, consistent with a meaningful pattern of intergovernmental relations? This is what I propose in the next section.

Playing by the Rules — or Not

WHETHER THEY ARE STATES IN THE INTERNATIONAL ARENA, UNIONS AND EMPLOYERS in industrial relations, or partners in intergovernmental relations, social actors create rules and institutions to reduce uncertainty. The idea is not to eliminate conflicts, which are inherent to such relationships, but rather to regulate them. More specifically, the purpose of social actors is to bind opponents or partners, to institutionalize — for the long term — concessions that have been accepted in the heat of conflict or commitments that have been made on a mutual basis. States constrain their own sovereignty when their neighbours accept a free-trade regime. Trade unions and employers define lasting rules for themselves through collective bargaining. In intergovernmental relations, the situation is similar: there would be no point reaching agreements if they did not constrain the different partners in one way or another. In a federation, relations are by definition unequal. Above and beyond differences in size and power, common in international relations, there is also a difference in kind between the central and sub-central governments. This specificity, however, does not affect the general logic presented here. There are, indeed, no cases where social actors are perfectly equivalent, and an infinite number of instances where differences between the parties in conflict are huge and fundamental.

Institutions matter because they constrain social actors. Institutional constraints, however, need not be evenly distributed. In an unequal relationship, they may be heavier for the weaker side. According to Michel Crozier and Erhard Friedberg, power lies precisely in an actor's capacity to maintain uncertainty, keep others guessing and avoid strong commitments.[39] Crozier and Friedberg capture an important dimension of strategic behaviour. In Canadian intergovernmental relations, for instance, governments usually "seek to maximize their freedom of action, and minimize external constraints, fiscal or regulatory."[40] The strategic perspective of these authors, however, does not grant sufficient importance to ideas and institutions. Institutional rules, in particular, are often created to mitigate power, and some arrangements may actually be more constraining for the powerful. Collective bargaining rules, for instance, constrain employers more than workers. This is their very purpose: they are created to even the chances, to limit the overwhelming power that employers have in a nonorganized labour market. In the same manner, in intergovernmental relations, effective institutional rules are likely to place more constraints on the central government, the actor least likely to demand formal constraints. In Canada, the social union process was initiated precisely to circumscribe the power of the federal government to change at will the rules of the game. Ottawa eventually signed SUFA because it settled a long debate without compromising much of its freedom and capacity for control. It also provided some gains through a recognition of the federal spending power, of the legitimacy of pan-Canadian objectives and of new mobility rules.[41]

From the point of view of conflicts and institutions, the balance sheet presented in the previous section makes perfect sense. Consider, first, fiscal federalism. In this case, Ottawa's determination to maximize control and to remain free of any institutional constraints is transparent.[42] True enough, with the CHST most federal transfers to the provinces have become nominally unconditional. The implicit, or notional, composition of these transfers, however, is indicative of federal priorities. In 1999–2000, the health care component of CHST for the first time became more important than the social assistance component, and the gap is likely to widen over time.[43] Ad hoc, earmarked increases in transfer payments have been provided for health, early childhood development and post-secondary education, but not for social assistance and social services.[44] For both notional and earmarked health transfers, the *Canada Health Act* still applies. The principles of the act are quite general and largely accepted, even by provincial governments. Still, in health care the conditions in place after the CHST and SUFA are basically the same as they were in 1984, and there has been no opening about a possible joint interpretation and implementation of the rules.[45] The sudden interest in Alberta and Quebec private clinics during the 2000 electoral campaign indicated how arbitrary and fickle federal oversight could become. Beyond the *Canada Health Act*, ad hoc increases in funding make long-term planning and reform difficult and distort provincial priorities.[46] Over the years, federal contributions to provincial health care spending have dropped, from

27 percent of the total in 1977–78 to somewhere between 10 and 15 percent now. Meanwhile, the weight of health expenditures has risen for the provinces, to the point that in 1999–2000 it represented around 40 percent of total program expenditures in many provinces.[47] Eventually, it could threaten the overall fiscal position of many governments.[48] As a consequence, provincial governments face a more difficult situation in health care, with the same old rules, the increased uncertainty brought by ad hoc funding and reaffirmed federal ambitions to govern the sector without funding it adequately. More generally, the fiscal imbalance between the federal and the provincial governments has increased, and it is likely to worsen in the years to come, because Ottawa collects a larger share of the most rapidly growing revenues while the sharpest rises in expenditures occur at the provincial level.[49] In spite of these fiscal trends, which would allow the federal government to accept more solid financial commitments, one would be hard-pressed to find the stability and predictability in funding that is expected with collaborative federalism.

A similar picture can be drawn for other areas of intergovernmental relations, where unilateral federal policies are simply too numerous to be treated as anomalies. The reverse may, in fact, be true. Collaboration has succeeded in areas where the federal spending power previously had been less significant and where there were fewer pre-existing patterns of hierarchy, standards and control. This was the case with child benefits, disability policy and, to a lesser extent, job training.[50] Otherwise, unilateral policies prevailed. In the core spending sectors of health care and post-secondary education, many federal initiatives actually seem driven by the will to circumvent the provinces. In social assistance and social services, the intention seems more related to a desire to shift from invisible and unpopular spending to more visible and politically palatable spending. The federal government prefers supporting children to unemployed adults, supporting low- and middle-income families to the poor, and supporting visible homelessness initiatives to stodgy social services.[51] As for the new, extended parental benefits associated with employment insurance, it is hard not to see in this initiative an attempt to pre-empt the Quebec government's long announced and popular proposal to claim the employment insurance funds associated with parental leave in order to improve coverage and benefits for parents. Jean Chrétien was clear on this count: "They're too late," he said, "that's not my fault!"[52] There is something like a mission statement in Ottawa, but it is not very collaborative.

The use of a new policy instrument such as the ad hoc, earmarked transfer is, of course, consistent with the picture presented here. SUFA does not constrain the federal government with respect to transfers, and policies implemented since February 1999 suggest that there are now fewer, not more, constraints on Ottawa's choices. Ad hoc transfers are, by definition, less structured and predictable than block grants.[53] Interestingly, the same can be said of the relationship between the federal government and citizens. In the past, federal programs for individual Canadians were entitlements, associated for instance with age, family or employment status, or earlier contributions. In the 1990s, most of these entitlements became, at least in part, targeted on the basis of income. This was the case with old age and child-related programs, but also with employment insurance.[54] There are advantages to such an approach, in that it allows government to better target those most in need.[55] There are also risks, however. Poverty and economic insecurity increased in Canada in the 1990s, and to a large extent this can be attributed to changes in income security programs.[56] The Child Tax Benefit itself may not be as useful a tool against poverty as is generally assumed.[57] Beyond the impact of the different measures, which are likely to change over time, the transformation of entitlements into targeted benefits raises important questions, because it replaces institutionalized social rights with more precarious benefits, which may be modified with every budget, often without preliminary public debate. Tax benefits tend to be obscure, technical and difficult to appraise. They make public engagement difficult and retrenchment by stealth easy.[58] Hence, with respect to citizens as well as to provincial and territorial governments, the federal government chooses policies that lessen its commitments and that leave as much flexibility as possible. The result, for individual Canadians as well as for provincial governments, is increased insecurity. Again, the pattern is clear and consistent. It does not correspond, however, to the promises of institutionalized collaboration.

Adjusting to Suboptimal Cooperation

I F THE SITUATION IS SO ONE-SIDED, WHY DID ALL PROVINCIAL AND TERRITORIAL GOVERN- ments except Quebec accept the agreement? Why do they participate so earnestly in collaborative efforts on a range of social policy issues (for instance, early childhood development, benefits and services for persons with disabilities, housing and labour market policy)? A number of explanations can be offered concerning these choices. Many accounts associate the signature of SUFA to the increased (equal per capita) transfers offered at the time by the federal government. Though undoubtedly relevant, these financial incentives are not sufficient to explain what happened. New investments could be expected in any case. More importantly, a pure logic of incentives cannot explain why provincial and territorial governments participated actively in collaborative efforts. These governments were not forced into signing SUFA. The agreement fell far short of their initial common position, but it incorporated some of their demands, albeit in a diluted version. It also institutionalized a pan-Canadian vision that they, and their electorates, considered valuable.[59]

SUFA merely consolidated an evolution that was already under way, as a result of federal fiscal and social policies. Provincial-territorial initiatives on the social union did not emerge from an inner desire to collaborate on social policy. They were, first and foremost, reactions against the CHST and the reduction in cash transfers it entailed. Provinces and territories wanted constraints on the federal spending power that would be in line with the decreasing value and reliability of the transfers that came from Ottawa. The Quebec government also reacted to a moving situation. It joined the other provincial governments after witnessing the adoption, by the federal government and the other provinces, of the National Child Benefit. In both instances, new rules were sought not to change the status quo, but rather because the status quo had changed already. This pattern is indicative of the causal mechanism at play. Provincial and territorial governments were prompted to act more to protect themselves than to transform the federation.

Collaboration, or cooperation, as it is usually called in the social sciences, does not preclude conflict. As suggested above, cooperation is a regulated and institutionalized form of conflict. Stable cooperation structures emerge when social actors succeed in constraining each other. When this happens, the outcome is often positive for all participants. Cooperation, however, is not always beneficial. There may well be suboptimal results, situations that produce losers as well as winners. This possibility is often neglected in the social science literature, because cooperation is primarily understood as a public good. Social actors are assumed to face a collective action problem, which they can solve only through cooperation. Cooperation, even when it is driven by a hegemonic power, is thus perceived as a gain for all. In a recently published book on international institutions, Lloyd Gruber suggests that in some cases cooperation may also be detrimental, at least for specific actors. The argument is simple. It starts from the idea, neglected in conventional rational choice representations, that some actors may prefer not to cooperate, because they want to maintain their autonomy or have preferences distinct from those of the dominant group. They end up cooperating, however, when stronger actors go ahead and change the choices that are available. When the status quo is no longer an option, argues Gruber, actors may favour a cooperative outcome that they would have rejected otherwise.[60] In an article on SUFA, Christopher Dunn quotes a British Columbia municipal affairs minister who nicely conveyed this general idea 35 years ago in a public address about a new regional district system. "You will either get what you want," he said to his audience, "or come to want what you get."[61]

Assessing the preferences of social actors is notoriously difficult. At best, preferences can be inferred from choices, and when social actors decide to cooperate, it is risky to argue that they would have preferred otherwise. However, if one follows the evolution of a process, such as the social union negotiations, it is possible to argue that preferences have been modified and adjusted along the way.

For the Quebec government, this evolution is unmistakable. In Saskatoon, in August 1998, the Bouchard government compromised on principles stated explicitly in the months prior, and it did so precisely because the status quo ante no longer existed.[62] Likewise, to agree with the September 2000 health accord, this government accepted some of the language of SUFA it previously had rejected, albeit with a strong clause on the division of powers. For other provincial governments the evaluation is not as straightforward, but there was undoubtedly a shift downward in expectations and demands. As explained above, provincial governments reacted after the fact to a moving situation and they mainly asked to be consulted and involved in future changes. In SUFA, they obtained modest responses to these concerns, but even these limited gains were not respected fully in the following months, with unilateral federal initiatives on transfers, homelessness and health care. Given their underlying preference for cooperation, the expectations of their electorates and the additional transfers they received, provincial governments basically adjusted their expectations rather than held on to their initial positions. They decided to want what they got.

In summary, provincial and territorial governments accepted SUFA and collaborative federalism, in part because they did not demand as much autonomy and freedom as the Quebec government and in part because they came to accept the options defined by the federal government as the only options available. Two readings of this outcome can be proposed. One would be that the provinces were dominated by a more powerful actor, which was able to define and impose the rules of the game. The other would stress the commonality of views between the federal and the provincial-territorial governments, and present the Quebec government as defeated by what Gruber calls a strong "enacting coalition." Both explanations convey part of the truth. The provinces failed to impose genuine constraints on the federal government, but they also joined Ottawa to define the final, suboptimal outcome, without the only government that held the line. In other words, provincial and territorial governments did not achieve their initial objectives but adjusted rapidly to a new situation they considered unavoidable, not so damaging and useful in some respects.

This evolution of preferences explains why provincial and territorial governments accepted SUFA and remained involved in collaborative federalism even though, as discussed above, these institutional arrangements left more freedom and control than expected to the federal government.

Conclusion

The Canadian government does not need a mission statement. Its social and intergovernmental policies may appear ad hoc, fickle or unpredictable, but this is not a sign of weakness or lack of purpose. The cultivation of uncertainty is a prerogative of power. More than ever, in Ottawa, political power is centralized around the prime minister, who governs by "bolts of electricity," reacting in a more or less coherent way to the issue of the day.[63] "Sometimes," quipped Jean Chrétien in the days before SUFA was signed, "on Monday I feel like giving the provinces more money, and then on Tuesday not."[64] For all this uncertainty, however, there is a clear pattern in intergovernmental relations which is apparent in fiscal federalism, in policy-making and in the federal government's choice of policy instruments.

Fiscal federalism in the late 1990s was defined not only by the decline of social transfers but also by their transformation. Transfers for health, post-secondary education, and social assistance and social services were curtailed severely after 1995, and they gradually but only partially recovered after the 1999 budget. Most critical were the shift to block funding and equal per capita entitlements (which disconnected Ottawa's fiscal contribution from provincial social needs), the rise of health care and post-secondary education as federal priorities at the expense of social assistance and social services, and the introduction of ad hoc, earmarked funds. These changes have numerous implications. First, they create new types of inequities and increase the vulnerability of smaller provinces. If the per capita rule had applied in 1998, Ottawa would have contributed 4.4 times more money for a person receiving social assistance in Alberta than for one in Newfoundland.[65] Second, the relative growth of health-related transfers increases the clout of the *Canada Health Act* as a federal tool to oversee the management of health services. Third, the adoption of ad hoc transfers increases even more the level of uncertainty in future funding. In other areas of intergovernmental relations, federal unilateralism also has remained important, either to circumvent the provinces in sectors such as health care and post-secondary education, or to prevail in particular policy sectors and establish federal visibility. Finally, the new policy instruments privileged by the federal government all preserve Ottawa's flexibility and control. Even measures aimed at individual citizens now share this characteristic. Targeted benefits are gradually displacing universal entitlements. Social rights are increasingly folded into the tax code.

Except for the Quebec government, which is necessarily penalized by its marginal position and lack of influence in this process, the provincial and territorial governments have adjusted their expectations and their demands downward. They accept the precepts of what is now called collaborative federalism, and play a defensive game that mixes unheeded demands for more predictable relationships and efforts to have a say in jointly defined policies. As for individual citizens, most of them remain unaware of issues that appear arcane and are poorly covered in the media. In this context, a call for a new mission statement appears unlikely to make a difference. The situation is structured not by a lack of vision, but rather by an uneven relationship, which is solidly rooted in a sharp and growing vertical fiscal imbalance between the two orders of government.

Provincial and territorial governments could alter the course of events by taking advantage of the SUFA review and renewal process to re-establish a common stance and put forward simple but forceful demands. Seeking increases in social transfers and redress in the fiscal imbalance would constitute an obvious rallying point. So would an attempt to give meaning to the statement of principle in SUFA regarding ensuring "adequate, affordable, stable and sustainable funding for social programs." This approach would not be convincing, however, without a clear proposal in favour of more provincial autonomy and flexibility in the core areas covered by the CHST. Provincial governments must reaffirm their constitutional jurisdiction over social policy and see that it is recognized by the federal government. New demands would have a greater chance of succeeding, as well, if the provinces could convince the Quebec government to enter this new round. This is certainly a tall order, but the satisfactory results of the September 2000 health care negotiation indicate that a genuine Quebec participation cannot be excluded.

Provincial and territorial governments also have to convince citizens that, as much as the federal government, they are Canadian governments, and can be trusted to put forward an appealing social policy agenda. Obviously, this would mean very different things in the different provinces. Public preferences are not the same across the country and the demand for social programs probably differs significantly from one region to the next. One way to initiate this discussion would be to underline the limitations of current federal orientations. Poverty and economic insecurity have increased in Canada, health care is a universal source of worry and post-secondary education remains underfunded. Our self-proclaimed "social investment" state takes little risk and makes few commitments.[66] It does not "invest" in persons and in social programs: it targets and spends, for one purpose and one budget at a time. This unreliable and often unilateral approach appears basically at odds with the idea of a social union. These choices and orientations ought to be submitted to the public not through a shallow procedure of citizen engagement, but rather through a broad and open process of democratic deliberation.

I would like to thank Charles Blattberg, Sarah Fortin, Peter Graefe, Andrée Lajoie, Harvey Lazar and France St-Hilaire as well as participants in the IRPP workshop for their helpful comments and suggestions.

1   Lazar (2000a, p. 5); Courchene (2001, p. 154); Maxwell (2001).

2   First Ministers of Canada (2000).

3   The term "collaborative" is used here simply as the standard label; it does not imply that intergovernmental relations are harmonious or genuinely collaborative. The same is true for "cooperative" and "executive federalism." For an earlier discussion, see Noël (2000a).

4   Perry (1997, pp. 28-69).

5   Bird and Chen (1998, p. 56).

6   Lazar (2000a, p. 8).

7   Pal (1985, p. 8). In 1951, direct grants to universities were established, but they were openly contested by the Quebec government and left the federal government with difficult questions regarding the status of technical or composite post-secondary institutions, such as the CEGEPs in Quebec. In 1966, these grants were abolished and tax points and cash transfers for post-secondary education were conceded to the provinces. Dupré et al. (1973, pp. 21-25); Hobson and St-Hilaire (1994, pp. 30-31).

8   Banting (1995, p. 298).

9   Bird and Chen (1998, p. 66).

10 Granatstein (1982).

11 Simeon (1972).

12 Bird and Chen (1998, p. 56).

13 In 1966, the Quebec Pension Plan was also created, parallel to the Canada Pension Plan. Hobson and St-Hilaire (1994, pp. 27-33); Perry (1997, pp. 210-217).

14 McRoberts (1997, pp. 40-42, 141-142).

15 Bird and Chen (1998, p. 67).

16 Maioni (1999, p. 100).

17 Milne (1986).

18 Prince (1999, pp. 166-174).

19 The 1992 Charlottetown Accord had referred to a "social and economic union," but the idea was dropped after the referendum. Noël (1998, p. 27).

20 Bird and Chen (1998, p. 67).

21 Boucher and Vermaeten (2000, p. 132).

22 Cost sharing remains present in small transfer programs. Some of these programs are extremely small and local (the Canada-Manitoba Agreement to correct damage to provincial lands due to beavers in a national park was worth $20,000 in 1987-88). Overall, there are nevertheless more than 100 small transfer programs, not all cost shared, that together amount to about 15 percent of federal transfers to the provinces. See Vaillancourt (2000, pp. 196, 208).

23 Boychuk (1996, p. 16).

24 Faltering, because after 1990-91, with the "cap on CAP," the annual growth of CAP funding was limited to 5 percent for the provinces not eligible for equalization (Alberta, British Columbia and Ontario). In 1995-96, the year before the CHST came into effect, CAP transfers were also frozen to the level of the previous year for all provinces. Boucher and Vermaeten (2000, p. 136).

25 Boucher and Vermaeten (2000, p. 137).

26 Coulombe and Mérette (2000, pp. 340-355).

27 My calculations. Sources: Hobson and St-Hilaire (2000, p. 176); Treff and Perry (1997, pp. 9:9, 10:3, 11:2; 2001, pp. 9:10, 10:4, 11:2).

28 If one considers as transfers the provincial revenues derived from the tax points conceded in 1977, the share of transfers in provincial revenues still drops from 24 percent in 1971 to 19 percent in 1999. Lazar (2000a, p. 14).

29 Lazar (2000a, p. 16); Pal (1999, p. 10).

30 Cameron and Simeon (2000, p. 75).

31 Noël (2000a; 2000b, pp. 14-17). See also the other chapters in the Gagnon and Segal volume, as well as Robson and Schwanen (1999); Richards (1999, pp. 5-10); Dunn (2000, pp. 50-51).

32 Lazar (2000a, p. 15; 2000b, pp. 108, 115); Courchene (2001, p. 95); Cameron and Simeon (2000, p. 80); Maxwell (2001, p. 9).

33 Provincial and Territorial Ministers of Health (2000, pp. 9-10); Hobson and St-Hilaire (2000, p. 177).

34 Hale (2000, p. 72; 2001, pp. 36-38); Robson (2001, p. 20).

35 Provincial/Territorial Council on Social Policy Renewal (2000).

36 Lazar (2000b, p. 122); Courchene (2001, pp. 272-274).

37 Hale (2000, p. 87).

38 Greenspon and Wilson-Smith (1996), and the various contributions to the "Chrétien Legacy" issue of *Policy Options* (2000).

39 Crozier and Friedberg (1977, pp. 69-70). In the context of Canadian intergovern- mental relations, it is interesting to note that Stéphane Dion once criticized Crozier, his mentor, for ignoring the importance of credible threats in power relations. In some contexts, argued Dion, power lies not in maintaining uncertainty, but rather in the "efficient use of threat." Dion (1982, pp. 94-96).

40 Cameron and Simeon (2000, p. 86).

41 Lazar (2000b, pp. 114-115).

42 Hale (2000, pp. 59-94).

43 Hobson and St-Hilaire (2000, p. 176).

44 Hobson and St-Hilaire (2000, p. 177); Courchene (2000, p. 18); Boychuk (2001, pp. 126-127).

45 Lazar (1998a, pp. 118-121); Maioni, (2000, pp. 39-40).

46 Robson (2001, p. 20); Corriveau (2001, p. A1).

47 This was the case in Nova Scotia, Ontario, Manitoba and Saskatchewan. The Canadian average was 36 percent. Canadian Institute for Health Information (2000).

48 Provincial and Territorial Ministers of Health (2000, p. 3). Courchene (2001, pp. 188-189).

49 Ruggeri (2000); Commission on Fiscal Imbalance (2001).

50 Lazar (1998a, pp. 110-131; 1998b, p. 33).

51 Boychuk (2001, p. 126).

52 My translation. Chrétien is quoted in Toupin (2000, p. B1).

53 Robson (2001, pp. 19-20).

54 Myles and Pierson (1997, pp. 448-449).

55 Battle (1999, pp. 1219-1257; 2001, pp. 183-229).

56 Osber (2000); Osberg and Sharp (2001); Heisz, Jackson and Picot (2001, pp. 247-272).

57 Shillington (2000, pp. 62-67).

58 Myles and Pierson (1997, p. 467); Shillington (1999, pp. 1263-1269). More generally, see Howard (1997).

59 Noël (2000b, pp. 17-18); Lazar (2000b, pp. 104-105, 110-111).

60 Gruber (2000).

61 Quoted in Dunn (2000, p. 50).

62 Noël (2000b, pp. 22-23).

63 Savoie (1999, p. 359).

64 Quoted in Paquet (1999, p. 102).

65 Coulombe and Mérette (2000, pp. 343-344).

66 See Chrétien (2000); Saint-Martin (2000, pp. 33-57).

Banting, Keith G. "The Welfare State as Statecraft: Territorial Politics and Canadian Social Policy." In *European Social Policy: Between Fragmentation and Integration*, ed. Stephan Leibfried and Paul Pierson. Washington: Brookings Institution, 1995.

Battle, Ken. "Relentless Incrementalism: Deconstructing and Reconstructing Canadian Income Security Policy." In *The Review of Economic Performance and Social Progress, 2001. The Longest Decade: Canada in the 1990s*, ed. Keith Banting, Andrew Sharpe and France St-Hilaire. Montreal and Ottawa: Institute for Research on Public Policy and Centre for the Study of Living Standards, 2001.

——. "Child Benefit Reform: A Case Study in Tax-Transfer Integration." *Canadian Tax Journal*, Vol. 47, no. 5 (December 1999): 1219-1257.

Bird, Richard M., and Duan-jie Chen. "Federal Finance and Fiscal Federalism: The Two Worlds of Canadian Public Finance." *Canadian Public Administration*, Vol. 41, no. 1 (spring 1998): 41-74.

Boucher, Edith, and Arndt Vermaeten. "Changes to Federal Transfers to Provinces and Territories in 1999." In *Canada: The State of the Federation 1999/2000: Toward a New Mission Statement for Canadian Fiscal Federalism*, ed. Harvey Lazar. Kingston: Institute of Intergovernmental Relations, 2000.

Boychuk, Gerard W. "Aiming for the Middle: Challenges to Federal Income Policy." In *How Ottawa Spends, 2001–2002: Power in Transition*, ed. Leslie A. Pal. Don Mills, ON: Oxford University Press, 2001.

——. "Floor or Ceiling? Standards in Social Assistance." *Policy Options*, Vol. 17, no. 5 (June 1996): 15-17.

Cameron, David, and Richard Simeon. "Intergovernmental Relations and Democratic Citizenship." In *Governance in the Twenty-first Century: Revitalizing the Public Service*, ed. B. Guy Peters and Donald J. Savoie. Montreal and Kingston: McGill-Queen's University Press, 2000.

Canadian Institute for Health Information. http://www.cihi.ca/facts/nhex/provnhex/tableA4.html Revised March 14, 2000.

Chrétien, Jean. "The Canadian Way in the 21st Century." Speech delivered in Berlin, June 2-3, 2000.

Commission on Fiscal Imbalance. *Fiscal Imbalance: Problems and Issues*. Quebec: Gouvernement du Québec, 2001.

Corriveau, Jeanne. "Renouvellement des équipements en radiologie: Québec n'ap-précie pas qu'Ottawa lui pousse dans le dos." *Le Devoir*, July 26, 2001: A1.

Coulombe, Serge, and Marcel Mérette. "Fiscal Needs and the CHST Per Capita Division Rule." *Canadian Tax Journal*, Vol. 48, no. 2 (June 2000): 340-355.

Courchene, Thomas J. *A State of Minds: Toward a Human Capital Future for Canadians*. Montreal: Institute for Research on Public Policy, 2001.

——. "A Paul Martin, Sr., Budget." *Policy Options*, Vol. 21, no. 3 (April 2000): 18-21.

Crozier, Michel, and Erhard Friedberg. *L'acteur et le système : les contraintes de l'action collective*. Paris: Seuil, 1977.

Dion, Stéphane. "Pouvoir et conflits dans l'or-ganisation: grandeur et limites du modèle de Michel Crozier." *Canadian Journal of Political Science*, Vol. 15, no. 1 (March 1982): 94-96.

Dunn, Christopher. "FYI: SUFA? DOA." *Policy Options*, Vol. 21, no. 4 (May 2000): 50-51.

Dupré, J. Stefan, David M. Cameron, Graeme H. McKechnie and Theodore B. Rotenberg. *Federalism and Policy Development: The Case of Adult Occupational Training in Ontario*. Toronto: University of Toronto Press, 1973.

First Ministers of Canada. *Communiqué on Health*. News release, ref: 800-038-004. Ottawa: First Ministers' Meeting, September 11, 2000. Available at www.scics.gc.ca

Gagnon, Alain-G., and Hugh Segal, eds. *The Canadian Social Union without Quebec: Eight Critical Analyses*. Montreal: Institute for Research on Public Policy, 2000.

Granatstein, Jack L. *The Ottawa Men: The Civil Service Mandarins, 1935–1957*. Toronto: Oxford University Press, 1982.

Greenspon, Edward, and Anthony Wilson-Smith. *Double Vision: The Inside Story of* the Liberals in Power. Toronto: Doubleday, 1996.

Gruber, Lloyd. Ruling the World: Power Politics and the Rise of Supranational Institutions. Princeton, NJ: Princeton University Press, 2000.

Hale, Geoffrey E. "Priming the Electoral Pump: Framing Budgets for a Renewed Mandate." In How Ottawa Spends, 2001-2002: Power in Transition, ed. Leslie A. Pal. Don Mills, ON: Oxford University Press, 2001.

——. "Managing the Fiscal Dividend: The Politics of Selective Activism." In How Ottawa Spends, 2000–2001: Past Imperfect, Future Tense, ed. Leslie A. Pal. Don Mills, ON: Oxford University Press, 2000.

Heisz, Andrew, Andrew Jackson and Garnett Picot. "Distributional Outcomes in Canada in the 1990s." In The Review of Economic Performance and Social Progress, 2001. The Longest Decade: Canada in the 1990s, ed. Keith Banting, Andrew Sharpe and France St-Hilaire. Montreal and Ottawa: Institute for Research on Public Policy and Centre for the Study of Living Standards, 2001.

Hobson, Paul A.R., and France St-Hilaire. "The Evolution of Federal-Provincial Fiscal Arrangements: Putting Humpty Together Again." In Canada: The State of the Federation 1999/2000: Toward a New Mission Statement for Canadian Fiscal Federalism, ed. Harvey Lazar. Kingston: Institute of Intergovernmental Relations, 2000.

——. Reforming Federal-Provincial Fiscal Arrangements: Toward Sustainable Federalism. Montreal: Institute for Research on Public Policy, 1994.

Howard, Christopher. The Hidden Welfare State: Tax Expenditures and Social Policy in the United States. Princeton, NJ: Princeton University Press, 1997.

Lazar, Harvey. "In Search of a New Mission Statement for Canadian Fiscal Federalism." In Canada: The State of the Federation 1999/2000: Toward a New Mission Statement for Canadian Fiscal Federalism, ed. Harvey Lazar. Kingston: Institute of Intergovernmental Relations, 2000a.

——. "The Social Union Framework Agreement and the Future of Fiscal Federalism." In

Canada: The State of the Federation 1999/2000: Toward a New Mission Statement for Canadian Fiscal Federalism, ed. Harvey Lazar. Kingston: Institute of Intergovernmental Relations, 2000b.

——. "The Federal Role in a New Social Union: Ottawa at a Crossroads." In Canada: The State of the Federation 1997: Non-Constitutional Renewal, ed. Harvey Lazar. Kingston: Institute of Intergovernmental Relations, 1998a.

——. "Non-Constitutional Renewal: Toward a New Equilibrium in the Federation." In Canada: The State of the Federation 1997: Non-Constitutional Renewal, ed. Harvey Lazar. Kingston: Institute of Intergovernmental Relations, 1998b.

Maioni, Antonia. "The Social Union and Health Care." Policy Options, Vol. 21, no. 3 (April 2000): 39-40.

——. "Decentralization in Health Policy: Comments on the ACCESS Proposals." In Stretching the Federation: The Art of the State in Canada, ed. Robert Young. Kingston: Institute of Intergovernmental Relations, 1999.

Maxwell, Judith. "Toward a Common Citizenship: Canada's Social and Economic Choices." Reflexion, Canadian Policy Research Networks, no. 4 (January 2001).

McRoberts, Kenneth. Misconceiving Canada: The Struggle for National Unity. Toronto: Oxford University Press, 1997.

Milne, David. Tug of War: Ottawa and the Provinces under Trudeau and Mulroney. Toronto: Lorimer, 1986.

Myles, John, and Paul Pierson. "Friedman's Revenge: The Reform of 'Liberal' Welfare States in Canada and the United States." Politics and Society, Vol. 25, no. 4 (December 1997): 448-449.

Noël, Alain. "Without Quebec: Collaborative Federalism with a Footnote?" Policy Matters, Vol. 1, no. 2 (March 2000a).

——. "General Study of the Framework Agreement." In The Canadian Social Union without Quebec: Eight Critical Analysis, ed. Alain-G. Gagnon and Hugh Segal. Montreal: Institute for Research on Public Policy, 2000b.

——. "Les trois unions sociales." *Policy Options*, Vol. 19, no. 9 (November 1998): 26-29.

Osberg, Lars. "Poverty in Canada and the USA: Measurement, Trends and Implications." Presidential Address to the Canadian Economics Association, Vancouver, June 3, 2000.

Osberg, Lars, and Andrew Sharpe. "Labor-Market Trends in North America: Has Economic Well-Being Improved?" Paper presented at the conference Labour in a Globalising World: The Challenge for Asia, City University of Hong Kong, Hong Kong, January 4-6, 2001.

Pal, Leslie A. "Shape Shifting: Canadian Governance Toward the 21st Century." In *How Ottawa Spends, 1999–2000. Shape Shifting: Canadian Governance Toward the 21st Century*, ed. Leslie A. Pal. Don Mills, ON: Oxford University Press, 1999.

——. "Federalism, Social Policy, and the Constitution." In *Canadian Social Welfare Policy: Federal and Provincial Dimensions*, ed. Jacqueline S. Ismael. Montreal and Kingston: McGill-Queen's University Press, 1985.

Paquet, Gilles. "Tectonic Changes in Canadian Governance." In *How Ottawa Spends 1999-2000: Shape Shifting: Canadian Governance Toward the 21st Century*, ed. Leslie A. Pal. Toronto: Oxford University Press, 1999.

Perry, David B. *Financing the Federation, 1867 to 1995: Setting the Stage for Change.* Canadian Tax Paper no. 102. Toronto: Canadian Tax Foundation, 1997.

Policy Options. "Chrétien Legacy," various authors, Vol. 21, no. 9 (November 2000).

Prince, Michael J. "From Health and Welfare to Stealth and Farewell: Federal Social Policy, 1980-2000." In *How Ottawa Spends, 1999-2000. Shape Shifting: Canadian Governance Toward the 21st Century*, ed. Leslie A. Pal. Don Mills, ON: Oxford University Press, 1999.

Provincial/Territorial Council on Social Policy Renewal. *Progress Report to Premiers No. 5*, Presented at 41st Annual Premiers' Conference, Winnipeg, August 9–11, 2000.

Provincial and Territorial Ministers of Health. *Understanding Canada's Health Care Costs: Final Report.* Presented at 41st Annual Premiers' Conference, Winnipeg, August 9-11, 2000.

Richards, John. "A Successful Counter-Reformation." *Inroads*, no. 8 (1999): 5-10.

Robson, William B.P. "Will the Baby Boomers Bust the Health Budget? Demographic Change and Health Care Financing Reform." *C.D. Howe Institute Commentary*, no. 148. Toronto: C.D. Howe Institute, February 2001; pp. 1-29.

Robson, William B.P., and Daniel Schwanen. "The Social Union Agreement: Too Flawed to Last." *C.D. Howe Institute Backgrounder.* Toronto: C.D. Howe Institute, February 8, 1999.

Ruggeri, G.C. "A Federation Out of Balance." Background paper commissioned by the Western finance ministers and presented at the 41st Annual Premiers' Conference, Winnipeg, August 9-11, 2000.

Saint-Martin, Denis. "De l'État-providence à l'État d'investissement social: Un nouveau paradigme pour enfanter l'économie du savoir?" In *How Ottawa Spends, 2000–2001: Past Imperfect, Future Tense*, ed. Leslie A. Pal. Don Mills, ON: Oxford University Press, 2000.

Savoie, Donald J. *Governing from the Centre: The Concentration of Power in Canadian Politics.* Toronto: University of Toronto Press, 1999.

Shillington, Richard. "Two Casualties of the Child Tax Benefit: Truth and the Poor." *Policy Options*, Vol. 21, no. 9 (November 2000): 62-67.

——. "Assessing Tax-Transfer Programs: Comments on the Paper by Ken Battle." *Canadian Tax Journal*, Vol. 47, no. 5 (1999): 1263–69.

Simeon, Richard. *Federal-Provincial Diplomacy: The Making of Recent Policy in Canada.* Toronto: University of Toronto Press, 1972.

Toupin, Gilles. "Congé parental : 'trop tard'." *La Presse*, June 8, 2000: B1.

Treff, Karin, and David B. Perry. *Finances of the Nation 2000.* Toronto: Canadian Tax Foundation, 2001.

——. *Finances of the Nation 1997.* Toronto: Canadian Tax Foundation, 1997.

Vaillancourt, François. "Federal-Provincial Small Transfer Programs in Canada, 1957-1998: Importance, Composition and Evaluation." In *Canada: The State of the Federation 1999/2000: Toward a New Mission Statement for Canadian Fiscal Federalism*, ed. Harvey Lazar. Kingston: Institute of Intergovernmental Relations, 2000.

Restoring   the
Federal   Principle:
The   Place   of
Quebec   in   the
Canadian   Social
Union

Introduction

T HE BACKDROP FOR THIS PAPER IS THE LAST SECTION OF THE SOCIAL UNION
Framework Agreement (SUFA) reached between the federal government and
all provinces and territories except Quebec on February 4, 1999. This section states
that, before the end of the third year of the agreement, the "governments will jointly
undertake a full review of the agreement and its implementation and make adjustments as required." More generally, now, six years after the 1995 Quebec referendum and 20 years after the adoption of the *Constitution Act, 1982*, is an opportune
moment to examine some of the major trends in Canadian federalism, both in general and as they relate to Quebec.

It is by no means clear that SUFA will actually undergo a real re-examination,
much less a thorough one. Indeed, for the agreement to be renewed the parties would
merely need to hold a meeting, at the end of which the agreement would be declared
as having been "re-examined." This would avoid the need to renegotiate the agreement, a process that might prove difficult (not least for Ottawa) and cast doubt upon
the supposed success of three years ago. Paradoxically, it can be argued that it is the
very flaws in the agreement — which will be discussed below — that make a genuine
re-evaluation and subsequent improvements highly improbable. A real review and
revision would be more plausible if SUFA rested on a stronger foundation.

Even if a genuine review were to take place, it is even less likely now than it was
in February 1999 that this process would lead Quebec to join in. In point of fact, SUFA
is, in the sphere of intergovernmental relations, the most recent manifestation of a deep
and longstanding impasse between Quebec and Canada. Because the problem is essentially political rather than technical in nature, the present analysis is also largely politi-

cal. Indeed, one of the few things that stand out clearly in this muddled picture is that we will get nowhere by deluding ourselves about the true nature of the problem at hand. In this paper I shall seek to put some of these unavoidable truths in context.

That said, it is entirely possible in light of the Canadian federal system's history of alternating periods of centralization and decentralization that the deterioration in Canada-Quebec relations, which we have witnessed for decades, will give way to a new phase in which the functional aspects of those relations will come to the fore. In this spirit, I will suggest a number of ways to break the current impasse and will identify areas of discourse that point to solutions which, although not in the cards now, might eventually become possible. I will examine the nature and evolution of Canada-Quebec relations over the past two decades and in particular highlight the opportunities as well as the inherent dangers that have emerged more recently in the context of the social union. Finally, I will attempt to show that, independent of SUFA's serious flaws, Quebec cannot remain on the sidelines of Canadian intergovernmental relations in the field of social policy. After all, the fact that Quebec has not signed the agreement does not mean that it is not part of Canada, that it is not a party to Canadian federalism or that it should not be involved in federalism as it is applied to social policy.

From Saskatoon to SUFA: The Third Round in the Canada-Quebec Impasse

AFTER QUEBEC JOINED THE PROVINCIAL/TERRITORIAL CONSENSUS AT THE ANNUAL premiers' conference held in Saskatoon in August 1998, it seemed for a time that the social union debate might bring about a new beginning in Canada-Quebec relations.[1] This consensus on ways of cooperating with regard to the social union was in line with Quebec's view of Canadian federalism, especially with respect to its opting-out provisions. Until then, Quebec had chosen not to take part in the discussions initiated by the other provinces in the wake of the significant cuts in social spending announced by Ottawa in 1995, only attending the provincial-territorial meetings as an observer.

Those who are unfamiliar with Quebec, or who have forgotten why so many Quebecers who are attached to Canada have become sovereignists over the last 30 years, might well ridicule the idea of Quebec signing an agreement on the basis of a provision allowing it to opt out of any arrangements made under the said agreement. Such a blinkered perspective misses the key point — the openness and goodwill that Quebecers have always shown toward Canada, as long as they felt that the vision that lies at the core of their membership in the federation was being respected. Indeed, Quebec's participation earlier in the SUFA process might have changed the dynamics of the discussions. Its representatives undoubtedly would have suggested to their counterparts that they thought more in terms of social federalism than in terms of a social union, making it easier for the provinces to find common ground. Moreover, Quebec not only constitutes the francophone pole of the Canadian duality, but it is also one of the country's main regions. Its participation could have served to bolster the regionalism that has spread throughout English-speaking Canada over the last 30 years, in Ontario as well as in other wealthy and powerful provinces like Alberta and British Columbia.

In any event, it should also be noted that the provincial-territorial consensus reached in Saskatoon was not limited to the right to opt out. The consensus also dealt with different ways of managing interdependencies and promoting cooperation on social policy. Moreover, it recognized that the federal government plays an important role in social policy, even though the provinces should continue to be primarily responsible for core programs. Thus by joining the provincial-territorial consensus (albeit only because there was a clear-cut and broad-based right to opt out), Quebec implicitly accepted the implications of a Canadian social union, which meant it had adjusted its own position.

Unfortunately, in early February 1999 the provincial-territorial common front, which Quebec had joined after having made unprecedented concessions, fell apart in just a few hours.[2] It is true that in the months following Quebec's decision to join, the position of its premier, Lucien Bouchard, had considerably weakened. During the fall 1998 Quebec election campaign, Bouchard had stressed to voters the importance of granting him a strong mandate to negotiate on the issue of the social union following the Saskatoon consensus. The subsequent re-election of the Parti Québécois government with a plurality of seats in the National Assembly but with fewer votes than the Liberals significantly weakened Bouchard's hand, in relation to both his own party and his federal and provincial/territorial counterparts in the ensuing negotiations on the social union agreement.

Nevertheless, the political reversal that followed and led to the swift conclusion of an agreement (i.e., SUFA) between the federal government and the other provinces and territories constituted an abandonment of Quebec by its provincial partners. It was also a lost opportunity at a broader level. This event confirmed and deepened the Canada-Quebec impasse, a situation that goes back to the repatriation of the Canadian Constitution in 1982 without Quebec's consent, exacerbated by the failure of the Meech Lake Accord in 1990.[3]

These three events — constitutional change in 1982, constitutional tinkering in 1987–90 and an administrative agreement in 1999 — are part of a pattern, for they demonstrate the structural inability of the Canadian political system to incorporate part of its historical and geopolitical heartland with its own particular vision of federalism and of the country. The problem is that the rest of Canada has never truly recognized the legitimacy of Quebec's distinct vision of Canadian federalism, and the presence of a sovereignist government now serves as an excuse for ignoring that vision. But the impasse is also due to a Quebec secessionist movement which refuses to engage seriously with Canada and which the rest of the country tends to identify with Quebec as a whole.

Beyond the substantive issues, the processes that led to all three agreements were also similar. In all three cases, interprovincial alliances that included Quebec eventually crumbled, with the "French province" finding itself isolated within Canada. The events leading to the signing of SUFA inevitably increased Quebec's distrust of interprovincial alliances, a distrust that was already well ingrained following the failure of the Meech Lake Accord.

The SUFA episode, among others, also serves to demonstrate that the Canadian intergovernmental system has become significantly biased against Quebec and its particular concerns, which have become more marginalized than ever before in Canadian history.

Federalism and the Social Union

AS ONE OF 14 PARTNERS IN INTERGOVERNMENTAL DISCUSSIONS, IT IS VERY DIFFICULT for Quebec to defend or impose a vision that differs, in fundamental respects, from the one that tends to prevail in the rest of the country.

Canadian duality now exists only at a formal linguistic level and is no longer linked to the reality of Quebec. There is currently no desire to give real meaning to Quebec's distinct character; the concept of equality among the provinces has become a dogma, thwarting both the growth of Canadian regionalism and recognition of the Canadian duality. The fact that Quebec public opinion has over time grown more sympathetic to some form of independence for the province, which is seen in the rest of the country as a threat to Canada's very survival, has done nothing to improve this situation.

It is important to recall these things because the issue of "national unity," as it is called in the rest of Canada, clearly influenced the SUFA negotiations — although this is not openly acknowledged. It manifested itself in a deep distrust of Premier Bouchard, who was seen in the rest of Canada as an unparalleled negotiator prepared to play the Canadian intergovernmental game without renouncing his "separatist" ambitions. Also, the other regions of Canada, being more homogeneous than Quebec, aspire whether consciously or not to a more unitary regime. The principles of sovereignty and equality of each level of government in its own jurisdictions and the need for clear jurisdictional boundaries are often seen as less important than ensuring cooperation, dialogue and partnership between the two levels of government. From this perspective, a national, *senior* level of government should work in concert with a provincial, *junior* level, in jurisdictional areas that are becoming increasingly interwoven. The fact remains, however, that by signing SUFA the provinces gave up significant authority in social policy in exchange for Ottawa's promise to grant additional dollars for health care.

As for the federal government, one of its main goals in seeking a social union agreement was to counteract the forces threatening to rupture the country. It sought to reinforce Canadian identity and promote national unity by showing Quebecers that Canadian federalism is capable of change. It is hard to imagine a more ill-suited approach to the problem. The federal government was making itself out to be a promoter of change, even though the changes it proposed were the very opposite of what Quebecers wanted. Indeed, they weaken what is considered an absolute minimum for Quebec — the maintenance of a strong federal principle wherein each level of government is sovereign within its areas of jurisdiction.

Federalism is a system that provides for the *sharing* but also the *separation* of powers between two levels of government. The objective is to govern communities that are both similar and different, allowing them to live together in harmony. The very nature of the federal principle implies a fundamental degree of separation that has always been vital for Quebec. That is why federalism should not be confused, as it often is, with subsidiarity, partnership or decentralization. These concepts are undeniably important, but they apply as much to a unitary system of government as to a federal system. Federalism is based on cooperation, certainly, but also on a diversity of visions and communities. That is why Canada must maintain a strong federal principle if it is to keep Quebec in the fold.

Indeed it is largely because of Quebec that Canada is a federation. The government of Quebec, the only government in Canada to be controlled by a majority of francophones, has always been a greater advocate than the other provinces of a strong federal principle. On the other hand, it could also be argued that since the 1976 rise to power of the Parti Québécois through to the 1995 referendum, Quebec's de facto withdrawal from this system has contributed to a weakening of the federal principle in Canada.

In its most recent and misguided effort to deal with the Quebec question, Ottawa has failed to recognize the fact that an ill-conceived social union that was artificially agreed upon in an effort to thwart the "separatists," far from solving the problem, would only make matters worse. In the long run, the real problem is not the existence of Quebec sovereignists per se, but the corrosive effects of Quebec's poor integration within Canada. This situation can only be exacerbated by defining a social union that does not take into account Quebec's distinct vision of federalism. Indeed, a parallel can be drawn between this situation and the 1982 enshrinement of the Canadian Charter of Rights and Freedoms, a process that cast aside Quebec's specificity and consent and thus caused a rift between Quebecers and other Canadians, even though they basically share the same values.

Furthermore, an artificial social union agreement alienates not only Quebec but also other regions, particularly the West, which do not entirely share Ottawa's vision in social policy. As will be seen below, however, positive developments may well result from this situation.

The Social Union Framework Agreement

BEYOND THE POLITICAL OBSTACLES, BOTH OLD AND NEW, WHAT ARE THE LIKELY CONsequences of the framework agreement itself for Quebec and the rest of Canada?

To begin with, SUFA's mobility provisions certainly appear incompatible with the maintenance of a strong federal principle. By definition the existence of two levels of government, each sovereign within its own jurisdictions, implies that either level of government may at times chose to exercise its powers in its own way. There is a growing tendency, however, to consider every difference an unacceptable barrier to the mobility of citizens, a disparity that must be corrected to conform to a pan-Canadian standard. Over and above the laudable objective of eliminating unnecessary barriers, SUFA's provisions on mobility would have the effect of creating an unrealistic number of all-encompassing commitments, in addition to affecting many programs in which there are significant differences between Quebec and the other provinces. As Claude Ryan aptly put it: "I also doubt that, in the areas directly linked to its distinct character, Quebec will be willing to cede to an outside authority its constitutional jurisdiction in education, health and social services."[4]

As for the rest of the agreement, it is a typical product of old-style executive federalism with its emphasis on technical and bureaucratic aspects.[5] It focuses on improving intergovernmental processes, not on questions of substance; it relates to issues that are usually discussed behind closed doors and neither concern directly nor interest the public. Thus the agreement's aim of ensuring "effective mechanisms for Canadians to participate in developing social priorities and reviewing outcomes" borders on the surreal.[6] More generally, this also makes it difficult to ascertain what has really happened over the past three years at the intergovernmental level regarding the social union.

Even from a federalist perspective, for Quebec to endorse the agreement would have been a fundamental and damaging political about-face, as the Quebec Liberal leader, Jean Charest, who was originally in favour of such an agreement, admitted regretfully. This was also the view of a number of experts, including former adviser to the Trudeau and Mulroney governments André Burelle, who concluded that SUFA amounted to putting the provinces under trusteeship.[7]

Even leaving aside the Quebec issue, SUFA has significant shortcomings. It is certainly not the major historical development for Canada that many had hoped it would be. Paradoxically, these shortcomings have been best described by Harvey Lazar, a well-known expert on intergovernmental relations and one of the agreement's main advocates.[8]

Lazar highlights the many contradictions that lie at the heart of SUFA. These include disputes over the interpretation of the agreement, its degree of formality, the implications of the provisions for citizen participation and intergovernmental cooperation, and the vision of Canada's future as implied in the agreement — in short, disagreements over the very essence of the agreement. It is evident that these problems go well beyond the normal tensions and contradictions inherent in any political agreement, especially when one considers the fact that some of the SUFA signatories (Premiers Klein and Harris come to mind) were elected on an ideologically right-wing platform that is very different from the values promoted by Ottawa in social policy.

In fact, the contradictions are so deep and fundamental that one might legitimately ask what the agreement is or whether an agreement even exists. What is clear, on the other hand, is why there was an agreement. Two circumstantial but powerful factors came into play: the urgent need for the provinces to obtain additional health-care funds from Ottawa, and a Canadian nationalist reaction against the "separatist" Quebec government. But the more one thinks about it, the more the agreement appears to be short-sighted, incomplete and riddled with contradictions and flaws.

SUFA is weighted in Ottawa's favour and, as currently written, does not significantly constrain the federal government's ability to intervene in social policy, even though this was what the provinces intended when they initiated the SUFA process. Considering that the new political climate which has emerged in some regions of the country, particularly the West, is undermining the political foundations of the agreement in those regions, it comes as a relief that SUFA is only an administrative document, with no legal clout, and that Quebec did not sign it.

Canada-Quebec Relations in a State of Flux

IT SHOULD BE POINTED OUT AT THE OUTSET THAT THERE IS NOTHING IN THE EVENTS that have occurred since 1999 to suggest that Quebec was mistaken in its decision not to take part in SUFA. In fact, three years later, it is more apparent than ever that this was its only option. The situation was difficult enough after the signing of SUFA when Quebec was abandoned by the other provinces for a third consecutive time, but it has deteriorated even more over the past year as a result of two major political developments, the first in Ottawa and the second in Quebec City. However, there may be a ray of hope on the horizon.

The first development, in Ottawa, was the triumphant re-election in November 2000 of Jean Chrétien's Liberal government, with a majority of the votes in Quebec.[9] The Liberal victory has reinforced the federal government's hard stance on the Quebec issue and a tendency to consider the case closed. The fact that the Liberal Party of Canada received more votes in Quebec than the Bloc Québécois, two years after the Liberal Party of Quebec won more votes than the Parti Québécois in the Quebec election, is widely seen in Ottawa as a vindication of the Chrétien government's policies and attitudes towards Quebec, on the issue of the social union as well as others. That said, Prime Minister Chrétien, viewed by some as the national political figure who represents the greatest obstacle to the normalization of relations between Canada and Quebec, may be serving his last mandate and should be leaving the stage in the next two to three years.

The second development, in Quebec City, was the sudden and unexpected resignation in January 2001 of Premier Lucien Bouchard, which also helped pave the way for a potential changing of the guard in terms of political actors historically linked to the Canada-Quebec impasse. The immediate effect, however, was to harden the discourse of the Parti Québécois government. Indeed, the PQ has reverted to a more hard-line sovereignist position under the leadership of Premier Bernard Landry, who has made it clear that he intended to adopt a more active stance in promoting Quebec sovereignty.

However, Premier Landry may prove to be another example of the "Nixon effect."[10] After an initial return to his sovereignist roots, Bernard Landry the realist might come to play the Canadian federalism game more effectively than his péquiste predecessors in a context where the achievement of Quebec sovereignty becomes very unlikely.

In the fall of 2000, Quebec's minister of intergovernmental relations, Joseph Facal, stated that the social union and fiscal imbalance were the two most important intergovernmental issues facing Quebec. Facal's reappointment to his portfolio in the new Landry government, on March 9, 2001, suggested that there would be little change in these priorities. This was confirmed a few months later when Premier Landry announced the creation of a task force to study the issue of fiscal imbalance between the two levels of government.

Quebec's desire to participate actively was also evident at the annual premiers' conference in Victoria on August 3, 2001. The issue of fiscal imbalance was among the main topics on the agenda under the sponsorship of Ontario Premier Mike Harris. Premier Harris' position received support from a surprisingly outspoken Premier Bernard Lord of New Brunswick, a province that is usually more likely to side with the federal government. At the conference, Premier Landry argued in favour of a transfer of tax points to ensure a permanent source of revenues to meet increasing provincial health-care needs, and the other premiers agreed to explore this option. Since then, the very existence of a fiscal imbalance has been strongly contested by the federal government, specifically by three senior ministers — Paul Martin, Allan Rock and Stéphane Dion. (It is revealing that no mention of SUFA was made at the premiers' conference, even though a major subject clearly linked to the agreement — the financing of health care in Canada — was the main topic of discussion.)

It is also the case that the resignation of the charismatic Lucien Bouchard as premier of Quebec has greatly increased the possibility of Jean Charest's Liberals taking over the reins of power within two years. This outcome will be even more likely if Premier Landry is unable to accept what promises to be a failure of his sovereignist offensive. Although a change of government would immediately boost Quebec's credibility in intergovernmental relations, it would not automatically resolve the Canada-Quebec problem, which, after all, is not a sovereignist invention. In other words, although the current political landscape is not at all conducive to a break in the impasse, this situation is likely to change rather quickly — but that in itself will not solve the basic problem.

One further political development that appears to be negative for the West but could perhaps have positive repercussions in terms of Canada-Quebec relations is also an outcome of the last federal election. The election revealed the inability of the Canadian Alliance to win significant support east of Manitoba. The party was clearly unable to present itself as a credible alternative to the reigning Liberal Party. Over the past year, the disarray within the Canadian Alliance and the forced resignation of its new leader, Stockwell Day, combined with the unlikely prospects of reorganizing the Canadian Right under Joe Clark's Progressive Conservative Party, has for all intents and purposes put the country under a one-party Liberal regime.[11]

One may recall that it was the creation, a decade ago, of a sovereignist party at the federal level that initiated this whole process. Following the failure of the Meech Lake Accord in 1990, Lucien Bouchard, then a federal Conservative cabinet minister, immediately created the Bloc Québécois, whose very existence was seen as a threat in the rest of the country. This, in turn, fuelled the rise of another regional party — this time in the West — the Reform Party, later to become the Canadian Alliance.[12] A dozen years on, we find ourselves with a one-party regime in Ottawa: the Liberals are the only party capable of winning power, a situation that has unhealthy consequences from every point of view. Once a governing party is no longer worried about losing the next election, the prime minister's powers — already substantial in a Westminster-style government like Canada's — become virtually unlimited.

So far, Bloc Québécois members of Parliament have kept out of the political process that was triggered by the creation of their party. This inertia on the part of sovereignists sitting in the House of Commons is all the more regrettable because such a historic opportunity may not present itself for some time, resulting as it does from a deepening of Western alienation. This alienation certainly has its own specific causes and dynamics, but it could be argued that it has been accentuated as a result of a failure to integrate Quebec and Quebec nationalism into the political life of Canada.

The provincialism in which the rest of Canada has managed to imprison itself in order to avoid recognizing Quebec's distinct character has, in some respects, backfired.[13] It has made Canadian political culture excessively provincial, in the strict sense of the word, while at the same time preventing the institutional and political expression of Atlantic and Western Canadian regionalism.

During the hearings of the Pepin-Robarts Commission in the late 1970s, regional alienation, particularly in Western Canada, emerged as one of Canada's two main political problems, the other being the Quebec question. Prime Minister Pierre Trudeau eventually shelved the commission's report, but 25 years later the sense of alienation in the West is deeper than ever. For instance, instead of pursuing efforts to achieve greater political power at a national level through Senate reform or a federal government dominated by the Canadian Alliance, a number of credible representatives from the West are now advocating a very different approach which consists of building strong provincial powers, particularly in Alberta and British Columbia. Public figures from Alberta have even suggested as a model the Quebec of the Quiet Revolution, with its theme of *maîtres chez nous* (masters in our own house), its Caisse de dépôt (deposit and investment fund) and its Régie des rentes (pension board).[14]

Perhaps we are witnessing a return to the convergence of Quebec-Western interests that provided Brian Mulroney's Conservative government two strong political mandates between 1984 and 1993, allowing him to conclude a free trade agreement with the United States and to almost succeed at reintegrating Quebec into the Canadian Constitution through the Meech Lake Accord. However, there is an element that is fundamentally new and positive in the present context, particularly in Alberta, where the environment is increasingly favourable to the right to opt out, a stance that is similar to Quebec's traditional position. Ralph Klein's return to the Alberta legislature on March 12, 2001, for a third mandate as premier, has certainly not hampered this movement. This could increase the potential for greater constitutional asymmetry applied to Quebec and other large provinces.[15]

Finally, recent changes in the political leadership in a number of other provinces should also be noted: Lorne Calvert became premier of Saskatchewan in January 2001, followed by Liberal Roger Grimes in Newfoundland in February and Liberal Gordon Campbell in British Columbia in June. Some of the consequences of these changes could already be seen at the 2001 annual premiers' conference, such as the support of the new premier of British Columbia for the position of Ontario's Mike Harris on fiscal imbalance. The premier of Alberta remains at the head of a Conservative government that has chosen a different path from the traditional Canadian social democracy that Ottawa promotes in the field of social policy. However, the departure of Mike Harris, announced in October 2001, will perhaps pave the way for a renewed role of the state and public administration in that province. This would be a welcome turn of events given that Quebec is always affected by what happens in Ontario and such a change could eventually serve to narrow the gap in the vision and values of these two neighbouring provinces.

Intergovernmental Developments since the Signing of SUFA

IT IS DIFFICULT TO IDENTIFY, LET ALONE PROPERLY ASSESS, THE DEVELOPMENTS THAT have taken place at the Canadian intergovernmental level since the signing of SUFA. Nevertheless, a number of points are worth noting. First, the Ministerial

Council on Social Policy Renewal, the body responsible for implementing the agreement, has made virtually no progress on a number of issues of particular interest to the provinces, such as the mechanisms for avoiding and resolving disputes and the monitoring and evaluation of the agreement. The Ministerial Council has met only three times since SUFA was signed and, tellingly, has not met at all since the signing of the health accord in September 2000.

It should also be noted that SUFA was not mentioned once in Premier Gordon Campbell's five-page letter of August 30, 2001, to Prime Minister Chrétien in which he reported on the results of the annual premiers' conference. Yet the letter makes a number of references to the First Ministers' Meeting held in September 2000, including a query about how Ottawa planned to follow up on its agreement to develop, in conjunction with the provinces, a mechanism for resolving disputes in the health care field. On that subject, the federal minister of health, Allan Rock, responded unequivocally that Ottawa did not intend in any way to abandon all or any of its exclusive powers to interpret and apply the *Canada Health Act*.[16]

It will be recalled that at the First Ministers' Meeting of September 2000 the alliance between the premiers of Canada's two largest provinces, Quebec and Ontario, scored a political victory, effectively forcing Ottawa's hand in amending the conditions to be attached to the transfer of additional health care funds. This showed that, despite the new political and constitutional context created by, among other things, the *Constitution Act, 1982*, Canadian geopolitics are still influenced by the "old" Canada, in that it is difficult to impose anything on the former Upper and Lower Canadas when they join forces to oppose it.

Ultimately, the impact of SUFA has been more noticeable in the sectoral-level forums such as the Meeting of Ministers of Social Services and in sectoral initiatives such as the Health Action Plan (the 2000 health accord) and the agreement on Early Childhood Development, which resulted from the First Ministers' meeting on September 11, 2000. Strengthened by an agreement that gives it a new legitimacy in social policy matters, especially through the clear and unprecedented recognition of its spending power, Ottawa now appears to attach less importance to the work of the Ministerial Council on Social Policy Renewal than to the sectoral-level forums. This could have something to do with the fact that the council membership includes representatives of the central agencies, who are more likely than representatives of their respective provincial departments to want to reconsider some of the concessions made by the provinces.

Thus, when it is not taking unilateral action, the federal government seems to rely on the sectoral-level forums made up of provincial ministers and technocrats. The latter are more inclined to accept Ottawa's leadership in social policy, as was the case during the era of cooperative federalism and cost-shared programs that ran from the beginning of the postwar period to the mid-1960s. Ottawa's ultimate aim appears to be to establish a uniform accountability framework from coast to coast and to harmonize evaluation standards. Nevertheless, some of the representatives of the large provinces in the sectoral-level forums often try to dampen Ottawa's zeal, either because they do not agree completely with the federal government or because they distrust it.

Prospects for the Future

THERE IS REASON TO BE UNEASY ABOUT THE ONGOING NEGATIVE EFFECTS ON Canadian politics of Quebec's non-participation in the 1982 Constitution and, more recently, the Social Union Framework Agreement. Indeed, the fact that Quebec is politically poorly integrated into Canada prevents Canadian democracy from functioning effectively. The results of the fall 2000 federal election are the most recent demonstration of this. It also has pernicious effects on the intergovernmental system as a whole, as witnessed by the hasty and artificial way in which SUFA was concluded.

Nevertheless, given that the main problem with the Canadian political system in regard to Quebec is its systematic refusal to recognize Quebec's distinct character, the province's non-participation in SUFA — besides being defensible and legitimate from a federalist point of view — could lead paradoxically to greater openness on this fundamental issue in the rest of the country. Not only does the agreement run counter to the interests of some provinces, but Quebec's non-participation clearly renders it deficient as a framework from which to chart a renewed national project.[17]

Claude Ryan has identified three possible ways of solving this problem, which can be summarized as follows: greater decentralization of powers to the provinces, similar to what is being proposed by the Canadian Alliance; a return to a more classic type of federalism (recommended by, among others, André Burelle) centred on clear and rigorous respect for the respective jurisdictions of each level of government and on joint decision-making in matters of common interest; and, finally, clear and effective recognition of the distinct character of Quebec.[18] I have also focused on the latter two approaches — strengthening of the federal principle and affirmation of Quebec as a robust, distinct society within Canada — in a recent analysis.[19]

It must be admitted that all of these avenues appear to be blocked at present, and it is highly unlikely that any of them could be seriously considered in the context of the SUFA review. However, as I have pointed out, circumstances may well change and it is important to be prepared for such an eventuality.

Paradoxically, Quebec's refusal to sign an administrative agreement that binds it neither constitutionally nor politically affords it more power and room to manoeuvre than did its decision not to ratify the *Constitution Act, 1982*, which nevertheless applies in every respect to *la belle province*. However, Quebec will only continue to enjoy this advantage if it adopts a more proactive approach to Canadian intergovernmental relations in the field of social policy.

Quebec's dynamic and innovative approach to social policy in recent decades gives it more than enough credibility to defend its views in an effective manner in intergovernmental forums.[20] In this regard the present circumstances are fundamentally different from those of the 1945–60 period, when Quebec complained about Ottawa's incursions into its areas of jurisdiction but did not have the wherewithal to act.

That said, Quebec needs to adapt its traditional constitutional position to better reflect the needs of the distinct society that it has become at the beginning of the 21st century. In particular, it must acknowledge the fact that constitutional jurisdictions are not self-contained as they once were. Indeed, even though Quebec's vision of federalism remains relevant, it has become outdated in some respects. For instance, its steadfast opposition, on principle, to any federal involvement in provincial areas of jurisdiction ignores the reality of the last 50 years, a period during which the federal spending power has been used in Quebec with sometimes positive consequences for its citizens — an example is the housing provided by the Canada Mortgage and Housing Corporation in the postwar years; of course, had the Meech Lake Accord been accepted, Quebec would have been more willing to acknowledge this reality.

However, Quebec should be careful not to become party to SUFA until it obtains a clear right to opt out with financial compensation, a *sine qua non* for its ability to interact effectively with the rest of Canada. This recommendation is particularly addressed to any future Liberal government that might be tempted to sign the agreement without obtaining the necessary concessions. Ultimately, this would only make the problem worse.

The Quebec Liberals' most recent position on SUFA is presented in detail in the final report of the Special Committee of the Quebec Liberal Party on the Political and Constitutional Future of Quebec Society. The agreement is deemed unclear and deficient in many respects, in particular with regard to the length of notice before the implementation of new federal pan-Canadian programs and the method of consulting with the provinces about these; the limits on the federal spending power in terms of direct, unilateral federal payments to individuals and organizations as well as transfers to the provinces; the mobility provisions; redress mechanisms for citizens; the respective roles and responsibilities of the federal and provincial governments in the sectors covered by the agreement; and the method for preventing and settling disputes. As for the measures that are most problematic from Quebec's point of view — public accountability, evaluation of the provinces, identification of best practices and the development of comparable indicators for measuring results — the Liberals suggest that the SUFA provisions seem promising but that it might be worthwhile referring to the wording used in the September 2000 health accord. The overall assessment is that "it should be up to the provinces to agree on mechanisms for developing the necessary convergence in areas of provincial jurisdiction."[21]

The tone of the report, which concludes that the issue of the Canadian social union is evolving and that "the agreement still needs to be tried and improved," seems overly optimistic about the future of SUFA, notwithstanding the Quebec issue. As for the latter, it would be naïve to think that Quebec's refusal to sign the agreement was simply due to easily resolved technical issues such as the design of an appropriate opting-out formula. In fact everything suggests that the federal refusal to allow Quebec the right to opt out is rooted in the long-standing impasse between Quebec and Canada.

In terms of broader strategy, it is important to recognize the links between the two principal structural problems facing Canada: Quebec nationalism and Western alienation.[22] For Quebec in particular, the experience of three consecutive failures to achieve broad interprovincial consensus, as well as the success of its alliance with Ontario in September 2000, should teach it to rely on circumstantial and temporary alliances with one or more provinces that have the means and motivation to oppose Ottawa's centralizing aims.

Naturally, the larger provinces of Ontario, Alberta and British Columbia immediately spring to mind. Quebec should take advantage of Western Canada's current focus on provincial autonomy as an opportunity to promote asymmetrical federalism as a potential solution to both the Quebec problem and Western alienation. On the other hand, the impressive performance of the New Brunswick premier on the subject of fiscal imbalance at the August 2001 premiers' conference in Victoria is a reminder that Quebec should not *a priori* exclude any province. Indeed, the social union issue serves to illustrate the complexity of the relationship between Quebec and the rest of Canada. Although the convergence of interests between Quebec and a region like the West is evident and appears to have great potential, important differences remain. For example, the Quebec government continues to espouse an essentially social-democratic orientation that garners wider support in Quebec than in the rest of Canada. Thus Quebecers are less interested perhaps than Albertans or Ontarians in having the federal government's social-democratic vision act as a counterweight in the social policy field. Differences in provincial wealth and resources are also a factor. In terms of per capita wealth, Quebec ranks somewhere in the middle, between the small Atlantic provinces, which are financially heavily dependent on Ottawa, and the large, wealthy provinces west of the Ottawa River. It is in Quebec's interest to have Ottawa maintain its role in the redistribution of Canada's wealth, and as such it cannot support the demand to have federal social transfers allocated purely on a per capita basis. The support of the small provinces may therefore be useful to Quebec, since, like them, it receives significant sums from the federal government. The key is for Quebec to be present, flexible and dynamic, but not to harbour any illusions about how solid alliances are.

Although alliances may be necessary, they can never resolve all of Quebec's problems. Quebec is an entity in itself and must be able to go its own way from time to time without this being seen as an aberration or as a sign of disloyalty to Canada.

In this spirit, it is important that governments and the public come to recognize that the Canadian intergovernmental system has become structurally biased against Quebec and its particular concerns. This bias is amply demonstrated by the fact that an intergovernmental agreement can be considered valid even though it has not been signed by the only province with a francophone majority.

The basic idea is to remind Canadians that Quebec has a distinct vision of Canada, one that is still relevant. As has been pointed out, this does not preclude the need for Quebec to adapt to a new context where constitutional jurisdictions are not as clearly delimited as they once were. On the other hand, Quebec's specificity has not prevented it from harmonizing its policies with those of the other provinces. It must be understood, nonetheless, that Canada's abandonment of a strong federal principle, combined with its refusal to recognize the true implications of Quebec's distinct character, can only result in a continuing deterioration of the Quebec problem, with negative consequences for the entire country.

Quebec, for its part, should express its willingness to cooperate in good faith with the other provinces and the federal government on social policy matters as long as mechanisms can be put in place to take into account its distinct character in this field, thus following up on the Calgary Declaration and the December 1995 federal motion on the distinct society. The other provinces should have recognized, for example, that Quebec's desire to opt out of the Millennium Scholarship Fund was based on its specific needs in education matters, and should have supported its request to withdraw from this program.[23]

Finally, the question of fiscal imbalance that was raised at the premiers' conference in August 2001 is a key issue that should be kept on the agenda. The increasing imbalance between Ottawa's revenue sources and its constitutional responsibilities relative to those of the provinces needs to be addressed as it ultimately works against the maintenance of a strong federal principle in Canada.

Conclusion

SINCE THE 1995 QUEBEC REFERENDUM, THERE HAS BEEN A TENDENCY WITHIN THE Canadian political and intergovernmental system to ignore and even deny, despite all the evidence, that there even is a problem between Quebec and the rest of Canada. This tendency to hide one's head in the sand, which seems to have become the norm in Ottawa power circles and among the English-speaking intellectual elites, is of great concern for the future of the country. Indeed, without a problem there is no need for a solution. More fundamentally, such a mindset prevents us from turning the energy inherent in facing any problem toward finding a solution while there is still time.

Canadians must come to realize that there is something fundamentally wrong with a political process which is incapable of dealing with the concerns of all the consecutive governments of the only province with a francophone majority, home to the founding people (in terms of the construction of the Canadian identity) and a quarter of the Canadian population. The increasingly evident alienation of Quebec's francophone majority within Canada remains the greatest problem facing the country and one that should be uppermost in the minds of both citizens and political leaders.

Even among those who do believe there is a Canada-Quebec problem, the objective seems to be no longer the historical reconciliation of Quebec with the rest of Canada but, rather, the total defeat of the "separatists," who are, such people are convinced, the country's only real problem. According to this analysis, francophones who voted overwhelmingly "Yes" in the 1995 referendum simply did not know what they were doing. This fairy-tale view of the world is the mirror image of unrealistic sovereignist ideology. Such federalist illusions do not take Canada's or Quebec's reality into consideration. They do not reflect an understanding of the Quebec fact, a national phenomenon that is firmly rooted in the history of Canada and thus one that will not disappear simply because it cannot be expressed positively. Nations do not wither away in this manner, certainly not in an era of globalization marked by stronger local and national identities. An iron law of human history is that the greater the effort to deny the existence of a nation, the more gives rise to negative expressions of nationalism.

It is crucial that Canadians be better informed on these matters. The fact is that a sense of alienation as deeply felt and as well documented as that of the francophone majority in Quebec will not simply disappear with the defeat of the sovereignists, but will instead destroy the country from within. As is the case for other national identities, for Quebec society to remain an open society, certain points of reference that are specific to it must be respected. One such point is the clear predominance of French without excluding English. To reiterate, the ongoing deterioration of Canada-Quebec relations has increasingly negative effects on the entire country and constitutes a greater danger today than Quebec separation. As sovereignty becomes less a functional political project than an unrealizable dream, and as the problems and frustrations related to Canada-Quebec tensions increase without any prospect of solution, there is a risk that some individuals could get out of control. Every effort must be made to ensure that the situation of Quebec within Canada does not become another Ireland.[24]

One step in the right direction would be to confront the problem head-on — even if there is no immediate solution — instead of continuing to systematically ignore it. SUFA is useful in this respect, precisely because it is such a clear manifestation of the Quebec-Canada impasse and therefore serves to highlight a problem in a system that denies its very existence.

However, SUFA no longer has the historical importance once attributed to it. And it will have even less importance in the future if Quebec decides to become actively involved on the intergovernmental scene. The 2000 health accord might be a good starting point for discussion in this regard. It has been approved by both the premier of Quebec and the leader of the Quebec Liberal Party, on the premise that it is up to the provinces to agree on mechanisms for convergence in areas of provincial jurisdiction. There is some indication that Quebec might be able to see to it that SUFA falls to the wayside, even if it is not formally abolished.

Quebec is different from the other provinces and, as long as it is not recognized and treated as such, Quebec society will have a greater tendency to keep its distance and try to withdraw from Canada. Only as a strong, distinct society will Quebec be able to participate effectively in strengthening the Canadian social union and to share its dynamism with the rest of the country.

1   In this regard, I should note that in early
    June 1998 I was asked by the Secrétariat
    aux Affaires intergouvernementales canadi-
    ennes du Québec to write a report "on the
    proposed Social Union in relation to
    Quebec's view of Canadian federalism." In
    that report, I analyzed, among other things,
    the potentially positive consequences of
    Quebec's joining the interprovincial consen-
    sus and recommended that it do so. See
    Dufour (1998).

2   See Noël (2000, p. 9).

3   The content of this agreement, which was
    entirely reasonable in the Canadian context,
    had been reached under ideal conditions:
    the Quebec government of the time was
    federalist, the federal government was will-
    ing to recognize Quebec's distinct character,
    and it was a period of prosperity that fos-
    tered a spirit of generosity and openness.

4   Ryan (2000, p. 209). On the subject of
    mobility, see also Frémont (2000).

5   "Executive federalism" refers to the specifi-
    cally Canadian system of federal/provincial
    and interprovincial agreements and confer-
    ences, at all levels and in most fields, which
    has become an important arena of power in
    Canada.

6   On this subject, see the thoughtful analysis
    by Susan Phillips in this book. Phillips is
    skeptical about the effect of the agreement's
    provisions on citizen participation and
    whether they will be implemented, noting
    that their success depends largely on federal
    grants to citizens' groups whose concerns are
    by definition more likely to resemble those
    of Ottawa than those of the provinces. In his
    chapter, Roger Gibbins writes even more
    pointedly of the decisive victory of intergov-
    ernmentalism over populism.

7   Burelle (1999); see also Gagnon and Segal
    (2000), Noël (2000), Frémont (2000),
    Binette (2000) and Ryan (2000).

8   See Lazar (2000a, b).

9   However, the sovereignist Bloc Québécois
    again won the majority of votes among
    francophone Quebecers.

10 It took someone as far to the Right as
    Richard Nixon, with his diehard anti-
    communist beliefs, to be the first American
    president to visit Red China.

11 According to Massicotte (2001), given the
    current alignment of political parties, the
    Canadian electoral system prevents changes
    from taking place at the federal level; the
    system undermines Canadian unity by
    accentuating regional variations in party
    representation, leaving the impression that
    the country is more polarized than it is.
    Massicotte argues that an electoral system
    based on proportional representation would
    have more advantages than drawbacks, but
    concludes that such a change appears
    unlikely in the foreseeable future.

12 The Reform Party was formed just prior to
    the Bloc Québécois. However, the BQ's suc-
    cess was such that it quickly acquired the
    status of Official Opposition, to the indig-
    nation of many English-speaking
    Canadians. This gave further impetus to the
    Reform Party to become a national party.

13 Dufour (1990).

14 See Harper et al. (2001) and Roger Gibbins'
    chapter in this book.

15 See also Spector (2001).

16 "Rock Rules Out Independent Medicare
    Referee" (2001).

17 This emerged from several of the papers
    presented at the conference "Perspectives
    and Directions: The Social Union
    Framework Agreement" on February 3-4,
    2000. See McIntosh (2002).

18 Ryan (2000).

19 Dufour (2000).

20 Quebec's dynamism in the social policy
    field is well documented. See, for example,
    Noël (1997, p. 241) as well as Yves
    Vaillancourt's chapter in this book.

21 Quebec Liberal Party (2001, pp. 87-91).

22 Aboriginal and multicultural issues are not
    structural in the sense used in the Pepin-
    Roberts report.

23 It was essentially to avoid penalizing
    Quebec students that the province finally

reached an agreement with Ottawa.
Quebec now has to live with an agreement
that does nothing to solve the underlying
problem.

24   On this subject, see Dufour (1998; 2000,
      pp. 76-79).

Binette, André. "Principles." In *The Canadian Social Union without Quebec: 8 Critical Analyses*, ed. Alain-G. Gagnon and Hugh Segal. Montreal: Institute for Research on Public Policy, 2000.

Burelle, André. "Union sociale: mise en tutelle des provinces." *Le Devoir*, February 15, 1999: A7.

Dufour, Christian. *Lettre aux souverainistes québécois et aux fédéralistes canadiens qui sont restés fidèles au Québec*. Montreal: Stanké, 2000.

———. *Rapport sur le projet d'union sociale en regard de la vision québécoise du fédéralisme canadien*. Quebec: Secrétariat aux Affaires intergouvernementales canadiennes du Québec, July 1998.

———. *A Canadian Challenge: Le défi québécois*. Lantzville, BC: Institute for Research on Public Policy/Oolichan, 1990.

Frémont, Jacques. "Mobility Within Canada." In *The Canadian Social Union without Quebec: 8 Critical Analyses*, ed. Alain-G. Gagnon and Hugh Segal. Montreal: Institute for Research on Public Policy, 2000.

Gagnon, Alain-G., and Hugh Segal, eds. *The Canadian Social Union Without Quebec: 8 Critical Analyses*, Montreal: Institute for Research on Public Policy, 2000.

Harper, Stephen, Tom Flanagan, Ted Morton, Rainer Knopp, Andrew Crooks and Ken Boessenkool. "Open Letter to Ralph Klein." *National Post*, January 26, 2001: A14.

Lazar, Harvey. "The Social Union Framework Agreement: Lost Opportunity or New Beginning?" Working Paper 3. Kingston: School of Policy Studies, Queen's University, August 2000a.

———. "The Social Union Framework Agreement and the Future of Fiscal Federalism." In *Canada: The State of the Federation, 1999-2000: In Search of a New Mission Statement for Canadian Fiscal Federalism*, ed. Harvey Lazar. Kingston: Institute of Intergovernmental Relations, 2000b.

Massicotte, Louis. "Changing the Canadian Electoral System." *Choices*, Vol. 7, no. 1 (February 2001).

McIntosh, Tom, ed. *Building the Social Union: Perspectives, Directions and Challenges*. Regina: Canadian Plains Research Center, University of Regina, 2002.

Noël, Alain. "General Study of the Framework Agreement." In *The Canadian Social Union without Quebec: 8 Critical Analyses*, ed. Alain-G. Gagnon and Hugh Segal. Montreal: Institute for Research on Public Policy, 2000.

Noël, Alain. "The Federal Principle, Solidarity and Partnership." In *Beyond the Impasse: Toward Reconciliation*, ed. Roger Gibbins and Guy Laforest. Montreal: Institute for Research on Public Policy, 1997.

Quebec Liberal Party. *A Project for Quebec: Affirmation, Autonomy and Leadership*. Report of the Special Committee of the Liberal Party of Quebec on the Political and Constitutional Future of Quebec Society, October 2001.

"Rock Rules Out Independent Medicare Referee." *The Gazette* (Montreal), November 14, 2001: A10.

Ryan, Claude. "The Agreement on the Canadian Social Union as Seen by a Quebec Federalist." In *The Canadian Social Union without Quebec: 8 Critical Analyses*, ed. Alain-G. Gagnon and Hugh Segal. Montreal: Institute for Research on Public Policy, 2000.

Spector, Norman. "Klein et Landry sont faits pour s'entendre." *Le Devoir*, March 13, 2001: A7.

SUFA and Citizen
Engagement:
Fake or Genuine
Masterpiece?

Introduction

T HE IDEA OF A RENEWED SOCIAL UNION IS AS MUCH ABOUT BUILDING STRONGER RELA-
tionships between citizens and governments as it is about building more collaborative relationships among governments. One widely used definition of social
union is that which "embodies our sense of collective responsibility (among citizens),
our federalism pact (between and across regions), and our governance contract
(between citizens and governments)."[1] The Social Union Framework Agreement
(SUFA) marks the first time that the federal and provincial governments have made a
joint commitment to engage citizens in the governing process. It not only is committed, according to its statement of principles, to ensuring that Canadians have "meaningful input into social policies and programs," but commits governments to report
publicly on the outcomes of social programs and to provide "effective mechanisms for
citizens to participate in developing social priorities and reviewing outcomes." Is
SUFA a genuine move toward a deliberative form of democracy in which citizens are
actively and meaningfully engaged in policy-making? To what extent are Canadian
governments living up to the SUFA principles and promises on citizen engagement?

To fully understand the significance of SUFA, we must reject the traditional
typologies used to describe federal-provincial relations, which focus on the degree
of underlying conflict or cooperation.[2] We need to conceive of a new approach to
federalism, one that involves citizens as well as governments, and does so in an
instrumental manner. "Instrumental federalism," which emerged in the late 1990s
and became enshrined in SUFA, focuses on the ability of governments to solve
problems that matter to Canadians and to enhance policy learning through evaluation — and on the accountability of governments in these two respects. These goals

derive directly from the philosophy of New Public Management (NPM). The notion of instrumentality is captured nicely by the Treasury Board Secretariat in its comment that the essence of SUFA is "doing what works for Canadians," rather than — it is implied — concentrating on (or being limited by) jurisdictional authority.[3] The approach embodied in SUFA is instrumental not only in getting results, but also in ultimately increasing the visibility and relevance of government and public trust in government. More importantly, all of these goals can serve to protect and promote the interests of individual governments within the federation.

Citizens are key to this process. Respect for the federal principle makes it difficult for governments to hold each other directly accountable for spending or for public policy. This is a particular concern for Ottawa, because the shift from cost-sharing and conditional funding to block transfers diminished its ability to influence provincial use of federal money. In instrumental federalism, citizens can hold governments to account based on public reporting of policy outcomes. They serve as a foil against encroachment or inaction by other governments: for instance, vigilant citizens, armed with the knowledge that the federal government has unilaterally cut transfer payments, or that a provincial government is improperly allocating federal dollars earmarked for early childhood development, for example, can exert political pressure to force compliance. Another motivation for this new approach to federalism is the recognition that trust and confidence in government are declining and that Canadians want to be engaged in policy-making but feel excluded.[4] SUFA does include provisions for engaging citizens in policy at the level of each individual government, yet it makes no commitment with respect to opening up intergovernmental decision-making to greater public involvement.

So citizens are to be the third force in federalism — not so much as a means of creating a social union that truly addresses the democratic deficit that has been so widely deplored, but as a third-party barrier to the actions of one government against another.[5] For this reason, the citizen engagement and accountability provisions of SUFA go hand in hand. Although citizens were brought into SUFA first and foremost to act as watchdogs, their role was expanded by more positive commitments around public involvement in policy-making. Neither the federal nor provincial governments had any concrete plan at the time, however, as to how these commitments would be met. Therefore, these broader promises around citizen engagement can be read as largely symbolic — nice if they could be kept, but no effort expended to develop a strategy to do so.

Still, the fact remains that commitments to citizen engagement are set out in SUFA and, if met, could have a positive impact on the relationship between civil society and government. The reality, as we will see, is that both levels of government have failed miserably in keeping their promises.

Although governments have not, so far, lived up to their SUFA commitments, enormous benefit would be derived from expanding the role of citizens in the social union. We therefore begin by exploring the potential of meaningful citizen engagement that is based on a model of deliberative democracy. What does this concept mean, and what kinds of institutions and practices are needed to implement it? In particular, how might intergovernmental decision-making be made more accessible to citizens and their organizations? We then turn from the potential to the reality of SUFA, first examining its actual promises around citizen engagement, then attempting to explain why they are part of a new model of instrumental federalism. The third part of the paper focuses on implementation: after almost three years, what have governments done to meet the commitments made under SUFA to engage citizens? The National Children's Agenda (NCA), which has been declared a priority by federal and provincial governments alike and which represents the first SUFA-influenced collaborative social policy effort, presents an opportunity to see how citizens and voluntary organizations have been engaged. Interestingly, although the engagement practices under the NCA fall far short of SUFA commitments, civil society has not been standing still, waiting to be asked to participate. In spite of limited publicity about SUFA, voluntary organizations have been improving their networks and orchestrating a greater role for citizens in the social union. The paper concludes that better organization and stronger leadership within civil society may make it increasingly difficult for governments to ignore their SUFA responsibilities even though, at present, they appear quite content to do so.

The Potential: Citizen Engagement and Intergovernmental Relations

I N THE CONTEXT OF INTERGOVERNMENTAL RELATIONS, IT MATTERS BOTH HOW AND where the public is involved in policy-making. "How" refers to the goals and methods of such involvement, while "where" refers to its location — in individual jurisdictions or at the intergovernmental level.

From Consultation to Citizen Engagement

Citizen involvement in policy-making has long been seen as a continuum, ranging from the token one-way provision of information (for example, written material describing a proposed policy and soliciting comments) to an interactive, iterative two-way dialogue that has a genuine influence on policy. The term "citizen engagement" is now generally used to describe practices at this latter end of the continuum. Citizen engagement is informed by a conceptual model of "deliberative democracy." It is an interactive, deliberative dialogue between citizens (and/or their organizations) and government officials that contributes meaningfully to specific policy decisions in a transparent and accountable manner.[6] Somewhere between tokenism and citizen engagement lie the various types of episodic public "consultation" that both federal and provincial governments regularly host. They include public meetings, legislative hearings, multistakeholder roundtables and other one-off events. The problem with most of these mechanisms is that they are lopsided: government usually determines who is invited, there are few opportunities for a real exchange of views and genuine dialogue, and participants receive limited information on how the results are used. In addition, these forms of consultation seldom make an impact on civil society in terms of developing leadership skills, mobilizing the community or building social capital. Moreover, traditional consultation has gained a reputation in many communities as being little more than a "telling and selling" exercise — telling people about the government's policy choice and selling them on it.[7]

Citizen engagement is meant not simply to reproduce traditional forms of consultation, but to promote a more deliberative form of democracy. Cohen defines deliberative democracy as "a framework of social and institutional conditions that facilitates free discussion among equal citizens — by providing favourable conditions for participation, association and expression — and ties the authorization to exercise public power (and the exercise itself) to such discussion."[8] This concept has several implications for reform. First, deliberation does not entail just any discussion but refers to "free public reasoning among equals who are governed by the decision."[9] *Reasoning* is interactive and iterative by nature; the participants are prepared to be moved by reason and to abide by the results.[10] The notion of free reasoning suggests that the process is inclusive and participatory and that the parties are treated as equals. But citizen engagement as part of deliberative democracy goes further than reasoning, and it is this aspect that gives governments the most difficulty. The concept also suggests that the results of the process be given weight in collective decision-making and be used to guide subsequent action. This does not imply, in my view, that citizens (rather than elected officials) have the final say on policy, but it does require established and credible mechanisms, processes or protocols, in order for the results of such deliberation to have an institutionalized impact on political decision-making. In addition, citizens need to know they have influence and the extent of that influence.

Citizen engagement based on the deliberative democracy model has three distinct benefits for a renewed social union. First, it is capable of producing better policy. Over the past decade, the nature of governing has changed from the top-down, command-and-control model to a more horizontal style of governance that involves collaboration among governments and with the private and voluntary sectors in planning, designing and implementing policy.[11] Increased horizontality is not a passing fad but an adaptive response to a more diverse population with differing needs and expectations of the state — and with less trust in the state — and to a more complex policy environment where government is only part of the solution. Given that this transition from government to governance is taking place at the end of a fiscal crisis, not only has the process of governing changed, but so too has its scope. Even in an era of budget surpluses, governments are choosing to do less than they used to; they are sticking to their defined "core business" and leaving many societal needs to be met by families and communities.

By necessity, then, the contemporary style of governance is more embedded in civil institutions than the top-down style of governing. It requires that policy-makers be knowledgeable about the needs and wants of partners and communities, that policy design benefit from the knowledge and expertise of the delivery agents (increasingly likely to be voluntary organizations), and that both the substance and the process of policy-making be seen as credible by the partners, who may share some of the risks or be responsible for implementation.[12] Acquisition of such knowledge and credibility hinges on meaningful involvement of the partners and citizens at all stages of the policy process.

The second distinct benefit of citizen engagement is a more active citizenry and more vibrant civil society. As Anne Phillips notes, deliberation matters only because there is difference. The free reasoning involved in deliberation builds pressure for the inclusion of differences, thus contributing to a spirit of revived pluralism.[13] Deliberative democracy, it is argued, promotes active citizenship because it requires individuals and organizational representatives to become informed about issues, rather than merely taking immutable positions or offering ill-conceived opinions, and to participate in the dialogue. The act of participation fosters the honing of citizenship skills and the building of horizontal networks based on trust.[14]

The third distinct benefit accrues to government directly. Citizen engagement raises the visibility and, potentially, the credibility of the government among its governing partners and among the public. It may also enhance democratic practices within political institutions by opening up legislative and other decision-making processes to public scrutiny.

Truly deliberative forms of democracy cannot be created in an ad hoc manner but require several kinds of infrastructure. An obvious prerequisite is institutions or fora run by and for the public. A problem with existing forms of consultation is that the state usually reserves the power to determine who will be consulted. In deliberative fora, such as citizen panels or juries, participants are selected at random or, on a representative basis, by a third party.[15] In other models, such as the newly formed Civic Forum in Scotland, representatives of civil society associations are self-selected and thus have a sense of ownership of the engagement process and the deliberative institution.[16]

Even if the goal is to engage individual citizens, the process is facilitated by strong associational democracy — that is, by extensive and active networks of voluntary organizations that are run democratically and have well-developed memberships.[17] Voluntary organizations are critical to citizen engagement because they are expert in service delivery and know their communities. If voluntary organizations embody internal democracy and have active memberships, they are themselves sites of deliberation that allow citizens to acquire and practise citizenship skills. However, voluntary organizations can be effective only if they have the capacity to participate actively and to undertake their own policy analysis, which in turn requires access to information, appropriate human and financial resources, and policy and technical expertise.[18] Finally, if indeed the goal of institutionalized citizen engagement is not to simply feed public opinion into the policy process, but to improve the relationship between governments and civil society, the state of that relationship must be monitored and made public.

Citizen Engagement in the
Intergovernmental Context

Since citizen involvement can take various forms and take place at various levels, it is useful to view it as on a continuum (table 1). From an intergovernmental perspective, participation can range from a process that is independent and contained within a single jurisdiction to one that is fully integrated within the machinery of intergovernmental decision-making. As Seidle observes, tentative steps have been taken in the direction of jointly led approaches to public involvement, with governments either establishing a common framework for engagement but conducting their own exercises, or jointly sponsoring and participating in consultative exercises.[19]

In practice, however, most of these joint exercises have been episodic, traditional types of consultation.[20] Indeed citizen engagement in intergovernmental decision-making remains extremely rare in Canada. As Mendelsohn and McLean argue, Canada lags considerably behind other federations in involving its citizens and voluntary organizations in intergovernmental processes.[21] A combination of factors have contributed to this situation. With the exceptional power of Canada's first ministers, the relatively weak position of legislators and the emphasis on party discipline, the negotiation of institutional interests has been the dominant style of intergovernmental relations.[22] The intergovernmental agenda is thus shaped largely by territorial interests, which leaves little room for groups that are not territorially based to exert their influence. Within the Federal/Provincial/Territorial Ministerial Council, intergovernmental specialists are assuming greater prominence, which tends to give precedence to matters of process and protection of governmental interests over matters of substance. To some extent, as well, the organization of the voluntary sector has contributed to its own exclusion. There is no true peak association representing the sector, and in many policy fields there is both poor vertical integration of local, provincial and national organizations and poor cross-organizational contact at the regional level. This structure, coupled with a lack of resources, renders civil society unable to press governments sufficiently to open up intergovernmental relations to citizens and organizations.

Citizen engagement could be made integral to intergovernmental relations in a number of ways: civic fora comprising representatives of voluntary organizations engaged in policy development and service delivery[23]; citizen juries and panels; regular rather than one-off meetings with individuals and organizations on particular issues; involvement of representatives of national voluntary organi-

Forms of Citizen Involvement in an Intergovernmental Context

Independent	→			Intergovernmental
Individual government initiative: independent of others	Involve representatives of other government in independent processes	Agreed framework, independent processes	Jointly led processes	Intergovernmental mechanisms attached to intergovernmental machinery
Common	→			**Rare**
	National Forum on Health	Calgary Declaration	National Children's Agenda	National Children's Benefit Reference Group (now defunct)
			Canada Pension Plan Review	Aboriginal Working Group to the F/P/T Ministerial Council

zations in working groups under the Federal/Provincial/Territorial Ministerial Council[24]; and convening of regular meetings of the Ministerial Council and the Sectoral Tables with leaders from the voluntary sector on key issues. Effective citizen engagement requires not only the means for participatory policy-making, but also a transparent process and ongoing review of the mechanisms to that effect. Lazar suggests an approach whereby each signatory would establish a legislative committee on the social union — a process that would also involve federal and provincial legislators more effectively.[25] Each committee would be expected to hold regular public hearings to review its jurisdiction's compliance with SUFA. Another approach would be to follow the monitoring practices of the framework agreement, or "compact," as in the United Kingdom between the Blair government and the voluntary sector. Its innovation is to convene an annual joint meeting of senior ministers and leaders from the voluntary sector for the purposes of: (1) preparing, for presentation to Parliament, an annual report on government and voluntary-sector adherence to the compact and on the general state of the relationship; and (2) producing an action plan that sets out steps for improving the relationship in the coming year.

The creation of new institutions for citizen engagement in the intergovernmental realm would not strip ministers of their ability to bargain behind closed doors or their ultimate decision-making power. Nor would the input of citizens and voluntary organizations replace the expertise of government officials. Rather, executive bargaining would have the benefit of ongoing dialogue with *additional* experts — those who are knowledgeable about local communities and about service delivery in those communities.

The SUFA Promise on Citizen Engagement

S UFA IS A PRODUCT OF NEGOTIATIONS OVER AN 18-MONTH PERIOD AND THUS IS AN agreement forged of compromise. The process included both interprovincial discussions to develop a common position and federal-provincial negotiation. The provinces took the lead by creating the Provincial/Territorial Council on Social Policy Renewal in 1995 and by reaching a consensus that included Quebec, made public at the 1998 premiers' conference in Saskatoon (the

Saskatoon Consensus). The full details of this consensus were elaborated in the Victoria Proposal released in January 1999.[26] During this period the federal government also laid out some of its key positions, in a two-part document, *Working Together for Canadians*, released in July 1998 and January 1999. In closed-door negotiations, with an offer by the prime minister to boost health care funding, a final agreement was reached in early February 1999 that saw the provinces make major compromises — compromises that were too great for Quebec to accept. Although the negotiations were not open to the public, a sense of which parts of SUFA were critically important to whom, and how ideas evolved, can be gleaned by comparing the earlier positions with the wording of the final agreement.[27]

SUFA mentions or has implications for citizen engagement in five contexts. The most important and most concrete directly addresses participation in policy. This occurs in two places. The first is under the opening section on principles, which encourages governments, within their respective constitutional jurisdictions, to follow the principle of ensuring "appropriate opportunities for Canadians to have meaningful input into social policies and programs." This principle, which does not appear in earlier provincial statements, reflects Ottawa's concern with building social capital and social cohesion, a concern that dates from the mid-1990s when a few centrally placed individuals in the Prime Minister's Office, Privy Council Office and key departments saw the need to engage citizens as a way of building a stronger, more cohesive society and restoring trust in government.[28]

Although this provision could be a powerful means of enhancing citizen engagement, since it requires that such engagement be *meaningful*, its impact is diluted because it appears as only a guiding principle rather than a commitment to action. It is reinforced, however, by a subsequent commitment modelled on a clause in the Victoria Proposal, to "ensure effective mechanisms for Canadians to participate in developing social priorities and reviewing outcomes."[29] The strength of this statement lies in the agreement to provide actual mechanisms, not mere opportunities. Its limitation is that the commitment applies to only the front end of establishing priorities and the back end of reviewing outcomes, and says nothing about actually involving citizens in policy development, design or implementation. For the provinces, however, specifying participation in priority-setting may not have been seen as a limitation at all; such involvement could potentially be used as a counterweight against federal meddling in provincial matters through use of the spending power to establish programs desired by Ottawa.

Yet as a means of facilitating citizen engagement this clause does indeed have limitations. The reality of priority-setting is that it is always an inherently political process and thus one that executives are reluctant to give up. While governments frequently do consult to assess underlying public values, and regularly commission public opinion polls to determine "top of mind" issues, they are unlikely to put themselves in a position of being bound, even morally, to engage in a process of public engagement that has real influence in priority-setting. In the intergovernmental realm, the reality of collective priority-setting also reflects the dominance of a politics of pragmatism: the overall priorities are not set by a single jurisdiction, but are negotiated; they become what most governments are willing to accept both in principle and in practice, once funding and other strings are attached. At the end of this process, priorities may or may not mirror the issues of greatest importance to citizens.[30] In effect, then, the SUFA provision is probably limited to engaging citizens in the review process.

The statement of principles offers a second kind of support for citizen involvement, related to strengthening civil society more generally. Governments agree to "promote the full and active participation of all Canadians in Canada's social and economic life" and to "work in partnership with individuals, families, communities, voluntary organizations, business and labour."[31] Both statements signal a recognition that in collaborative forms of governance, now more than ever, governments need the voluntary and private sectors as partners, and that an active citizenry and a vibrant civil society contribute positively to governance. However, the wording of the first statement is sufficiently broad to be read as largely symbolic, while the wording of the second is so general as to be meaningless — it would be difficult to find an instance of a contemporary government *not* working in some kind of partnership.

The third way in which SUFA brings citizens into federal-provincial relations is through accountability, an idea that, in wedding NPM to federalism, has resonance with both the federal and provincial governments. Once Ottawa decided to come to the table, as Lazar observes, it bargained hard for public accountability as a way of pressing the provinces to fulfill their social policy obligations.[32] In principle, the provinces had already accepted — indeed developed — the idea of public accountability in the Victoria Proposal, albeit with significant differences in perspective from that of the federal government.[33] In both the federal and provincial takes on it, accountability requires a vigilant citizenry. Under the section "Informing Canadians," each signatory agrees to "monitor and measure outcomes of its social programs and report regularly to its constituents on the performance of these programs," and to use third parties, as appropriate, in assessing progress. It should be noted that the reporting is on outcomes, not mere outputs or activities, and that, in respect of constitutional jurisdiction, provinces are to report to their own constituencies, not to the federal government. As Lazar notes, "Over time, it is anticipated that different governments will use comparable indicators to measure progress so that this flow of information to the public will enable those who are interested to compare results in their jurisdiction to results in other jurisdictions."[34] Ottawa's initial intention, as laid out in *Working Together*, would have gone much further in standardizing and centralizing this process, by having sectoral ministers develop uniform accountability frameworks and comparable indicators, articulate best practices and methods for citizen participation, and establish third-party social audits.[35]

Ottawa's desire to embrace more results-based federalism is motivated by several factors. First, it is compatible with events within the federal government in recent years. In line with NPM philosophy, attention has been increasingly focused on outcomes and service standards, as demonstrated by the results-based management process led by the Treasury Board Secretariat.[36] The focus on public reporting of results, in the intergovernmental context, is a way of holding the provinces responsible for how they spend federal transfers. Although there was some accountability for social spending under the cost-shared Canada Assistance Plan (CAP) — the monies had to be spent on social assistance and spending had to meet a few minimal conditions — under block funding it is impossible for Ottawa to require that the provinces meet any particular standards of service, or indeed that they use the transfer for the nominally designated purpose at all. The SUFA accountability provisions are intended to give the public and civil society organizations the information on outcomes they require for vigilance, pressing underperforming provinces to direct spending toward social programs and to design more effective programs.

The provinces had also embraced the idea of public accountability in the Victoria Proposal, but with important caveats with respect to autonomy and independence. They would develop their own indicators, and accountability would be linked to a rationalization of responsibilities in the federation through reduction of overlap and duplication.[37] Their goals in supporting public accountability

were similar to those of the federal government — to use the threat of public cen-
sure to ensure that Ottawa lived up to its funding commitments. What the
provinces lost in the final agreement was a measure of reciprocal transparency: a
clause requiring the federal government to report publicly, on an annual basis, on
its provision of adequate and stable program funding did not survive.

The fourth provision is another dimension of promoting greater public
accountability. Under the heading "Ensuring Fair and Transparent Practices," governments committed "to have in place appropriate mechanisms for citizens to
appeal unfair administrative practices and bring complaints about access and service." If implemented, this measure would not only replace, but extend to other
areas, the appeal provisions of CAP that were lost when it was rolled into the
Canada Health and Social Transfer (CHST) in 1995. An appeals process is particularly important given the downloading of services to voluntary organizations
that has occurred over the past decade. In many service areas there are multiple
providers but no designated coordinator — and governments have in many cases
absented themselves from this role — so that a person in need of a service may
not know how to access it. With multiple service providers, there may also be
considerable differentiation in the way users are treated. As with public reporting, an appeals process is fully compatible with the NPM philosophy, which
espouses service standards (although not on a national basis) and government
accountability for failure to serve *consumers* according to their expectations.

The final element is an explicit promise to involve citizens and their organizations in a review of SUFA at the end of its initial three years, by ensuring "significant opportunities for input and feed-back from Canadians and all interested
parties, including social policy experts, private sector and voluntary organizations." So far, virtually nothing appears to be happening on this front. With just
a few months to go before renewal, any serious attempt at providing "significant
opportunities" should be underway and announced, to give individuals and organizations time to assess, reflect and respond.[38]

In all of these elements SUFA is carefully worded. Use of the ambiguous
term "Canadians" in the key commitments leaves one wondering whether this
means individual citizens only or organizations as well. Over the course of the
1990s, many Canadian governments attempted to reorient consultative participation away from organizations and toward individuals.[39] This shift was partly
driven by a desire to engage citizens in civic life. It also grew out of the populism

that led to the founding of the Reform Party and that favours direct relationships between citizens and elected officials, without the filter of intermediary organizations. A third impetus was the negative response to public-sector restructuring, which led many Canadian governments to conclude that they should neither fund nor provide opportunities for their critics.[40] Although it has recently been acknowledged that much can be learned from civil society organizations, governments are still struggling to engage individuals as well. The question is whether SUFA would, mistakenly in my view, limit engagement to citizens representing only themselves, or would also welcome representatives of organizations. Although pains have been taken to avoid specific mention of organizations, the language is sufficiently inclusive to embrace processes that involve either organizations and individuals or organizations exclusively.

Citizen Engagement Under Instrumental Federalism

The significance of SUFA's citizen engagement provisions should not be underestimated, because they are indicative of a shift to a new mode of federalism that I will call "instrumental federalism." This instrumental character derives from four elements. The first is problem-solving that may require greater collaboration among governments and that, from the federal perspective, should not be unduly hampered by jurisdictional boundaries. It also promotes policy learning through information sharing and identifying best practices among governments. Although the notion of governments "getting along and doing good" is an attractive one, problem-solving is potentially an abrogation of the federal principle, as Quebec quickly realized. Rather than constraining Ottawa's use of the spending power, as the provinces had intended, instrumental federalism has facilitated what Noël calls "politically palatable spending" — boutique programs for popular causes such as reducing homelessness or supporting innovations that can be controlled by the Finance Department and are often not subject to Cabinet decision-making.[41]

Perhaps even more important than actually fixing policy problems is being seen to do so. In the late 1990s, public opinion polls commissioned by various Canadian governments demonstrated quite dramatically that public trust and confidence in government (at all levels) were declining.[42] Gaining visibility and getting credit for programs that are important to Canadians, particularly health care, have thus become a major preoccupation of both federal and provincial governments.

The third element of instrumental federalism is accountability through outcomes-based measurement and public reporting. It was through this door of accountability that citizens were brought into the initial provincial and federal proposals put forward during the SUFA negotiations. The provinces saw public reporting as a means of ensuring that the federal government maintained stable and adequate transfers, while Ottawa saw it as a means of ensuring that the provinces spent transfers as intended. The main implication of the SUFA accountability provisions is to place the onus on citizens, unrealistically in my opinion, to review outcomes, assess their meaning, compare them across provinces and take political action to achieve better results. In effect, it makes social scientists of us all. This is unrealistic, not because citizens are apathetic or not up to the task. Outcome measurement is a complex task and public debate about it requires access to relevant data and technical information and the ability to assess the quality of measurement, as well as institutional venues for debate on the adequacy and policy implications of the data.

Finally, citizen involvement in policy-making has a key role in instrumental federalism because it is a means of both building trust in government and facilitating policy learning. Citizen participation is of particular interest to Ottawa because it is a way of establishing direct relations with Canadians, without mediating them through provincial governments. Given that the federal government's role in social policy is based on funding rather than direct service delivery, it appears remote and irrelevant to citizens in most parts of the country. By engaging citizens in policy, Ottawa gains a degree of public relevance, which could have positive effects for national unity should relationships with provincial governments sour or should Quebec sovereignty become an immediate issue once again.

The form of federalism embedded in SUFA differs from collaborative federalism in that citizens are the essential third force. The primary objective in elevating citizens to a new status is not to enhance democratic practices directly, and it is surely not to open up intergovernmental relations to greater public involvement. Rather, the goals of citizen engagement are instrumental — that is, to serve the interests of governments in protecting themselves and their responsibilities in the federation against the actions of other governments.

When Potential
Meets Reality

To what extent have the SUFA provisions, as a package, contributed to the development of genuine, institutionalized forms of citizen engagement? Although some are evidently limited in scope due to compromise, the commitments could, if properly and enthusiastically implemented, promote deliberative forms of citizen engagement and stronger relationships between civil society and governments. There is little likelihood of this happening, however, for several reasons.

Neither Ottawa nor the provinces have shown any enthusiasm for keeping the SUFA promise to ensure meaningful public input into social policy. After almost three years under SUFA there are still no concrete plans to develop the requisite institutions or mechanisms for meaningful citizen engagement. As Lazar observed shortly after SUFA was announced, there is "no evidence that signatory governments have a blueprint up their sleeves for improving democratic processes in relation to the social union."[43] Nor is there any evidence that governments have attempted to involve citizens in "developing social priorities" under SUFA. The initiative on early childhood development announced in late 2000, for example, was determined to be a priority through the normal mechanisms of executive federalism, rather than being a product of dialogue with citizens. Nor has there been any progress in establishing transparent processes of public appeal against unfair administrative practices or lack of access to services.

The provinces are not highly motivated to comply with or tie their citizen engagement activities to SUFA: with jurisdiction over social policy, they have many opportunities to interact and build partnerships with the voluntary organizations that deliver services and with the users of those services; they do not need SUFA to engage citizens in policy or to form relationships with them. Arguably, provincial governments are involved in more innovative and effective citizen engagement, but not in ways that are directly connected to or prompted by SUFA. The extent of provincial interest in enhancing citizen engagement and establishing partnerships with voluntary organizations varies enormously, however.[44] At one end of the spectrum are Newfoundland, which has recently developed a Strategic Social Plan that embodies partnership with community organizations and that provides for a social audit, and Quebec, which has developed a comprehensive plan for the engagement and funding of community organizations.

Other provinces have mechanisms for the participation of individuals and voluntary organizations in policy development in particular areas. Saskatchewan's advisory council on children and family services, for instance, brings together
representatives of community service providers and consults regularly with the
provincial government.[45] At the other extreme is Ontario, whose government has
a highly centralized political decision-making process concentrated in the
Premier's Office and has displayed little interest in engaging civil society in policy. Given these differences, we are unlikely to see any united provincial front in
implementing SUFA citizen engagement commitments or holding governments
accountable for their failure to do so.

The federal government has a greater need for the type of citizen involvement suggested by SUFA, because one of its goals in a renewed social union is to
build stronger direct relationships with citizens and in the process bypass provincial governments. Such direct links are expected to not only promote trust in the
federal government, but also buttress national unity regardless of its relations with
the provinces. Yet the federal government's progress on citizen engagement has
been impeded by a lack of both time and imagination and by an increased mobility within the public service that makes relationship-building with citizens difficult
to sustain. Innovation on a procedural level is hindered by the grip of the Ottawa
communications industry on the means of consultation: there is a more or less
entrenched template for conducting consultations that in recent years has not
prompted much innovation. To the extent that effective citizen engagement requires
new mechanisms or institutions, or the reform of existing ones, the process is hampered by the Chrétien government's firm resistance to institutional change.[46]

In contrast, the accountability aspects of SUFA have been taken more seriously, although a few consecutive years of budget surplus have significantly
altered both the incentive to involve citizens in accountability exercises and the
consequences of doing so. The particular set of political circumstances that motivated the provinces to enter into a federal-provincial agreement in the first place
centred on the need to constrain the use of the spending power, so that Ottawa
could not entice the provinces into new spending programs and then, in times of
restraint, unilaterally cut funding and leave them holding the financial bag and
dealing with public criticism.[47] In this context, the idea of public reporting and
rendering of accounts for the modification of existing programs and their funding, coupled with commitments to clearly state the roles and responsibilities of

each order of government, was attractive to the provinces.[48] The federal government was even more strongly disposed to outcome-based accountability, reflecting its internal push for results-based management led by the Treasury Board Secretariat. Now that federal transfers have been restored, however, the provinces have less to gain through such reporting than Ottawa. With the CHST topped up and additional resources in place for special initiatives, it would be easy for the federal government to say, "We put up the money as promised; if things did not turn out as expected, blame the provinces."

Although many provinces are set on developing their own outcome measures and some, such as Alberta, are far ahead of the federal government, there is a reluctance to provide truly comparable measures if there is a possibility these will be used by Ottawa to redistribute transfers or impose standardized measurement in a way that violates provincial autonomy and ignores local differences.[49] In addition, outcome measurement of social policies has proven to be much more complex in practice than in concept, and citizens and voluntary organizations are extremely limited in their ability to be effective watchdogs. Even for those jurisdictions that favour outcome measurement, at least on their own terms, such assessment has so far succeeded largely in measuring outputs, not outcomes. In addition, the difficulty of relating outcomes to particular programs should not be underestimated. For instance, it is one thing to collect data on literacy rates or child health and quite another to make the case that changes in these rates are the result of specific programs for early childhood development. Furthermore, many complicating factors, such as degree of urbanization and basic demographic profiles, might render the comparison of broad population-based measures a poor indicator of the effectiveness of provincial spending and programming. Consequently, while measurement and public reporting mechanisms are being established, the process is taking longer than initially imagined.

Finally, it can be argued that some of the disappointment in SUFA is the result of the expectations it had raised. It was widely assumed that SUFA would impel an opening of the intergovernmental process to citizens and civil society organizations (although this was never actually promised). Virtually no movement has occurred in this direction. In particular, with the exception of some participation by national Aboriginal organizations, the Ministerial Council and the Sectoral Tables remain as closed as ever to nongovernmental actors. This can be attributed to the longstanding fear on the part of ministers and the inter-governmental specialists who are part of the machinery of executive federalism that citizen involvement will limit their ability to set priorities and bargain effectively. It is my contention, however, that citizen engagement will not reach its full potential until it takes place in the intergovernmental realm as well as within individual governments.

Where does this leave the process of implementation of SUFA's commitments to citizen engagement? Far from its potential. It leaves the review of outcome measures and the possible involvement of citizens in the three-year review of SUFA itself as the most likely prospects. Four elements are required for effective use of outcome measurement and establishment of a related deliberative dialogue. First, voluntary organizations must have the opportunity to draw on their expertise in service delivery and knowledge of local communities and help define appropriate measures. Second, the measures must be open to public scrutiny. This implies that voluntary organizations or other third parties have the means to collect independent data or have access to government data and methods of collection and analysis for the purposes of review, and also possess the expertise to conduct their own assessment. Few civil society organizations and even fewer individuals have such expertise and resources. Third, a way has to be found to link outcome measurement to programming and funding, which involves access to additional information on program inputs and activities and requires sophisticated analysis. Finally, even if appropriate outcome measures are achieved, fora will have to be established for discussion and deliberation of their implications. In sum, reviews of outcomes may be possible in theory, but they are extremely difficult to achieve in practice.

Whether Canadian governments will scramble at the last minute to involve individuals and voluntary organizations in the three-year review remains an open question, but they have done nothing so far to provide the "significant opportunities" promised. A few regional meetings, a toll-free phone line and some workbooks do not constitute meaningful engagement. Rather, they are a poignant illustration of how ill-prepared governments are to take citizen engagement seriously in the intergovernmental context. Further, given that few serious efforts have been made to fulfill the commitments made under SUFA, no rational government is likely to be enthusiastic about a meaningful, open review process. Nor are citizens likely to have much to say, since so little has happened.

A Test Case:
The National
Children's Agenda

T HE NATIONAL CHILDREN'S AGENDA (NCA) THAT WAS ANNOUNCED IN 1999 AND the subsequent Early Childhood Development Initiative (ECDI) that flows from it represent the first test of the impact of SUFA on social policy.[50] They are also a good test of the real interests of Canadian governments in citizen engagement under SUFA, because in most provinces the delivery of child and family services is largely the responsibility of voluntary organizations and because parents, who may well count themselves as experts on the matter of children, have a great deal to contribute to policy discussion on the subject. This is also an area in which federalism accommodates highly divergent systems of service delivery across provinces, especially in the provision of child care.[51] The provinces not only vary greatly on the mix of state, not-for-profit and commercial provision of services, but have a range of mechanisms for engaging providers and citizens in policy dialogue, with some provinces — notably Saskatchewan and Quebec — producing extensive engagement and other provinces very little.[52]

Admittedly, the initial steps toward the development of the NCA predate SUFA. In January 1997 the Ministerial Council requested that governments begin exploring possibilities for jointly developing a broad agenda and comprehensive strategy aimed at improving the well-being of children.[53] The premiers expressed strong support for this initiative at their annual summer meeting. In December 1997 the first ministers, with the exception of the Quebec delegation, affirmed their commitment to developing a National Children's Agenda and agreed to fast-track the groundwork through the Ministerial Council. In May 1999 their commitment was formalized by the Ministerial Council with the release of the statement *Developing a Shared Vision*.[54] This document sets out broad values and four goals with respect to children: promoting health, ensuring safety and security, fostering successful learning, and encouraging social engagement and responsibility.[55] However, it does not offer specific means for meeting these goals.

In the spring and summer of 1999 the federal and provincial/territorial governments sponsored a nationwide consultation on the NCA, coordinated at the national, provincial and territorial levels.[56] The process consisted of round-tables (of selected voluntary organizations and researchers) and focus groups (including members of the public) in five cities; a toll-free phone number; a workbook to provide feedback; a national workshop of professionals, academics and representatives of the five national Aboriginal organizations to discuss outcome measurement and monitoring; and additional meetings organized by individual jurisdictions. In other words, it was a consultation as conventional as any other in the previous decade, and the results — or "what was said" — were reported in the federal government's usual vague manner.[57] Initial feedback from voluntary organizations and individuals on the vision was generally positive. Lacking detail, however, it could not go very far.

The federal government signalled its continued support for the NCA in the 1999 Speech from the Throne, indicating that a federal/provincial/territorial agreement on a national action plan on early childhood development, consistent with SUFA, would be in place by December 2000.[58] Ottawa and the provinces (without Quebec) issued a communiqué on their intention to pursue what would become the ECDI two months early, backed by a federal commitment of $2.2 billion (about $100 per child) over five years starting in 2001–02.[59] Under the agreement, the provinces/territories have undertaken to invest in four general areas: promotion of healthy pregnancy, birth and infancy; improved parenting and family supports; strengthening of early childhood development, learning and care; and strengthening of community supports.[60] Within these areas, the provinces/territories will determine their own priorities and configuration of services. Congruent with SUFA, they have agreed to establish a baseline of current expenditures and activities on early childhood development, report annually to their publics on their investments, and develop a shared framework for reporting on outcomes that includes comparable indicators of both outputs (such as the growth of programs) and outcomes (such as the proportion of children who are ready to learn when they start school).[61] The agreement clearly states that the amount of federal funding provided to any jurisdiction will not be based on performance.

How does the NCA score on SUFA's citizen engagement components? In terms of priority-setting, it cannot be said that under the NCA citizens were effectively engaged in the process. To be fair, the NCA was well underway before SUFA was finalized. Nevertheless, the announcement, a year and a half into the SUFA era, that the priority would be early childhood development came not from the consultation process but from governments directly. They had already determined that this would be the focus, partly because research findings showed the

importance of children's early years for long-term outcomes.[62] An additional political advantage of this decision is that the focus on early childhood development
enables governments to submerge or even sidestep direct discussion of child care
as a priority, since some provincial governments want no part of a national strategy for child care. It was unlikely that even if child care had emerged as a major
concern in the consultations it would have been embedded in the ECDI as an
explicit priority. In sum, priority-setting has, evidently, remained a political, executive process.

The NCA also gets failing marks on the SUFA principle of ensuring that
Canadians have meaningful input into policy. Although in its early stages the
NCA featured consultation, and although this was jointly sponsored — itself an
innovation — it was a traditional consultation rather than a truly deliberative
engagement. The results were badly analyzed and poorly reported, and could not
possibly have contributed in any meaningful way to policy or program development. Moreover, there is no sign that governments are interested in establishing
a civic forum or any other ongoing deliberative mechanism for engaging the voluntary organizations that are involved in service delivery. In public
accountability, however, real gains have been made. Although it is too early to tell
how enthusiastically the provinces/territories will pursue the development of
comparable indicators, particularly in the area of child care where the differences
are considerable, they have at least agreed to collect and report this information.
Appropriately, the ECDI makes it clear that the provinces/territories are reporting
the measures to their constituencies, not to the federal government. If outcome
measurement is to truly enable policy-learning and guide investment and policy
design, and if citizens are to be a central part of this process, the next step is to
create mechanisms for voluntary organizations, individuals and academics to discuss the meaning and implications of these measures. In addition, a joint feder-
al/provincial/territorial review process to determine how measures might be
gradually refined would facilitate good data collection.

More interesting than limited intergovernmental attempts at engagement
under the NCA is the quiet, behind-the-scenes work, assisted by federal funding,
to develop better civil society networks and improve public vigilance. The policy
community around children's issues historically has not been particularly cohesive, its membership fragmented by both geography and diversity of interests.
Child and family policy encompasses a wide range of policy issues, including

health, education, justice, child care and disability. Although most of these areas are served by national umbrella organizations, both policy development and service delivery are concentrated at the provincial and municipal levels. Given the sparse resources and the multitude of organizations involved, advocates have had difficulty mobilizing at all three levels of government as well as across policy fields. Although many children's advocacy groups received federal funding in the 1970s and 1980s under Secretary of State and National Health and Welfare programs, most of this support was withdrawn in the mid-1990s due to financial restraint and a reluctance by the state to fund its critics.[63] In the mid-1990s, following the failure of a second national child care strategy and after federal funding had begun targeting "children at risk," national organizations devoted to child and family issues saw that the only way to maintain support for the notion of universal access to services was to increase the bandwidth of the message — that is, to establish a more collective and comprehensive position.[64] They formed two broad coalitions, with some overlapping membership. Campaign 2000, comprising more than 70 national, provincial and community organizations, is concerned primarily with reducing child poverty. The National Children's Alliance (NCA) was formed by some 30 organizations in 1996 for the express purpose of advancing a broad-based children's agenda. As intergovernmental interest in a national children's agenda began to develop, Ottawa deemed it useful to have a sounding board and support for such an agenda in civil society — preferably a political actor with more of a professional than a radical approach to this issue. Its choice was the relatively conservative NCA, an organization that has since received substantial federal funding.

Federal support has enabled the NCA to hold its own series of consultations with regional and local organizations, to build nationwide networks, to increase the coalition's policy and analysis capabilities, and to become more institutionalized by hiring a full-time coordinator. Over the next few years the NCA intends to direct its energies toward having a voice in the government's choice of indicators, holding the government to account on measurement and reporting outcomes, and ensuring that individuals and voluntary organizations are engaged in implementing the EDCI.[65] This fits nicely with Ottawa's goal of using citizens as watchdogs — that is, of equipping civil society to do indirectly what, due to the sensitivity of intergovernmental relations, it could not do directly. Fortunately, there are benefits for civil society as well. It will be interesting to see whether the government remains willing to support the coalition should it become critical of federal funding and policy, or whether it will withdraw funding as it did in the 1980s and 1990s.

Conclusion

S INCE THE SIGNING OF THE SUFA IN 1999, THERE HAVE BEEN SIGNIFICANT DEVELOP-
ments in how Canadian governments relate to civil society and in the potential for citizen engagement in policy-making. None of these developments has taken place in the arena of intergovernmental relations, however, and none has been directly driven by SUFA. So far, SUFA's only real impact has been in the area of accountability. Its requirement that governments report on policy outcomes has been embedded in new federal-provincial agreements, such as the ECDI and 2000 health accord, negotiated under the SUFA banner. Although it is too early for governments to have actually produced results-based measurements, the eventual comparison of outcomes across jurisdictions will be of some benefit in facilitating public dialogue around social policy investment and in holding governments accountable for their commitments. Outcomes measurement cannot guarantee enhanced accountability and citizen engagement, however. If this exercise is to be meaningful and useful, it must be possible for outcomes to be linked to inputs and outputs — that is, to spending and specific programs. Measurement and interpretation of outcomes is a challenge in itself. If individuals and organizations are to have an effective role in reviewing outcomes, they will need considerable analytical expertise and access to provincial data on measurement methods, as well as data on spending and programming, in order to evaluate the appropriateness and accuracy of the measures and assess their implications for social policy. This is no small task. If citizens are to play the role of watchdog in instrumental federalism, the voluntary sector will have to be strengthened and fora will have to be established to accommodate dialogue on outcomes. On a positive note, in areas such as children's policy Ottawa has begun to once again provide civil society organizations the funding they need to participate in the debate on what in fact constitutes appropriate indicators.

In spite of the relative lack of citizen engagement under SUFA, many governments across the country have begun to develop more positive relationships with citizens and the voluntary sector. They have used means such as strategic social planning, citizen-based summits, framework agreements with the voluntary sector based on mutual expectations and strengthening of civil society organizations. Independent of government, the voluntary sector has, in many cities and provinces, begun to coalesce and to play a leadership role[66]; in the past year alone, for example, many coalitions representing a broad cross-section of organizations have emerged.[67] If civil society continues to organize and to develop its leadership capabilities, governments will find it increasingly difficult to ignore voluntary organizations and to walk away from their commitments to citizen engagement. Thus, pressure to fulfill the SUFA promises on citizen engagement is likely to come from the bottom up, financially supported and partly enabled by government. Such a process takes time, however, and the clock may run out on SUFA before any bottom-up influence can be exerted.

Since it is difficult for governments to reject public involvement, perhaps the best hope for the institutionalization of meaningful, deliberative citizen engagement in intergovernmental relations is if the existing provisions survive the three-year review of SUFA. This would give current efforts within civil society and current federal and provincial exercises in relationship-building with the voluntary sector time to pay off, and would give civil society time to develop the capability and connections necessary to see that the potential for a more inclusive, deliberative process of policy-making and of intergovernmental relations is reached. Only in this way will a masterpiece of deliberative democracy be created from the blank canvas of SUFA.

The insightful and detailed comments of Sarah Fortin, Matthew Mendelsohn, Alain Noël, F. Leslie Seidle, France St-Hilaire and participants in the IRPP workshop Back to the Table on the first draft of this paper are gratefully acknowledged.

1   Biggs (1996, p. 1).
2   For some of the classical work on this, see Smiley (1979, pp. 105-113) and Simeon (1972).
3   Treasury Board Secretariat (1998).
4   For a summary see Graves (1999, pp. 37-73). Public attitudes toward government and citizen participation became a hot topic in Ottawa when Ekos Research began conducting an annual panel survey, *Rethinking Government*, in the mid-1990s, followed by *Rethinking Citizen Engagement*. For a comparative analysis of levels of trust see Pharr and Putnam (2000).
5   On the democratic deficit, see Maxwell (2001).
6   Graham and Phillips (1998); Abele *et al.* (1998); and Mendelsohn and McLean (2002, p. 9).
7   Graham and Phillips (1998).
8   Cohen (1997, p. 412).
9   Cohen (1998, p. 186).
10 There is an active debate around whether deliberative democracy must be based solely on reasoning, or if other forms of communication can contribute legitimately. See Dryzek (2000, pp. 67-74). The emphasis on reasoning is, in my view, meant to indicate that deliberation, in the context of policy-making, involves problem-solving and thus persuasion through argumentation. I use the concept of reasoning not to stress the rationality of the process, but in terms of arriving at "public judgment," in Yankelovich's language, by connecting knowledge of trade-offs with underlying values. See Yankelovich (1992, pp. 102-108).
11 For this and similar definitions of governance, see Rhodes (1996, pp. 652-667); Paquet (2000, pp. 119-124).
12 Christiano argues that deliberative democracy has an impact at the societal level as well, because societies that engage in a great deal of sincere public discussion on the merits of alternative proposals tend to be more just and more protective of liberty. See Christiano (1997, p. 244).
13 Phillips (1995, p. 151); Schlosberg (1998, p. 605). The concept of social capital has been popularized by Putnam (2000).
14 Putnam (1993).
15 For an overview of citizen juries and panels see Abele *et al.* (1998). See also Fishkin (1995).
16 Phillips (2003).
17 For a discussion of "thick" democracy see Mansbridge (1983); Barber (1984). Concern about voluntary organizations without members is expressed in Skocpol (1999, pp. 66-73).
18 "Capacity" in the voluntary sector is described in Government of Canada/Voluntary Sector (1999).
19 Seidle (2000).
20 Julie Simmons argues that ministerial councils outside of social services, particularly the Canadian Council of Ministers of the Environment and the Canadian Council of Forestry Ministers, have gone further in encouraging citizen participation. Simmons (forthcoming).
21 Mendelsohn and McLean (2000, p. 23).
22 Mendelsohn and McLean (2000, p. 23).
23 For a discussion of the possible use of civic fora in intergovernmental relations, see Phillips and Echenberg (2000).
24 Such engagement is not without precedent in intergovernmental relations. Under the NCA, representatives of the five national Aboriginal organizations are included in a working group under the Ministerial Council, and in December 1999 the first ever joint meeting of the Ministerial Council and the national organizations was held. See Prince (2000, pp. 45-46). There is good reason for separate meetings with Aboriginal leaders given the distinctive issues of children's policy in their communities, and much could be learned through engagement of representatives and members of other communities as well.

25 Lazar (2000a, p. 109).
26 This period is recounted in more detail by Gagnon and Segal (2000, pp. 1-7) and by Simmons (forthcoming).
27 This comparison is made in a systematic way for various parts of SUFA in the collection of papers that appear in Gagnon and Segal (2000). Both the Saskatoon Consensus and the Victoria Proposal are reprinted in the appendices to that volume.
28 For instance, Evan Potter explains that when Peter Harder arrived at the Treasury Board in late 1995 as the new secretary, he saw the importance of countering the growing public distrust of government and was a strong proponent of public accountability. See Potter (2000, pp. 115-116).
29 The wording of the Victoria Proposal was "[to provide citizens with] appropriate opportunities for public input in developing priorities and objectives for social programs."
30 One example of this is the National Child Benefit (NCB), which is often heralded as an example of federal-provincial cooperation. As Boychuk observes, the NCB did not result from a public desire, nor was it sold to the public. Rather, it was the result of pragmatic politics, designed to sell the provinces on the agreement. Boychuk (2000, p. 47). See also Jenson (2000, pp. 48-50).
31 The former was not part of the Victoria Proposal while the latter was, in a section on promoting individual and collective responsibility.
32 Lazar (2000b, p. 4).
33 It should be noted that the Saskatoon Consensus made no mention of citizen accountability, leaving this issue to the regular mechanisms of accountability in a parliamentary democracy. See Otis (2000).
34 Lazar (2000a, p. 109).
35 Otis (2000, pp. 96-100).
36 This interest in results-based management was manifest both formally at the institutional level and informally at the personal level. It is interesting to note that Alex Himmelfarb, who had been deputy secre-

tary of the Treasury Board Secretariat when results-based management was being developed, became chief federal negotiator for SUFA.
37 See Otis (2000, pp. 103, 116-119). At the time, rationalization was a popular idea in several provincial jurisdictions, notably Alberta and Ontario, which had recently completed processes of streamlining or disentangling provincial-municipal relations.
38 The compact negotiated between the Blair government and the voluntary sector in England (with separate framework agreements negotiated in Scotland, Wales and Northern Ireland) includes a code of good practice for consultation. It stipulates that a minimum of 12 weeks be allowed for replies in written consultations, to accommodate the work cycles of voluntary organizations. Were the English code applied to citizen engagement in the review and renewal of SUFA, and assuming that governments would need at least a month to analyze and publish the results of such a consultation, they would have had to produce the questions and documents on which they are inviting comment no later than September 2001. See Home Office and Working Group on Government Relations (2000).
39 There have been several attempts, both positive and negative, to involve citizens as individuals. The economic summits in Alberta and Quebec were constructive exercises in building a broad base of participation. See Abele et al. (1998). The federal government's Task Force on Violence Against Women in the early 1990s was a less positive exercise: individual women recounted their experiences of violence at length, while representatives of rape crisis centres, shelters and women's groups had limited input, yet their extensive expertise in service delivery would have contributed greatly to the discussion.
40 Jenson and Phillips (1996, p. 124).
41 See Alain Noël's chapter in this book, as well as Savoie (1999, pp. 344-350).

42 See Graves (1999, pp. 38-39).

43 Lazar (2000*a*, p. 110).

44 These differences are independent of the
    ideology of the governing party, as both
    New Democratic (e.g., Saskatchewan) and
    Conservative (e.g., Alberta) governments
    have been attempting to improve their rela-
    tionships with the voluntary sector and
    with citizens. The critical factors seem to be
    the degree of centralization of power in the
    Premier's Office and the premier's view of
    the role of citizens and civil society.

45 Thompson with Maxwell and Stroick
    (1999, pp. 12-15).

46 Savoie (2000, pp. 10-11).

47 See Roger Gibbins' chapter in this book.

48 Otis (2000, pp. 100-113).

49 Perhaps the two provinces that have taken
    outcome measurement the furthest are
    Alberta and Ontario. Alberta has been a
    leader in developing indicators for its
    health care system, and Ontario is in the
    process of producing outcome-based mea-
    surement for education.

50 The National Child Benefit is often cited by
    Ottawa as what might be achieved under
    SUFA, but in fact it predates SUFA. The
    accountability and reporting frameworks
    associated with the NCB were emulated in the
    National Children's Agenda which followed.

51 Jenson with Thompson (1999).

52 See Thompson with Maxwell and Stroick
    (1999).

53 See Government of Canada (1997).

54 There was also a supplementary document
    addressing measurement and indicators of
    children's well-being.

55 *Developing a Shared Vision*, produced in col-
    laboration with the five national Aboriginal
    organizations, also includes an Aboriginal
    perspective on children's issues.

56 The $1 million cost of the consultations was
    covered jointly as well: half was paid by the
    federal government and half was divided
    among the provinces and territories accord-
    ing to a formula. For a discussion of the
    consultation see Seidle (2000, pp. 11-13).

57 For a description of the process and report
    of results, see Government of Canada
    (1997). This has become a standard formu-
    la for federal consultations. See Phillips
    (1991); Mendelsohn and McLean (2002).

58 In commitments announced in the 1999
    Speech from the Throne, the federal gov-
    ernment has undertaken a number of spe-
    cific initiatives with regard to children and
    families. These are outlined on the HRDC
    Website: www.hrdc-drhc.gc.ca/minister/
    hrdc/ invest.shtml

59 Quebec did not sign because sections of the
    agreement infringe on its constitutional
    jurisdiction over social matters. It should
    be noted that Quebec is a leader in pro-
    grams for children and families.

60 First Ministers of Canada (2000).

61 The agreement sensitively notes that the
    different starting points of provinces should
    be taken into account when reporting on
    these indicators.

62 The most influential of these was McCain
    and Mustard (1999).

63 See Pal (1995); Jenson and Phillips (1996).

64 Mahon and Phillips (2002).

65 Personal communication.

66 The largest ongoing exercise in relation-
    ship-building is the Voluntary Sector
    Initiative (VSI) launched by the federal gov-
    ernment in June 2000, a commitment of
    almost $95 million to a variety of programs
    whose objective is to strengthen the sector
    itself and its relationship with government.
    Implementation is overseen by an array of
    Joint Tables that are themselves experi-
    ments in collaboration. See Phillips (2001).
    Almost a third of VSI's funding is allocated
    to short-term projects aimed at equipping
    voluntary organizations to better engage
    with the federal government and encourag-
    ing departments to involve these organiza-
    tions. When SUFA was being negotiated
    most provinces ignored the voluntary sec-
    tor except as a contractor of services. Over
    the past two years, however, a number of
    provinces and municipalities have under-

taken major initiatives toward building
more effective state-sector partnerships. In
several provinces these initiatives have
already begun to generate more innovative
means for involving voluntary organizations
in the policy process.

67   These include, for instance, loose, diverse
      coalitions in British Columbia, Manitoba
      and Ontario and local chambers of volun-
      tary organizations in Calgary, Edmonton
      and Ottawa. Quebec has long-standing
      mechanisms for dialogue within the volun-
      tary and community sectors, resulting in
      much greater cohesion and organization at
      those levels than exists in the other
      provinces. See White (2001) and Yves
      Vaillancourt's chapter in this book.

Abele, Frances, Katherine Graham, Alex Ker, Antonia Maioni and Susan D. Phillips. *Talking with Canadians: Citizen Engagement and the Social Union*. Ottawa: Canadian Council on Social Development, 1998.

Barber, Benjamin. *Strong Democracy: Participatory Politics for a New Age*. Berkeley, CA: University of California Press, 1984.

Biggs, Margaret. *Building Blocks for Canada's New Social Union*. Ottawa: Canadian Policy Research Networks, 1996.

Boychuk, Gerard W. "SUFA, the Child Benefit and Social Assistance." *Policy Options*, Vol. 21, no. 3 (April 2000): 46-47.

Cohen, Joshua. "Democracy and Liberty." In *Deliberative Democracy*, ed. John Elster. Cambridge: Cambridge University Press, 1998.

——. "Procedure and Substance in Deliberative Democracy." In *Deliberative Democracy: Essays on Reason and Politics*, ed. James Bohman and William Rehg. Cambridge, MA: MIT Press, 1997.

Christiano, Thomas. "The Significance of Public Deliberation." In *Deliberative Democracy: Essays on Reason and Politics*, ed. James Bohman and William Rehg. Cambridge, MA: MIT Press, 1997.

Dryzek, John S. *Deliberative Democracy and Beyond*. Oxford: Oxford University Press, 2000.

First Ministers of Canada. *Communiqué on Health*. News release, ref: 800-038-004. Ottawa: First Ministers' Meeting, September 11, 2000. Available at www.scics.gc.ca

Fishkin, James. *The Voice of the People: Public Opinion and Democracy*. New Haven, CT: Yale University Press, 1995.

Gagnon, Alain-G., and Hugh Segal, eds. *The Canadian Social Union without Quebec: 8 Critical Analyses*. Montreal: Institute for Research on Public Policy, 2000.

Government of Canada. 1997. "Background Information on the National Children's Agenda." Available at www.socialunion.gc.ca

Government of Canada/Voluntary Sector. *Working Together: Report of the Joint Tables*. Ottawa: Privy Council Office and Voluntary Sector Roundtable, 1999.

Graham, Katherine A., and Susan D. Phillips. "Introduction." In *Citizen Engagement: Lessons in Public Participation from Local Government*, ed. Katherine A. Graham and Susan D. Phillips. Toronto: Institute of Public Administration of Canada, 1998.

Graves, Frank L. "Rethinking Government As If People Mattered: From 'Reagonomics' to 'Humanomics'." In *How Ottawa Spends 1999–2000: Shape Shifting: Canadian Governance Toward the 21st Century*, ed. Leslie A. Pal. Toronto: Oxford University Press, 1999.

Home Office and Working Group on Government Relations, 2000. *Consultation and Policy Appraisal: A Code of Good Practice*. Available at www.ncvo-vol.org.uk

Jenson, Jane. "Regarding the SUFA through Policies for Children: Towards a New Citizenship Regime." *Policy Options*, Vol. 21, no. 4 (May 2000): 48-50.

Jenson, Jane, with Sherry Thompson. *Comparative Family Policy: Six Provincial Stories*. Ottawa: Canadian Policy Research Networks, 1999.

Jenson, Jane, and Susan D. Phillips. "Regime Shift: New Citizen Practices in Canada." *International Journal of Canadian Studies*, no. 14 (fall 1996): 111-136.

Lazar, Harvey. "The Social Union Framework Agreement and the Future of Fiscal Federalism." In *Canada: The State of the Federation 1999/2000*, ed. Harvey Lazar. Montreal and Kingston: McGill-Queen's University Press, 2000a.

——. "The Social Union Framework Agreement: Lost Opportunity or New Beginning?" Working Paper no. 3. Queen's University School of Policy Studies, August 2000b.

Lemieux, Vincent. "Government Roles in Governance Processes." In *Modernizing Governance: A Preliminary Exploration*. Ottawa: Canadian Centre for Management Development, 2000.

Mahon, Rianne, and Susan D. Phillips. "Dual Earner Families Caught in a Liberal Welfare Regime? The Politics of Child Care Policy in Canada." In *Child Care Policy at the Crossroads: Gender and Welfare State Restructuring*, ed. Sonya Michel and Rianne Mahon. New York: Routledge, 2002.

Mansbridge, Jane. *Beyond Adversary Democracy*. Chicago: University of Chicago Press, 1983.

Maxwell, Judith. "Toward a Common Citizenship: Canada's Social and Economic Choices." *Reflexion*, no. 4. Ottawa: Canadian Policy Research Networks, January 2001.

McCain, Margaret N., and Fraser J. Mustard. *Preventing the Real Brain Drain: The Early Years Study. Final Report*. Toronto: Government of Ontario, 1999.

Mendelsohn, Matthew, and John McLean. "Getting Engaged: Strengthening SUFA through Citizen Engagement." In *Building the Social Union: Perspectives, Directions and Challenges*, ed. Tom McIntosh. Regina: Canadian Plains Research Center, University of Regina, 2002.

——. "Reconcilable Differences: Public Participation and Intergovernmentalism in Canada." Paper presented at the conference "The Changing Nature of Democracy and Federalism in Canada," Winnipeg, April 2000.

Otis, Ghislain. "Informing Canadians — Public Accountability and Transparency." In *The Canadian Social Union without Quebec: 8 Critical Analyses*, ed. Alain-G. Gagnon and Hugh Segal. Montreal: Institute for Research on Public Policy, 2000.

Pal, Leslie A. *Interests of State*. Montreal and Kingston: McGill-Queen's University Press, 1995.

Paquet, Gilles. "Tectonic Changes in Canadian Governance." In *How Ottawa Spends 1999–2000: Shape Shifting: Canadian Governance Toward the 21st Century*, ed. Leslie A. Pal. Toronto: Oxford University Press, 1999.

Pharr, Susan J., and Robert D. Putnam, eds. *Disaffected Democracies: What's Troubling the Trilateral Countries?* Princeton, NJ: Princeton University Press, 2000.

Phillips, Anne. *The Politics of Presence*. Oxford: Oxford University Press, 1995.

Phillips, Susan D. "Voluntary Sector-Government Relations in Transition: Learning from International Experience for the Canadian Context." In *The Nonprofit Sector in Interesting Times*, ed. Kathy Brock and Keith Banting. Montreal and Kingston: McGill-Queen's University Press, 2003.

——. "From Charity to Clarity: Reinventing Federal Government-Voluntary Sector Relationships." In *How Ottawa Spends 2001–2002: Power in Transition*, ed. Leslie A. Pal. Toronto: Oxford University Press, 2001.

——. "How Ottawa Blends: Shifting Government Relationships with Interest Groups." In *How Ottawa Spends 1991–1992: The Politics of Fragmentation*, ed. Frances Abele. Ottawa: Carleton University Press, 1991.

Phillips, Susan D., with Havi Echenberg. *Simon Says Take a Giant Step Forward: Advancing the National Children's Agenda*. Paper prepared for the National Children's Alliance, 2000.

Potter, Evan H. "Treasury Board as a Management Board: The Re-Invention of a Central Agency." In *How Ottawa Spends 2000-2001: Past Imperfect, Future Tense*, ed. Leslie A. Pal. Toronto: Oxford University Press, 2000.

Prince, Michael J. "Aboriginals Are Securing a Role." *Policy Options*, Vol. 21, no. 3 (April 2000): 45-46.

Putnam, Robert D. *Bowling Alone: The Collapse and Revival of American Community*. New York: Simon & Schuster, 2000.

——. *Making Democracy Work*. Princeton, NJ: Princeton University Press, 1993.

Rhodes, R.A.W. "The New Governance: Governing without Government." *Political Studies*, Vol. 44 (1996): 652-667.

Savoie, Donald J. "The Managerial Prime Minister." *Policy Options*, Vol. 21, no. 9 (November 2000): 10-11.

——. *Governing from the Centre: The Concentration of Power in Canadian Politics*. Toronto: University of Toronto Press, 1999.

Schlosberg, David. "Resurrecting the Pluralist Universe." *Political Research Quarterly*, Vol. 51, no. 3 (September 1998): 585-616.

Seidle, F. Leslie. "Executive Federalism and
Public Involvement: Integrating Citizens'
Voices." Paper presented at the conference
"The Changing Nature of Democracy and
Federalism in Canada," Winnipeg, April
2000.

Simeon, Richard. *Federal-Provincial Diplomacy:
The Making of Recent Policy in Canada.*
Toronto: University of Toronto Press, 1972.

Simmons, Julie M. "Ministerial Council Decision-
Making and Executive Federalism." In *The
Changing Nature of Democracy and
Federalism in Canada*, ed. Paul Thomas.
Winnipeg: University of Manitoba Press,
forthcoming.

Skocpol, Theda. "Associations without
Members." *American Prospect*, Vol. 10, no.
45 (July–August 1999): 66-73.

Smiley, Donald V. "An Outsider's Observations of
Federal-Provincial Relations among
Consenting Adults." In *Confrontation and
Collaboration: Intergovernmental Relations in
Canada Today*, ed. Richard Simeon.
Mississauga: Institute of Public
Administration of Canada, 1979.

Thompson, Sherry, with Judith Maxwell and
Sharon Stroick. *Moving Forward on Child
and Family Policy: Governance and
Accountability Issues.* Ottawa: Canadian
Policy Research Networks, 1999.

Treasury Board Secretariat. 1998. "Analysis of the
Social Union Initiatives: Staff Working
Paper." Available at: www.tbs-sct.gc.ca

White, Deana. "Harnessing a Movement, Taming
an Ideology: On the State and the Third
Sector in Quebec." *Isuma*, Vol. 2, no. 2
(summer 2001): 40-50.

Yankelovich, Daniel. "How Public Opinion Really
Works." *Fortune*, Vol. 126, no. 7 (October
5, 1992): 102-108.

S U F A :
Sea Change or
Mere Ripple for
Canadian Social
Policy?

Introduction

A SSESSING THE SIGNIFICANCE OF SUFA IS IMPORTANT FOR TWO REASONS. FIRST, IT has been presented, in both a positive and a negative light, by various commentators, as a consequential development for the role of the federal government in social policy, for the place of Quebec within the federation and for the overall nature of intergovernmental relations in Canada.[1] Second, understanding the character and effectiveness of SUFA is relevant to its scheduled review and to the natural question of whether there should be a successor agreement. While these questions and issues have obvious bearing on all levels of government in Canada, they are addressed here primarily with a focus on the federal government. Additionally, the focus of this chapter is both SUFA and the social union, two phenomena not always properly recognized in the literature as separate entities. SUFA refers to the administrative agreement signed by the federal government, nine provinces and the territories. The social union is a broader concept, encompassing SUFA along with other agreements and activities over a longer period.

The social union, as a multidimensional phenomenon, refers to three matters. First, it is *a series of processes and structures*, initiated by the annual premiers' conference in 1995 and the subsequent formation, in 1996, of the Provincial/Territorial Council on Social Policy Renewal, which the federal government joined shortly thereafter. Second, it is *a procession of policy decisions and intergovernmental arrangements*, including action plans, budget allocations, fiscal federalism and program changes. Third, it is *a cluster of perspectives* on federalism and social policy, to be sure, but perhaps more deeply, it embodies belief systems concerning the roles of, and relationships among, states, the economy, families and communities. In this sense, the social union refers to the long-term ideas and infrastructure of Canadian social policy.

In all three dimensions, the social union is a continually contested bundle of political bargains, concessions and consensus, as well as intergovernmental partnerships and, at times, partings of the way. Moreover, SUFA is part of a larger and, in most respects, more longstanding set of factors in transforming social programs in Canada. Some common elements are recognizable in recent social policy developments. On balance, recent documents and decisions point to marginally more space for Aboriginal self-determination and relatively greater provincial/territorial autonomy and diversity in social policy priorities, program design and delivery.

This chapter proceeds in five sections. The first section sets out the conceptual framework. This consists of placing SUFA in relation to recent trends in Canadian social policy and setting out a number of analytical propositions. The next three sections illustrate these propositions by examining recent federal and intergovernmental decisions in the following social policy fields: children and families, disability issues, and health care. From this, the final section considers the contribution of SUFA to the restoration and reform processes that several social programs are now undergoing. It is argued that SUFA's impact on recent social policy developments has been modest, more a gentle ripple than a large swell transforming the social union like "a sea-change into something rich and strange."[2] The operation and evolution of the social union are conditioned by several factors and dynamics, only one of which is administrative agreements among first ministers such as SUFA. Other critical factors include recent federal elections, public concerns about health care, and the markedly improved financial status of the federal and most provincial governments. Moreover, the ideas and underlying trends in contemporary social programs were evident prior to SUFA and derive from both new public management and attempts to implement more active and robust social programs.

Ongoing and Emerging Trends in Canada's Social Union

C ANADIAN SOCIAL POLICY OVER THE PAST 20 YEARS CAN BE DIVIDED INTO FOUR phases of development, corresponding roughly to government mandates and dominant strategies of policy change apparent at the national level.[3] The four phases are: maintaining the social safety net, 1980–84; restraining social program costs, 1984–88; restructuring the social role of government, 1988–97; and repairing the social union, 1997 and beyond. This last phase corresponds to the emergence of budget surpluses at the provincial and federal levels. The second and third Chrétien governments have injected additional resources into health care, family policy and post-secondary education. This latest phase is characterized by a reparation agenda, which entails making amends and adjusting programs or transfers felt to be lacking in scope or funding.

Certainly, reparation has been a central dynamic in federal and provincial social policy debates and within the arena of intergovernmental politics. Many program developments can be interpreted as reform processes through which competing notions of federalism, offloading, and citizenship are expressed and negotiated. Provinces and territories, Aboriginal governments and groups, community organizations, and families and individuals have constantly expressed the desire for stable, predictable, and adequate funding of social transfers and programs. The restoration of previously frozen and cut federal funding is apparent in our case study of health care under the Canada Health and Social Transfer (CHST) and, to a lesser extent, in the case study of transfers to the provinces for programs for persons with disabilities.

A major example of restoration is the reintroduction, in the 2000 federal budget, of full indexation of income-tax brackets, numerous tax credits and income thresholds for eligibility for benefits. This move, not so much an innovation as a rejuvenation, reversed a policy introduced in 1986 by the Mulroney Conservative government and maintained by the first two Chrétien Liberal governments. The restoration of full indexation is immensely significant, because "it halts the stealthy slide in the value of a number of important tax benefits, including those for seniors, and solidifies ongoing increases to the Canada Child Tax Benefit (CCTB)."[4] The CCTB is another example of restoration of increased funding for programs for low- and middle-income families with children, to be sure, but also of the principle of universality in child benefits. By 2004–05, due to benefit increases and indexation, more than 95 percent of Canadian families with children will be eligible for the CCTB, a major incremental increase from the 80 percent coverage by federal child benefits in the early 1990s. The result is that federal child benefits are almost universal again.[5]

At the same time, there are signs that social policy is going beyond repairing programs through restored funding to taking new approaches.[6] Traces of such fundamental change can be found in disability policy, with the new vision articulated by *In Unison* and the numerous reforms in tax measures for Canadians with disabilities.[7] Substantial innovation is suggested also by the National Child Benefit (NCB) and the National Children's Agenda (NCA), the financing reforms to the Canada Pension Plan introduced in 1998, the increased attention to early childhood development by all governments — an interest now embedded in the CHST — and the growing inclusion of national Aboriginal organizations in the discussion, design, and review of federal and intergovernmental social policy-making. Across several social policy fields, recurrent elements in practice can be identified. These trends — some new, some old — reflect all three dimensions of the social union, namely processes and structures, policy decisions and intergovernmental agreements, and multiple perspectives on the public good. Prominent trends include the following:

Developing a shared vision and policy framework of principles and objectives to guide negotiations and programming. Such intergovernmental visions are more developed in areas such as disability and the children's agenda than in contentious and disputed areas such as health care. These intergovernmental visions may be with or without the direct participation of Quebec. In various policy fields — labour market and social-housing agreements are two instances — other provinces are excluded from the agreements, thus creating a wider pattern of asymmetry in Canadian federalism and the social union.

Governments are working together more than they have in the recent past, and with other sectors such as the Aboriginal and voluntary sectors and specific client constituencies such as the disability community. This includes public commitments, contained in agreements, to include mechanisms for Canadians to participate in developing and reviewing vision, priorities, programs or outcomes. For example, several national Aboriginal organizations are increasingly involved directly in multilateral and bilateral arrangements with federal and provincial/territorial governments, including consultations and delivery of health and social services. Despite these gains at the program level, national Aboriginal leaders still struggle to gain access to, and a regular place within, the structures and processes of executive federalism.[8]

After several years of restraint in social spending, governments are introducing incremental increases to selected areas of funding. This is occurring at both orders of government, through unilateral actions and intergovernmental processes. A related trend is the increasing use of the tax system, perhaps most notable at the federal level, to deliver social benefits. Examples of social policy through the tax system include the recently introduced Medical Expense Supplement for Earners (1997) and the Caregiver Tax Credit (1998) in disability policy, as well as the federal child tax benefit, the NCB (1998).

A growing, grudging acknowledgement by Ottawa that primary authority and responsibility for most health, educational, and social programs and services rest with the provinces. This acknowledgement is reflected in the adoption of broad intergovernmental agreements within which a wide range of options concerning the provision of programs and services is possible or has been adopted. That it is a grudging acknowledgement is revealed by continued federal social policy initiatives in areas of provincial jurisdiction with little or no prior consultation, and by the move toward earmarked transfers for early childhood development and health care under the CHST.[9] Yet, at the same time, scope for policy and program diversity and discretion by provincial and territorial governments is evident in the Early Childhood Development (ECD) initiative and the 2000 health accord. As a result, we will, in all likelihood, be seeing more social policy divergence across jurisdictions in Canada over the next five to 10 years.

A greater commitment to enhancing the knowledge base of policy sectors and to disseminating research results and sharing information on administrative practices and policy lessons. Closely connected to this pledge is the adoption of results-based accountability frameworks for the joint setting of targets and monitoring of performance, and for each government to report results to its constituency. Should targets not be met, however, there are no financial penalties in transfer payments. Accountability frameworks are a feature of the multilateral and bilateral Employability Assistance for Persons with Disabilities (EAPD) agreements, SUFA itself, the ECD agreement and the Health Renewal Accord, among other accords in additional policy fields. The ECD agreement commits governments to begin reporting publicly on results by September 2001, and the 2000 health accord has a reporting target date of September 2002.

Despite some of the above trends, which are in the early stages of development, there is the enduring custom in Canada of executive dominance over the governmental process with a minor role played by legislatures. First ministers may not be autocrats, but they certainly enjoy a great deal of authority and influence, perhaps nowhere more than in the intergovernmental arena. This concentration of power within Canadian executive federalism has been remarked upon for decades, and there is a growing range of proposals for democratizing policy-making institutions.[10]

After withdrawing from most social policy fields for a decade or more, Canada's senior governments are restoring funds to retrenched programs, notably in health care, education, training, and certain child and family services. Furthermore, governments are exploring ways of reforming the relationship between political systems and civil societies and the approach to public problems in the face of new issues and past lessons.

Children and Families: A Rising Priority for All Governments

THE CURRENT FEDERAL INITIATIVES FOR CHILDREN AND FAMILIES ARE LISTED IN FIGure 1. This package includes a broad set of policy instruments, notably transfer payments to other governments through the ECD agreement; direct expenditures to persons and community organizations through Healthy Family Programs; transfers to Aboriginal communities, agencies and families through the Aboriginal Head Start program; tax relief and tax expenditures to households; research on children and youth; and regulatory measures on child custody, access and support. While a number of these instruments and areas fall squarely within federal jurisdiction, all have implications for provincial and territorial governments and thus for intergovernmental relations.

During the Chrétien government's second mandate, from 1997 to 2000, as the fiscal situation of Ottawa improved spectacularly while poverty stubbornly persisted, measures to support families and their children emerged as a prominent policy area. It appears that children and families will continue to be a priority in the Liberals' third mandate. In the 2001 Throne Speech to preview the mandate, the Chrétien government boldly promised: "A generation ago, Canadians took up the challenge of eliminating poverty among seniors. And ensuring no Canadian child suffers the debilitating effects of poverty is a top priority of our government." The Throne Speech articulates three goals for child and family policy at the federal level:

A n   O v e r v i e w   o f

F e d e r a l   I n i t i a t i v e s

f o r   C h i l d r e n   a n d

F a m i l i e s ,   2 0 0 2

- Aboriginal programming: Aboriginal Head Start
- Child custody, access and support law and guidelines
- Early childhood development initiatives
- Education funding increased to support children on reserves who have special needs at school
- Extended maternity and parental benefits
- Healthy Family Programs:
  Community Action Program for Children
  Canada Prenatal Nutrition Program
  Fetal Alcohol Syndrome/Fetal Alcohol Effects initiative
- National Child Benefit: Canada Child Tax Benefit and NCB Supplement
- Research:
  National Longitudinal Survey on Children and Youth
  Understanding the Early Years
- Tax relief and tax expenditure measures

Source: www.socialunion.gc.ca

1. to help disadvantaged families with children break the cycle of poverty and dependency;
2. to ensure that all families have access to the services and supports they need to care for their children; and
3. to provide young Aboriginal Canadians with the basic tools they need to take greater advantage of the opportunities Canada has to offer.[11]

The Throne Speech identifies potential further action in all three areas. The first goal is a selective strategy for tackling poverty with a categorical approach to assisting welfare-poor and working-poor families with children. The NCB, introduced by Ottawa in 1998, has similar objectives.[12] The 2001 Throne Speech commits the Liberals to building on "successful employment support pilot programs [in British Columbia and New Brunswick] by working with the provinces and territories to develop new measures to help single parents overcome poverty and become more self-sufficient."

The second goal has a universalistic scope and an awareness of the instability and variety of family forms in contemporary Canada. Here, the Throne Speech indicates that the federal government will "work with the provinces to modernize the laws for child support, custody and access to ensure that they work in the best interests of the children in cases of family breakdown" and "to take steps to enable parents to provide care to a gravely ill child without fear of sudden income or job loss." Furthermore, with the expansion of the CCTB over the last four years, and with more enhancements planned, the Liberals are making this program available to more middle-income families, thus edging back toward a universal child and family cash benefit at the national level.[13]

The third goal expresses a crucial element of cultural recognition. According to the Throne Speech, the federal government will

> work with First Nations to improve and expand the early childhood development programs and services available in their communities...expand significantly the Aboriginal Head Start program, to better prepare more Aboriginal children for school and help those with special needs; [and adopt] measures to significantly reduce the number of Aboriginal newborns affected by Fetal Alcohol Syndrome...by the end of this decade.[14]

Does all this add up to a coherent package of policies and goals for children and families in Canada? In a federal system, that is not a question to be put to a single government, especially at a level at which the government does not have the constitutional jurisdictions that largely pertain to children and families. Questions that can be put to the federal government are whether the Liberals have placed children and families on the national policy agenda, have addressed a range of issues of real significance to children and their families, and have committed substantial resources over the long term. Various stakeholder and interest groups have different answers to these questions, with some disapproving, others remaining detached, still others commending the measures and plans. The present cluster of policies for children and families, supported by the NCA and the NCB, represents the most explicit and extensive family policy at the federal and intergovernmental levels in perhaps a generation. This is underscored by the ECD initiatives agreed to by the first ministers, with the exception of the Quebec premier, in September 2000. The main features of the ECD agreement are outlined in table 1.

The communiqué from the first ministers' meeting provides a context for the ECD agreement. It expounds:

> The early years of life are critical in the development and future well being of the child, establishing the foundation for competence and coping skills that will affect learning, behaviour and health. Children thrive within families and communities that can meet their physical and developmental needs and can provide security, nurturing, respect and love. New evidence has shown that development from the prenatal period to age six is rapid and dramatic and shapes long-term outcomes.
>
> Intervening early to promote child development during this critical period can have long-term benefits that can extend throughout children's lives. Governments and other partners currently provide a range of programs and services to effectively support early childhood development. The challenge is to build on existing services and supports, to make them more coordinated and widely available.[15]

The ECD agreement thus focuses on children and families and their immediate communities from the prenatal period to age six. It has two objectives: "to promote early childhood development so that, in their fullest potential, children will be physically and emotionally healthy, safe and secure, ready to learn, and socially engaged and responsible" and "to help children reach their potential and to help families support their children within strong communities."

The ECD echoes several features of SUFA and the NCA, suggesting that it constitutes a set of "ideas in good currency" in child and family policy and reflects the public and elite mood regarding how social policy and intergovernmental

Table 1   134

Initiatives under the Early Childhood Development Agreement, 2001–06

Key areas of action	Focus of supports	Programming examples
Healthy pregnancy, birth and infancy	Pregnant women New parents Infants Caregivers	Prenatal classes and information Infant screening programs
Parenting and family supports	Parents/guardians Caregivers	Family resource centres Parent information Home visiting
Early childhood development, learning and care	Young children	Child care centres Preschools Developmental programs for young children
Community supports	Formal support systems Informal helping networks	Community-based planning Service integration Healthy community initiatives

Source: Based on First Ministers of Canada (2000).

relations should be conducted today.[16] These ideas include a focus on early prevention and coordinated approaches that are inclusive of children with disabilities and children living in a variety of circumstances. From a governance perspective, ideas in good currency include an expansion of funding for services and programs over time in a predictable and sustained fashion; governments working together and with other groups, including Aboriginal peoples; governments reporting frequently and publicly on their progress to their respective constituencies; and governments investing in research and knowledge and sharing effective practices with others.

We can observe also what Alain Noël calls "collaborative federalism with a footnote"[17] — that is, Quebec's nonadherence to a federal/provincial/territorial document because it infringes on its constitutional jurisdiction in matters of social policy, and its nonparticipation judged to be problematic by other governments. Notwithstanding "sharing the same concerns on early childhood development," the ECD communiqué states in an endnote that Quebec "intends to preserve its sole responsibility for developing, planning, managing and delivering early childhood development programs. Consequently, Quebec expects to receive its share of any additional federal funding for early childhood development programs without any new conditions." This points to another social union feature — the federal government announcing further expenditures to support an intergovernmental agreement. In this instance, Ottawa is committing $2.2 billion to early childhood development over the five-year period 2001–02 to 2005–06. As described in table 1, the provinces and territories have agreed to use this increased funding in one or more of the four areas of action.

Disability Issues: A Bold Vision with Modest Results

INTERGOVERNMENTAL INITIATIVES AND PLANS RELATED TO DISABILITY POLICY ARE itemized in table 2. Employment Assistance for People with Disabilities (EAPD) represents a case of collaborative federalism, remarkable in that it took place in the fiscally constrained and intense politics of the immediate post-CHST and pre-SUFA period. Over the 1996 to mid-1998 period, there were

Table 2   136

Intergovernmental
Disability Policy
Initiatives and
Plans, 1997-2002

- First Ministers' Meeting identifies disability issues as a mutual priority in social policy renewal, June 1996 (reaffirmed December 1997)
- Multilateral Framework on Employability Assistance for People with Disabilities (EAPD), signed (with the exception of Quebec) in September 1997
- Bilateral agreements on EAPD signed by all provinces except Ontario, 1997–98; five-year agreements, from April 1998 to March 2003, with a review process in the third year
- Canada Pension Plan consultation process co-chaired by federal and provincial officials (1997) and reforms (1998) agreed to by eight provinces (British Columbia and Saskatchewan dissenting) and the federal government
- *In Unison: A Canadian Approach to Disability Issues*, a vision paper developed by federal/provincial/territorial social services ministers (except Quebec's), including consultation processes with disability and Aboriginal organizations, released in October 1998
- Disability Links, a joint initiative in support of *In Unison* to offer single-entry access to, and seamless connection among, federal/provincial/territorial programs and services for job seekers with disabilities and potential employers, 1998–99; implemented in early 2001
- Disability Accountability Framework, another joint venture under *In Unison*, "to monitor the implementation of *In Unison*, to measure its success and the challenges that continue to be addressed. The proposed accountability framework will guide the way governments report to the public on actions in support of *In Unison* for persons with disabilities. It will also enable governments to share information with each other."
- *In Unison 2000: Persons with Disabilities in Canada* released in March 2001 by federal, provincial and territorial ministers responsible for social services; provides information on effective practices and highlights continuing challenges and areas for further intergovernmental collaboration

Sources: Federal and provincial government
Websites, including www.socialunion.gc.ca/pwd/
unison/backgrounder_e.html

easily more than 40 intergovernmental meetings on replacing the Vocational Rehabilitation for Disabled Persons (VRDP) program, an intergovernmental agreement begun in the early 1960s and rooted very much in the social protection paradigm. Meetings on negotiating EAPD and related disability policy issues took place at all levels: First Ministers' Meetings, annual premiers' conferences, meetings of ministers responsible for social services, and working groups of officials on benefits and services for persons with disabilities. At times, the meetings involved all 13 governments, although more frequently they were bilateral or multilateral.[18]

The federal government, nine provinces and two territories agreed upon a multilateral framework on EAPD in October 1997. Although the Quebec government did not endorse the multilateral framework, its officials observed the proceedings and later undertook bilateral negotiations to secure a cost-shared arrangement with the federal government.

Like the VRDP program, EAPD funding is based on equal contributions from the province/territory and the federal government in each year of the agreement. Like VRDP and the Canada Assistance Plan (CAP), EAPD has two parts: an umbrella multilateral agreement and, within this, a series of bilateral administrative agreements. Unlike VRDP (until 1994) and CAP (until 1990), however, federal funding will be limited rather than open-ended. EAPD has an upper limit to the federal share of $193 million annually. Also unlike VRDP and CAP, it is intended to have a strong focus on employability and labour market activities; consequently, medical services as well as programs provided in sheltered workshops and work-activity programs that are not directly linked to meeting employability needs will not likely be cost-shared. Federal funding for previous VRDP programs inconsistent with EAPD will be phased out over a three-year period. Formal bilateral negotiations began in late 1997, and within two years all 10 provinces had signed bilateral agreements. The agreements are in effect for five years, until March 2003.

In late 1998, following two years of collaboration and consultations, ministers responsible for social services released a policy framework to guide governmental action in the field of disabilities. Called *In Unison: A Canadian Approach to Disability Issues*, it is the first substantial consensus among governments (with the exception of Quebec) on a national vision for disability policy. The shared vision proclaims:

> Persons with disabilities participate as full citizens in all aspects of Canadian society. The full participation of persons with disabilities requires the commitment of all sectors of society. The realization of the vision will allow persons with disabilities to maximize their independence and enhance their well being through access to required supports and the elimination of barriers that prevent their full participation.[19]

The vision is to be implemented through three interrelated building blocks: disability services and supports for daily living; education, training and employment; and income security programs. In policy directions to date the most progress made has been in emphasizing the employability of working-age persons with disabilities; likely the most challenging reforms are making benefits and services more portable and making program delivery more holistic and person-centred.

In July 1999 the federal government released its own vision document, *Future Directions to Address Disability Issues for the Government of Canada: Working Together for Full Citizenship*. Echoing themes in earlier documents as well as SUFA, *Future Directions* sets out several priorities for federal policy. These include increasing public accountability and improving policy and program coherence on disability issues, building a comprehensive base of knowledge in disability issues, and supporting the capacity of the disabled community to participate in the policy process.

If the 2001 Throne Speech is any guide, disability issues will figure more prominently in the Liberals' third mandate, not necessarily as an overarching policy sector such as children and families, but as a dimension of activities in a number of policy sectors across the federal government. In research and development, the government commits to increase investments to "support the development of new technologies to assist Canadians with disabilities." For Aboriginal peoples, the Throne Speech states that measures will be taken to significantly reduce the number of Aboriginal newborns affected by fetal alcohol syndrome by the end of this decade. For all children and families, the government commits to "improve the support available to parents and caregivers in times of family crisis" when caring for "a gravely ill child." On good health and quality care, the Throne Speech mentions that efforts will be strengthened "to prevent injuries and promote mental health." In the area of skills and learning, conceivably looking beyond the current EAPD agreements due to expire in

2003, the Throne Speech says the federal government "will work with the provinces and territories and other partners toward a comprehensive labour-market strategy for persons with disabilities."[20]

Table 3 outlines recent initiatives on the federal government's disability policy agenda. Notable policy instruments are legislative reforms dealing with rights of various kinds and tax measures. The federal tax system has several major disability-related programs dealing not only with income support and tax relief, but also with promoting independent community living, education, employment, family support and caregiving. Targeting tax assistance to groups deemed in need is not, of course, unique to persons with disabilities. What is distinctive is the comparatively greater federal tax expenditures for persons with disabilities, in recent budgets, than for most other client groups and social policy themes. Over the past decade, while tax measures in other areas have been under restraint, there have been numerous extensions to disability-related tax assistance and several new measures introduced.

The 1997–2000 Liberal government included three budgets and one mini-budget, and these fiscal plans introduced 17 tax measures related to disability policy, offering tax relief or addressing economic and social objectives. The October 2000 mini-budget was anything but "mini" for disability policy, providing more than twice the new tax spending of the February 2000 budget for people with disabilities.[21] This builds on the further tax assistance announced in the 1998 and 1999 budgets, generating a total of $1.6 billion in additional tax assistance for people with disabilities and their caregivers by 2004–05, arising from the second Liberal mandate.

Health Care Funding
and System Renewal:
Giving Back and
Moving Forward

I N OUR POST-DEFICIT ERA, "NEW" INVESTMENTS FOR HEALTH CARE ANNOUNCED IN FED-eral budgets are a frequent theme as well. After years of restraining the growth rate in health transfers to the provinces in the 1980s and early 1990s, the CHST delivered absolute cuts in transfer payments to the provinces. Announced in the

Federal Government
Initiatives and
Plans for
Disability Issues,
1 9 9 6 – 2 0 0 2

1996	*Equal Citizenship for Canadians with Disabilities: The Will to Act.* Report of the Federal Task Force on Disability Issues, a task force of Liberal MPs established by three cabinet ministers; involved extensive participation by more than 20 national disability organizations and major Aboriginal organizations
1997	Opportunities Fund for People with Disabilities introduced in the federal budget as a three-year pilot program but since extended
1997–2000	An estimated 17 tax-expenditure measures related to disability policy announced in three budgets and one economic statement
1998	Social Development Partnerships Program
1998, 2000	Amendments to *Criminal Code, Canada Evidence Act, Canadian Human Rights Act* and *Canada Elections Act* concerning people with disabilities
1998–2003	Canadian Heritage contribution agreement with the Court Challenges Program of Canada
1999	*Future Directions to Address Disability Issues for the Government of Canada: Working Together for Full Citizenship,* federal vision paper released by HRDC, the leading department on disability issues
2000	Extension of veterans' disability pensions and other benefits to various groups with previously little or no access
2001	Cross-sectional survey on people with disabilities to be conducted
2001	Including a longitudinal survey and other studies in future research; and creating a disability accountability and reporting framework; developing beyond an ''access and inclusion lens'' for policy processes; implementing Throne Speech commitments
2002	Canada Student Grants for persons with disabilities increased to cover exceptional costs of specialized services and equipment

Source: Based on Human Resources Development
Canada, *The Government of Canada's Record on
Disability* (Ottawa: HRDC, 1998). Available at
www.hrdc-drhc.gc.ca/common/news/9821b4.html

February 1995 federal budget, the CHST is among the most striking and unilateral developments ever in Canadian social policy and fiscal federalism.

The CHST is a child of federal deficit reduction and a cousin of provincial demands for greater autonomy in social policy. Within this national context of spending restraint and flexible federalism, especially in relations with Quebec, the CHST has three main elements. First, it replaces and consolidates the previous arrangements of federal transfer payments for social assistance and social services under CAP, as well as for health and post-secondary education under the Established Programs Financing (EPF) agreement, into a single program. Second, in the beginning the CHST involved a cut of $7 billion over the 1996–97 to 1997–98 period. Third, while the five conditions associated with the *Canada Health Act* remain in place and are enforced by Ottawa with respect to social assistance and social services, only one of the five conditions under the *Canada Assistance Plan Act* is retained.[22]

Given the secrecy and haste in crafting the CHST and the ministerial bargaining, the federal government did not decide upon a cash floor for the CHST until six months after the budget was announced. Finance officials favoured a transfer payment floor of $9 billion per year, while some ministers, particularly social Liberals, wanted a floor of $12.5 billion per year. The Prime Minister's Office settled for an annual cash floor of $11 billion.[23]

The CHST deeply aggravated and immediately provoked provinces and territories into developing a new process of interprovincial/territorial collaboration for social policy renewal. Federal unilateralism encouraged interprovincialism. While the provinces and territories were unable to prevent the implementation of the CHST, they have been partially successful in getting Ottawa to bolster the amount of cash payments to be transferred in each of the five years of the fiscal arrangement.

Prime Minister Chrétien established in 1994 a National Forum on Health to develop a vision of the health system, and the forum reported in early 1997. If nothing else in Canadian health policy and politics, the forum's report influenced the 1997 federal budget, which made the first of what has become a series of cash supplements to the provinces for health care. That budget provided $300 million over the subsequent three years for developing new approaches to home care and drug coverage and other innovations. Of that, $150 million was assigned to a Health Transition Fund, allocated by health ministers, and $50 million was allotted to the Canada Health Information System to develop a national system of health care information. The remaining $100 million was intended to increase funding for two existing programs, the Community Action Program for Children and the Canada Prenatal Nutrition Program.[24]

At the outset of the 1997 general election, the prime minister announced that a re-elected Liberal government would raise the CHST's cash floor from $11 to $12.5 billion. This announcement likely helped the Liberals keep the issue of medicare largely off the electoral agenda that summer, but it did not please the provinces or fulfill their demands for restoration of the cuts in transfer payments. As Ottawa's fiscal position improved rapidly from deficits to surpluses, public concerns about the state of Canada's publicly insured medical system persisted, as did calls by premiers for the restoration of full federal funding to the provinces for health care.

A year later, on the same day that nearly all first ministers signed SUFA, they all signed a much shorter document, the *Federal/Provincial/Territorial Health Care Agreement*. This accord contained four key points. First, the federal government committed to a "substantial increase" in health funding, through the CHST, in the approaching 1999 budget. Second, the provinces and territories agreed to devote all of this increase to health services "in accordance with the health-care priorities within their respective jurisdictions." Third, the provinces and territories additionally reaffirmed their commitment to the five principles of the *Canada Health Act*. Fourth, in language similar to that of SUFA, it was "agreed that governments would work together to develop ways of measuring the performance and effectiveness of health care services, and that this information will be developed and reported to Canadians."[25] Shortly thereafter, the February 1999 federal budget pledged an additional $11.5 billion to the provinces, through the CHST, over five years.

One year later, the next federal budget announced a further $2.5 billion to the provinces over four years for health care and post-secondary education. Still, the premiers contended — with merit — that federal funding had not yet restored the full extent of cuts made in the early 1990s. Then, for the fourth time since 1997, Ottawa announced another increase to the CHST for health care. In September 2000, amidst speculation of an election call that autumn, the prime minister convened a meeting of first ministers to discuss health care.

New federal funding commitments on health care through the CHST, for the period 1998–99 to 2005–06, are presented in table 4. Along with the $45 bil-

Table 4

New Federal Funding Commitments on Health Care through the CHST, 1998–99 to 2005–06

(Billions of dollars)

	1998-1999	1999-2000	2000-2001	2001-2002	2002-2003	2003-2004	2004-2005	2005-2006	Total
1998 Budget[1]	1.5	1.5	1.5	1.5	1.5	1.5	1.5	1.5	12.0
1999 Budget		2.0	2.0	2.5	2.5	2.5			11.5
2000 Budget[2]			1.0	0.5	0.5	0.5			2.5
2000 Health Accord				2.5	3.2	3.8	4.4	5.0	18.9
Total	1.5	3.5	4.5	7.0	7.7	8.3	5.9	6.5	44.9

[1] This increase was to the CHST cash floor, raising it from $11 billion to $12.5 billion a year. The other increases are supplements to the CHST rather than permanent enhancements to the cash floor.

[2] This increase was designated in federal budget papers as for post-secondary education as well as health care, although no proportions were specifically noted.

These amounts do not include federal investments in health care measures that lie outside the CHST. Over this same period, the federal government announced additional spending commitments of approximately $4.6 billion on health care renewal. Half of that was announced at the time of the September 2000 health accord, reflecting shared intergovernmental priorities on medical equipment, primary-care reform and health information technologies.

Source: Department of Finance Canada, various years. Available at http://www.fin.gc.ca

lion in additional funds to provinces and territories for health care, the federal government has committed approximately $4.6 billion to a host of targeted health measures, some to be expended in collaboration with other governments and other funds allocated directly though federal programs and agencies. Overall, about 90 percent of the new monies allocated to health care by Ottawa since the mid-1990s have been directed through the CHST.

After some hard bargaining, late-night negotiations and last-minute compromises, a deal was reached to which all first ministers agreed.[26] The main elements of the September 2000 *First Ministers' Agreement on Health System Renewal* (2000 health accord) are presented in table 5.

Premier Lucien Bouchard of Quebec explained why he had signed this health accord: "We have all the guarantees we need to make sure that no transfer of jurisdiction has been achieved, that provincial jurisdictions will be respected, and that it is a dynamic, positive agreement for the benefit of all citizens of our provinces, and of Quebec and Canada."[27] Indeed, the accord included an introductory statement declaring that nothing in the document "shall be construed to derogate from the respective governments' jurisdictions" and that the document should be "interpreted in full respect of each government's jurisdiction." The health accord noted: "Given their constitutional responsibilities, provincial and territorial governments play the primary role in the design, management and funding of the health services within their jurisdictions." Moreover, the action plan outlined several priority areas for collaboration "so that each government can be more effective in relation to its responsibilities for health."

In addition, on the topic of accountability and public reporting of program results, the federal principle, rather than the federal government, seems to have prevailed. In wording that goes beyond SUFA in this regard, the health accord state:

Respecting each other's responsibilities, all governments believe in the importance of being accountable to Canadians for the health programs and services they deliver. Clear public reporting, with appropriate, independent, third party verification will enhance the performance of health services, and is important for achieving the vision and accomplishing the priorities set out above.

The purpose of performance measurement is for all governments to be accountable to their public, not to each other. The amount of federal funding provided to any jurisdiction will not depend on achieving a given level of performance.[28]

Table 5

First Ministers'
Accord on Health
System Renewal,
September 2000

Priority areas	Policy aims	Governments involved
Access to care	To improve timely access to and quality of health services	Provincial and territorial (P/T)
Health promotion and wellness	To recognize the determinants of health, enhance disease and illness prevention and improve public health, including early childhood development	Federal, provincial and territorial (F/P/T)
Primary health care	To ensure timely access to services outside of emergency departments and to promote the establishment of interdisciplinary primary health care teams	F/P/T
Supply of doctors, nurses and other personnel	To coordinate efforts to ensure adequate supply of personnel with skills to provide appropriate levels of care and services	P/T
Home care and community care	To strengthen public investment in home and community care	P/T
Pharmaceuticals management	To develop ways to assess the cost-effectiveness of prescription drugs for inclusion in government plans	F/P/T
Health information	To strengthen a Canada-wide health info-structure	F/P/T
Health equipment and infrastructure	To invest in equipment, new technologies and facilities to improve access for Canadians	F/P/T

Source: Adapted from First Ministers of Canada (2000).

The health accord also commits governments to develop "a comprehensive framework using jointly agreed comparable indicators such that each government will begin reporting by September, 2002" to their respective publics on health status, health outcomes and service quality. This is an advance on the SUFA text, which is less specific on the nature of the reporting and lacks timelines for reporting to constituencies. Ottawa's next proposal on this process is contained in the January 2001 Throne Speech, in which the Chrétien government announces its intention to "work with the provinces and territories to create a citizens' council on health care quality, which will obtain the public's perspective on relevant and meaningful measures of health system performance."[29] Interestingly, this proposal was advanced by federal officials during the September 2000 negotiations on the health accord but was rejected by the provinces at the time.

To guide governmental commitments on health, the accord identifies a vision, seven principles and eight priority areas for action. The emphasis is on maintaining the five principles of the *Canada Health Act* and strengthening insured hospital and medical services by providing predictable and growing funding and by supporting innovations including research, information systems and performance measurement. Given recent controversies around two-tier medicare and the privatization of health care, the accord contains several references to our publicly funded and delivered system.

The eight areas of priority action (see table 5) reflect issues that have been the focus of the National Forum on Health; provincial royal commissions and task forces; numerous meetings of health ministers and deputy ministers; and positions of professional associations, expert viewpoints and expressed public anxieties. Rather than SUFA itself, it is these factors, what we may call part of the social union milieu, that have shaped the agenda of health care reform. And, of course, there is the matter of funding.

To secure provincial and territorial consent on the health accord, the prime minister announced a general cash increase to the CHST of $18.9 billion over five years (2001–02 to 2005–06). Further, outside of the CHST, the federal government is investing $1 billion over two years (2000–01 and 2001–02) for a Medical Equipment Fund; $500 million in 2000–01 in an independent corporation with a mandate to quicken the development and take-up of new information technology systems in health care; and $800 million over four years, beginning in 2001–02, in a renewed Health Transition Fund to support reform in primary care. These moves reflect priority areas in the health accord. The December 2001 federal budget did not add any new funds to health care through the CHST, but did confirm the full protection of the health accord decisions. It announced $175 million in spending, primarily for the Canadian Institute for Health Information and the Canadian Institutes of Health Research, with a small amount to Health Canada for data on First Nations people living on reserves.

The total CHST cash therefore rises from $15.5 billion in 2000–01 to $18.3 billion in 2001–02, and then grows more gradually over a number of years to $21 billion in 2005–06. To ensure stability in funding, the increases were legislated just prior to the October 2000 election. For subsequent predictability of funding, the federal government has promised to establish, by the end of 2003–04, the CHST cash transfers for 2006–07 and 2007–08. In addition, as earlier discussed, Ottawa is transferring to the provinces and territories $2.2 billion over five years for the ECD agreement, the first intergovernmental social policy agreement to emerge post-SUFA. The funds for this measure are earmarked for that purpose and provided for through the CHST. This signifies a new form of conditionality, although a modest form, within this funding instrument.

The prime minister sweetened the pot at the September 2000 meeting of first ministers by pledging to remove the $10 billion ceiling on the equalization program entitlements for 1999–2000, resulting in higher payments — an estimated $792 million — to the seven eligible provinces.[30]

Even with these injections of new funds, the future of the health care system and the federal government's role in that system remain under scrutiny and debate. The Senate Standing Committee on Social Affairs, chaired by Senator Michael Kirby, has been examining the state of Canada's health care system, with a focus on pressures, constraints and Ottawa's role. Over 2001 and 2002 the committee released five reports, and it has described the financing of health care as the most controversial health care issue in the country. In April 2001 the prime minister created the Commission on the Future of Health Care in Canada, with Roy Romanow, the former premier of Saskatchewan, as the sole commissioner. The commission's mandate is to address the long-term sustainability of a high-quality, universally accessible, publicly administered health care system. Mr. Romanow is also taking up the question of financing, an issue he has described as at the heart of the health care debate. His final report is expected at the end of 2002. Some premiers have said they cannot wait for these federal processes to conclude, and are thus commissioning their own studies and announcing various health care reforms. The provinces are asserting their primary responsibility for the provision of health services and the proper management of the health care system. They also argue that the federal government ought to fulfill its commitment to the premiers to work with the provinces and territories in developing a dispute avoidance and dispute resolution mechanism for disagreements related to the *Canada Health Act*. The management of federal-provincial disputes over national health standards is a difficult issue that predates SUFA, reflecting classic tensions between unity and diversity inherent to the social union.

Concluding Observations

THE ACTUAL AND POTENTIAL ROLE OF SUFA CANNOT BE UNDERSTOOD WITHOUT an appreciation of developments in the wider economic, social and political systems. Viewed in this context, SUFA's impact on social policy-making and the management of federalism is more akin to a ripple than a sea change. Table 6 provides a summary of the analysis and discussion. It shows the three dimensions of the social union and relates these to the three policy areas examined in the chapter. In a simple fashion, it reveals that SUFA is but one agreement among many and that the social union itself is an ever-changing multidimensional phenomenon. Table 6 also suggests that SUFA has not made a big splash nor provided a basic framework for the management of the social union. The ECD initiatives and the 2000 health accord make no mention of SUFA, for example. Discussions and decisions seem to be proceeding constructively on a sectoral basis in accordance with the history, issues and needs of particular policy areas.

That SUFA caught, rather than created, the wave of change is indicated by various factors. One is that a number of intergovernmental agreements crafted one, two or three years before SUFA contained nearly all the elements that would appear in that accord. In the policy fields of children, disability, labour markets and social housing, the paper trail was well established before SUFA was reached in 1999. A good example is the Multilateral Framework on EAPD

Table 6

Governmental
Initiatives in
Family, Disability
and Health Policy:
A Summary View

Dimensions	Child and family policy	Disability issues	Health care
Federal and intergovernmental processes and structure	◆ National Children's Agenda: developing a vision, consultations and revisions of vision (1996–98)	◆ Canada Pension Plan review and consultations (1995–97) ◆ Review and development of new employment strategy for persons with disabilities (1996–98) ◆ Income-tax systems (through the 1990s and into the 2000s)	◆ National Health Forum (1994–97) ◆ Romanow Commission on the Future of Health Care (2001–02) ◆ Numerous provincial commissions and task forces on health reform (through the 1990s and into the early 2000s) ◆ First ministers' meetings
Policy decisions and intergovernmental agreements	◆ Canada Child Tax Benefit (1998) ◆ Early Childhood Development initiatives (2000)	◆ EAPD (1997) ◆ *In Unison* (1998) ◆ Income-tax measures (various years)	◆ *Canada Health Act* (1984) ◆ CHST (1995–96) ◆ F/P/T Health Care Agreement (1998)

Table 6 150

Governmental Initiatives in Family, Disability and Health Policy: A Summary View (cont.)

Dimensions	Child and family policy	Disability issues	Health care
Policy decisions and intergovernmental agreements (cont.)	◆ Child Custody and Access (2001–02)		◆ First Ministers' Accord on Health System Renewal (2000)
Perspectives on federalism, social policy, political economy and civil society	◆ Collaborative federalism[1] ◆ Focus on prevention and early years of life, Aboriginal youth and communities	◆ Collaborative federalism ◆ Full citizenship for persons with disabilities, including employability	◆ Collaborative and classical federalism ◆ Pressure on federal government to restore funding ◆ Commitment to publicly funded and delivered health care and respect for provinces to set priorities within their own jurisdictions

[1] Refers to "federalism with a footnote" — that is, intergovernmental agreements without direct participation and acceptance by the Government of Quebec

agreed to in September 1997 by ministers responsible for social services. The framework contains a statement of purpose, an objective and principles to guide the bilateral agreements. One of the principles is flexibility — that is, within the broad objectives of the initiative, each province and territory has the flexibility to develop programs and services and deliver them in the manner that best responds to the requirements of people with disabilities and to labour market circumstances. Another principle is coordination, which dictates that programs and services for people with disabilities are designed and implemented so that they make "the best use of resources to empower citizens with disabilities." Moreover, people with disabilities are to be consulted on program design, implementation and evaluation. Still another principle is implementation of bilateral agreements within an accountability framework. The accountability process is to be annual, to be provided to consumers and the general public, and to include results-reporting based on quantitative and qualitative measures and indicators.[31]

Here we see a set of ideas that were rising on the agendas of public officials, community advocates and policy-makers through the 1990s, bolstered by the new public management and reinvention of government movements, as well as beliefs about "active" social programming.[32] Likewise, references to the five principles of the *Canada Health Act* in intergovernmental agreements and communiqués have been part of the medicare mantra of politicians for several years now. Through repeated chanting and buoyed by obvious public support, federal, provincial and territorial leaders have elevated the *Canada Health Act* to quasi-constitutional status, legitimizing the role of the federal spending power in relation to this area of provincial jurisdiction and the role of Health Canada to both interpret the principles and impose conditions on the provinces regarding health insurance programs. An ongoing issue for the social union is whether the *Canada Health Act*, in its present form, can or should continue to be the master narrative and the dispute resolution mechanism for health policy provision and innovation in the country.

Elections and public opinion have also been important variables in shaping the recent evolution of Canada's social policies. During the 1997 and 2000 election campaigns the prime minister announced new federal investments in health care through the CHST. The political calculus for Mr. Chrétien was clear, especially in September 2000:

> To campaign as the champion of medicare, Mr. Chrétien would have been forced to explain his role over seven years as Prime Minister in the decline of a once proud system. The public, thanks to Mr. Harris [the premier of Ontario] as much as anyone, understands that Ottawa carved billions out of their precious health-care system in bad times and dragged its feet in putting the money back when times turned good. A war over medicare, therefore, would have been messy... The point was to get health care off the table, to try to neutralize the issue by restoring cash transfers to their previous level.[33]

More generally, over the last five years there has been what pollster Allan Gregg calls "a profound change in the priorities and public-opinion agenda of Canada," with Canadians now citing social issues as the most important matter facing the country.[34] Gregg points out that it is not only the issues agenda that has shifted, but also the constituencies driving the concern on social matters; those pressing for greater action on social issues and the restoration of social programs tend to be women, people with low and moderate incomes, the young and the elderly. There are divisions, though, even within and among these groups, as to how best to restore social protection and the acceptability of promoting an agenda of diversity and cultural recognition in Canadian society.

The fiscal circumstances of governments have been a decisive factor in shaping the policy agenda, moulding public experiences and expectations and the dynamics of intergovernmental relations. Discussion of the use of the federal spending power took on greater significance as Ottawa went from a record deficit of $42 billion in 1993–94, to the first surplus in a generation in 1997–98, to a surplus of $12.3 billion in 1999–2000, with projections of further surpluses over the subsequent five years. Any influence SUFA may have is due in large part to the possibilities for restoration and new construction of social programs flowing from this rolling wave of budget surpluses.

More than an encore is required for SUFA. If there is to be a renewed agreement, it will have to capture the additional and refined ideas contained in more recent agreements on early childhood development and health care renewal. Furthermore, as a democratic process and political bargain, a SUFA sequel will have to be more respectful of differences, including the place of Aboriginal peoples and Quebec within the federation, and more engaging of community groups.

I would like to thank Sarah Fortin, France St-Hilaire, Michael Mendelson, Alain Noël and Denis Saint-Martin for their specific comments and suggestions.

1 For a range of views, see Cameron (1999, p. A17); Robson and Schwanen (1999); Gagnon and Segal (2000); and Courchene (2001, ch. 6).

2 The concept of sea change apparently originates from William Shakespeare's *The Tempest*, Act 1, scene 2.

3 For details on how these four phases are delineated and what each embraces, see Prince (1999, ch. 5).

4 Battle (2001, p. 207).

5 Battle (2001, pp. 187, 199). Also see Finance Canada (2001).

6 For a comparable view, see Battle, Torjman and Mendelson (2000).

7 Prince (2001a, ch. 7).

8 Prince and Abele (2000, ch. 12).

9 Recent examples of federal unilateralism in social policy include the Millennium Scholarship Fund, the homelessness initiative and the Canadian Innovation Fund. For an excellent survey of the role of fiscal arrangements under the social union, see Hobson and St-Hilaire (2000, ch. 6).

10 See, for example, Savoie (1999); Bakvis (2000-01); and Patten (2000-01, pp. 60-79, and 221-239).

11 Government of Canada (2001).

12 The NCB seeks to improve the economic security of low-income families with children. Two of its core goals are to help prevent and reduce the depth of child poverty and to help parents find and keep jobs by providing the benefits and services to support them. A third goal is to reduce overlap and duplication between governments in this field of social policy.

13 The CCTB is an income-tested benefit, delivered through the tax system, paid monthly to families with children. It has two parts: a CCTB base benefit for low- to middle-income families, and the NCB Supplement for relatively low-income families, specifically those with annual incomes of $32,000 or less.

14 Government of Canada (2001).

15 First Ministers of Canada (2000, p. 1).

16 On the concept of ideas in good currency, see the discussion in Pal (1997).

17 Noël (2000).

18 For dates and details of many of these meetings, see the social union Website: www.socialunion.gc.ca

19 Federal/Provincial/Territorial Ministers Responsible for Social Services (1998, p. 1). Available at www.socialunion.gc.ca

20 Government of Canada (2001).

21 Prince (2001b, pp. 487-501).

22 The five principles set out in the *Canada Health Act*, 1984, are accessibility, comprehensiveness, portability, public administration and universality. The conditions underlying the *Canada Assistance Plan Act*, 1966, are that need be the sole basis for determining eligibility for income support; that residency rules be prohibited for receipt of social assistance; that there be an appeals system on social assistance decisions; that the provinces and territories commit to reporting and sharing data; and that federal transfers support only the provision of nonprofit social services. Under the CHST, like the EPF before it, there are no federal standards for cost-sharing of post-secondary education.

23 For details on the origins of the CHST, see Greenspon and Wilson-Smith (1996).

24 Budget 1997, "Sustaining and Improving Canada's Health Care System." Available at www.fin.gc.ca/budget97

25 The Federal/Provincial/Territorial Health Care Agreement, February 4, 1999. This agreement was supported by a September 1998 intergovernmental agreement among health ministers, which set out a series of priorities and future directions for health care in Canada.

26 For an intriguing analysis of the tactics, see Adams (2000, p. A4). New federal funding for health was announced in the 1998,

1999 and 2000 budgets and as part of the September 2000 health accord. The cash floor of the CHST has been raised only once, to $12.5 billion in 1998.

27   Quoted in Bouchard (2000, p. A6).

28   First Ministers of Canada (2000, pp. 3, 4). Available at www.scis.gc.ca. The federal principle, sometimes called the "classical federalism model," holds that the powers of government are divided constitutionally so that the national and provincial orders are each coordinate and independent in particular policy spheres. See Wheare (1963).

29   Government of Canada (2001).

30   The official estimate of the benefits of removing the equalization ceiling for 1999–2000 is as follows (in millions of dollars): Newfoundland 36, Prince Edward Island 10, Nova Scotia 62, New Brunswick 50, Quebec 489, Manitoba 76, Saskatchewan 69 (for a total of 792) (Finance Canada: www.fin.gc.ca). For a recent justification of the equalization program from the federal government's perspective, see Dion (2001, p. A15).

31   For the full text, see Ministers Responsible for Social Services (1997).

32   Pal (1997, ch. 2 and 5). See also Noël (1999, pp. 195-219).

33   Greenspon (2000, p. A17).

34   Gregg (2000/2001, p. 34).

Adams, Paul. "Desperate Diplomacy Delivers Last-Minute Deal." *The Globe and Mail*, September 12, 2000: A4.

Bakvis, Herman. "Prime Minister and Cabinet in Canada: An Autocracy in Need of Reform?" *Journal of Canadian Studies*, Vol. 35, no. 4 (winter 2000–01).

Battle, Ken. "Relentless Incrementalism: Deconstructing and Reconstructing Canadian Income Security Policy." In *The Review of Economic Performance and Social Progress*, ed. Keith Banting, Andrew Sharpe and France St-Hilaire. Montreal and Ottawa: Institute for Research on Public Policy and Centre for the Study of Living Standards, 2001.

Battle, Ken, Sherri Torjman and Michael Mendelson. *Social Programs: Reconstruction Not Restoration*. Brief to the Standing Committee of Finance. Ottawa: Caledon Institute of Social Policy, October 2000.

Bouchard, Lucien. "Health-Care Quick Fixes Opposed." *The Globe and Mail*, September 12, 2000: A6.

Cameron, David. "The Social-Union Pact Is Not a Backward Step for Quebec." *The Globe and Mail*, February 12, 1999: A17.

Courchene, Thomas J. *A State of Minds: Toward a Human Capital Future for Canadians*. Montreal: Institute for Research on Public Policy, 2001.

Dion, Stéphane. "If It Ain't Broke." *The Globe and Mail*, July 13, 2001: A15.

Federal/Provincial/Territorial Ministers Responsible for Social Services. *In Unison: A Canadian Approach to Disability Issues*. Ottawa: Human Resources Development Canada, October 1998.

Finance Canada. *Canada Child Tax Benefit Increases by $300 a Year per Child in July 2001*. News release. Ottawa: Finance Canada, June 28, 2001. Available at www.fin.gc.ca/ news01/01-057e.html

First Ministers of Canada. *Communiqué on Health*. News release, ref: 800-038-004. Ottawa: First Ministers' Meeting, September 11, 2000. Available at www.scics.gc.ca

Gagnon, Alain-G., and Hugh Segal, eds. *The Canadian Social Union without Quebec: 8 Critical Analyses*. Montreal: Institute for Research on Public Policy, 2000.

Government of Canada. *Speech from the Throne to Open the First Session of the 37th Parliament of Canada*. Ottawa: Government of Canada, 2001.

Greenspon, Edward. "Why Chrétien Chose Health-Care Peace in Our Time." *The Globe and Mail*, September 12, 2000: A17.

Greenspon, Edward, and Anthony Wilson-Smith. *Double Vision: The Inside Story of the Liberals in Power*. Toronto: Doubleday, 1996.

Gregg, Allan R. "A Shifting Landscape." Maclean's/Global Poll. *Maclean's*, December 25, 2000/January 1, 2001: 34.

Hobson, Paul A.R., and France St-Hilaire. "The Evolution of Federal-Provincial Fiscal Arrangements: Putting Humpty Together Again." In *Canada: The State of the Federation 1999/2000, Toward a New Mission Statement for Canadian Fiscal Federalism*, ed. Harvey Lazar. Montreal and Kingston: McGill-Queen's University Press, 2000.

Ministers Responsible for Social Services. *Multilateral Framework on Employability Assistance for People with Disabilities* (1997). Available at www.socialunion. gc.ca/pwd/ multi_e.html

Noël, Alain. "Without Quebec: Collaborative Federalism with a Footnote?" *Policy Matters*, Vol. 1, no. 2 (March 2000).

——. "Is Decentralization Conservative? Federalism and the Contemporary Debate on the Canadian Welfare State." In *Stretching the Federation: The Art of the State in Canada*, ed. Robert Young. Kingston: Institute for Intergovernmental Relations, Queen's University, 1999.

Pal, Leslie A. *Beyond Policy Analysis: Public Issue Management in Turbulent Times*. Toronto: Nelson, 1997.

Patten, Steve. "Democratizing the Institutions of Policy-Making: Democratic Consultation and Participatory Administration." *Journal of Canadian Studies*, Vol. 35, no. 4 (winter 2000–01).

Prince, Michael J. "Tax Policy as Social Policy: Tax Assistance for Canadians with

Disabilities." *Canadian Public Policy*, Vol. 37, no. 4 (2001*a*): 487-501.

——. "Citizenship by Instalments: Federal Policies for Canadians with Disabilities." In *How Ottawa Spends 2001-2002: Power in Transition*, ed. Leslie A. Pal. Toronto: Oxford University Press, 2001*b*.

——. "From Health and Welfare to Stealth and Farewell." In *How Ottawa Spends 1999–2000. Shape Shifting: Canadian Governance Toward the 21st Century*, ed. Leslie A. Pal. Toronto: Oxford University Press, 1999.

Prince, Michael J., and Frances Abele. "Funding an Aboriginal Order of Government in Canada: Recent Developments in Self-Government and Fiscal Federalism." In *Canada: The State of the Federation 1999/2000, Toward a New Mission Statement for Canadian Fiscal Federalism*, ed. Harvey Lazar. Montreal and Kingston: McGill-Queen's University Press, 2000.

Robson, William B.P., and Daniel Schwanen. *The Social Union: Too Flawed to Last*. Toronto: C.D. Howe Institute, February 1999.

Savoie, Donald J. *Governing from the Centre: The Concentration of Power in Canadian Politics*. Toronto: University of Toronto Press, 1999.

Wheare, K.C. *Federal Government*. London: Oxford University Press, 1963.

The Quebec Model
in Social Policy
and Its Interface
with Canada's
Social Union

Introduction

I N CANADA, REFORMS WITHIN THE TWO FIELDS OF FEDERAL/PROVINCIAL RELATIONS AND social policy have been inextricably linked since the 1930s. Any examination of reforms within the former inevitably leads to central issues within the latter, and vice versa. Although some people may wish that this were not so, there is not much they can do about it.

Any study that aims to provide a balanced analysis of these two dimensions faces an enormous challenge. Indeed, in the literature and public debates on the social union, the "union" aspect is often emphasized to the detriment of the "social." This is an error. While the word "union" refers to the intergovernmental dynamics within the Canadian federation, "social" refers to the dynamics of the transformation of social policies. It is therefore important that we adopt a truly multidisciplinary and integrated approach, to consider not only the intergovernmental dynamics but also projects related to social policy reform. Here, the issue of the social union, more specifically the Social Union Framework Agreement (SUFA), adopted in February 1999, will be examined from a Quebec perspective, focusing on the social dimension (social policies) in the first two sections and on the union dimension (intergovernmental relations) in the third.

A number of seemingly innovative reforms of social policies and practices in Quebec will be examined, taking into account the fact that creative solutions based on similar principles exist in other regions of Canada and elsewhere in the developed and developing world. However, these innovative policies and practices, though neither invulnerable nor irreversible, have more substance in Quebec than in the rest of North America.

The text is divided into three parts. The first part identifies two distinct periods regarding the role of social policies in the Quebec model of development — the period 1960–80, when the welfare state was established, and the period 1980–2000, when it underwent crisis and transformation. The second part examines some of the innovative social policies and practices that have emerged in Quebec in recent years. Finally, the third part comments on a number of interfaces between the new model of social policies emerging in Quebec and the Canadian social union.

Social Policies and Quebec Models of Development

OVER THE PAST THREE YEARS THE DEBATE ON THE EXISTENCE OF A "QUEBEC MODEL of development" has been rekindled, raising a number of questions: Is there or is there not a Quebec model of development? If there is such a model, in what ways has it changed over the last 40 years? If changes are necessary, what direction should they take? In what respects is this model similar to or different from those found in other Canadian provinces and in other countries? How does the changing Quebec model fit within the Canadian, North American and international environments and within a context of globalization?

This debate concerns both the social and economic development models, although most commentators refer exclusively to the latter. Here, we are particularly interested in the role of social policies and the contribution of a number of innovations to the current redefinition of the Quebec model of development. It can be stated from the outset that, yes, there is a Quebec model of development; it emerged in the 1960s, underwent significant changes in the 1980s and 1990s, and will no doubt undergo further changes in the coming years. Finally, it is revealing to interpret the history of social policies in Quebec and Canada in the light of this Quebec model and its impact on the evolution of intergovernmental relations since 1960.

This history of the Quebec development model draws on Gilles L. Bourque's groundbreaking research on the development of industrial policy in Quebec over the last 40 years, including his detailed examination of the 1986–94 period when Robert Bourassa's Liberal Party was returned to power.[1] Bourque's analysis of economic development reveals that there was a first Quebec model during the 1960s and 1970s, which entered a transitional period in the 1980s and finally gave rise to a second model in the 1990s.[2] In economic terms, the first Quebec model corresponds to a vision of an entrepreneurial, hierarchical, nationalist and centralizing state. In contrast, the second model corresponds to a vision of the state as a "facilitator" and partner in its relationships with private enterprises, employer organizations and unions.

This paper is based on Bourque's work but includes a more in-depth analysis of the social dimension. Following Bourque's chronology, social policies can be assigned to one of three periods: (a) the first period, corresponding with the expansion of the welfare state in Quebec during the 1960s and 1970s; (b) a transitional period, corresponding with the crisis of the welfare state that prevailed in the 1980s; and (c) the second period, which began in the 1990s in the midst of the crisis of the welfare state and in which a reconfiguration was attempted, as reflected in a number of social innovations.[3] The policies of this period were more innovative than those of the preceding one, particularly when compared with the social policies that existed in the rest of Canada. Accordingly, it can be argued that the reform to the health and social services system initiated by Quebec health minister Marc-Yvan Côté between 1988 and 1993 and completed by his Liberal and Péquiste successors are something other than a neoliberal policy. The relationships that developed between the Quebec government and autonomous community health and welfare organizations as a result of this Côté-Rochon reform can be seen as characteristic of the second Quebec model of social development.[4]

As will be seen below, this division of the history of Quebec's social policy into two models — the 1960–80 model and the 1990–2000 model — is particularly useful for interpreting federal-provincial relations from a Quebec perspective.

Social Policies of the First Quebec Model

The reforms introduced in Quebec in the 1960s and 1970s in the fields of income security and social services were no more innovative than those introduced by the federal government and the more progressive provincial governments 15 years earlier. In terms of Fordist/welfarist[5] social innovations, in fact, Quebec often trailed behind. Saskatchewan, for example, had begun undertaking this type of initiative at the end of the Second World War.

Thus the social policies implemented during the Quiet Revolution in Quebec were not considered original in and of themselves. The vision of the architects of the social program was fundamentally the same, in terms of principles and content, whether they were based in Ottawa and Regina between 1945 and 1975 or in Quebec in the 1960s and 1970s. The politicians and senior officials shared a Keynesian and Fordist vision in which the government played a key role in planning, regulating, funding and administering social programs (distribution of benefit cheques and administration of services). In reality, the ideas contained in Ottawa's policy documents (e.g., the 1943 Marsh report, the 1970 Munro report and the 1973 Lalonde report) converged with Quebec's (the 1963 Boucher report as well as various volumes of the Castonguay-Nepveu report published between 1967 and 1971).

In short, the ingredients in the Quebec policy model strongly resembled those in the rest of Canada. Yet, Quebec's social policies were often perceived as original and innovative, as if they were part of a distinct model. This perception stemmed from the fact that they would be implemented not by Ottawa but by Quebec. In this respect, the viewpoints of Quebec reformers differed significantly not only from those of their federal counterparts but also from those of other provincial reformers (particularly those in social democratic governments in Manitoba, Saskatchewan and British Columbia in the 1960s and 1970s). The social democratic governments that pioneered reforms like hospital insurance in the late 1940s and health insurance in the early 1960s took these initiatives because Ottawa refused to do so. Nevertheless, they continued to believe that the federal government was in the best position to intervene in these fields. They therefore welcomed its introduction of cost-shared programs such as unemployment assistance in 1956, hospital insurance in 1957, the Canada Assistance Plan (CAP) in 1966 and health insurance in 1968.

From 1963 onwards, the social policies in place and those being pursued by the Quebec government were part of a set of coherent, integrated programs that fit a model of development adapted to Quebec society. Thus, while the 1963 Boucher report on public assistance[6] was a federalist document, it incorporated a modern nationalist vision of social policy. In philosophical, social and economic terms, it took up ideas that had been circulating for 10 years in other provinces as well as within the Canadian Council for Social Development (then the Canadian Welfare Council) and the federal health and welfare department.[7]

Nevertheless, the Boucher report was profoundly innovative on the political and constitutional plane, because it clearly stated that the Quebec government was in the best position to plan, develop, control and coordinate social policy.

Beginning in the summer of 1963, its authors (among them Claude Morin) appealed to the Quebec government to demand the right to opt out of these federal programs, arguing that federal cost-shared programs in areas of provincial jurisdiction had a structural effect on Quebec programs. In this regard, it is worth revisiting recommendation 14 of the Boucher report: "The Government of Quebec should pursue and intensify its efforts to have the Government of Canada withdraw from joint (or cost-shared) social assistance programs and compensate, through a broadening of taxation fields, the resulting accrued expenditures for Quebec."[8] The right to opt out of federal cost-shared programs was among the firmest demands of Jean Lesage's Liberal government during the tumultuous federal-provincial conference in March-April 1964, which also dealt with the Canada and Quebec pension plans.[9] In short, the fight to obtain the right to opt out of federal cost-shared programs began long before the constitutional conferences of the 1980s and 1990s.

Quebec made some progress at the outset, as Lester B. Pearson's government seemed willing to negotiate arrangements that might possibly lead to a form of asymmetrical federalism in which Quebec could carve out special status for itself, particularly in the social policy field. But this political openness was short-lived — Pearson was made to see reason and Quebec was expected to, once again, become a province like the others. However, the question of opting out would officially remain on the agenda for many years. Ottawa made outward concessions, but these were temporary and did not lead to any permanent changes. The way in which these temporary concessions were made in the 1960s — through "window dressing," as federal official Al Johnson described such tactics — served to muddle the issue over the years, preventing Quebec from obtaining any special status. Thus, Quebec's plan to withdraw from federal cost-shared programs failed, even though certain symbolic concessions created the opposite impression. Since 1963, Ottawa has continued to intervene indirectly in Quebec's social programs,[10] despite the inescapable footnotes in federal documents that chronically point out that Quebec enjoys special fiscal arrangements in one program or another.[11]

All of this means that the first Quebec model of social development and social policy was not really original. With the exception of the pension plan, the integrated approach in health and social services, the CLSCs (local community service centres), the less punitive approach in youth protection and the Parental Wage Assistance program (APPORT), introduced in 1979, Quebec social policies of the 1960s and 1970s were similar to those in the rest of Canada. Quebec's Quiet Revolution model was reflected less in the area of social policy than in its economic policy — for instance, in the creation of Hydro-Québec, the Quebec Deposit and Investment Fund and the General Investment Corporation of Quebec.

In brief, Quebec-Canada tensions in the 1960s and 1970s had less to do with the content of social programs than with control over them; perhaps this is why federal-provincial disputes were so intense. The fact that Ottawa was leading in social policy innovations gave it a strategic edge in its confrontations with Quebec. Its interventions, whether direct (unemployment insurance, family allowance, social housing programs administered by the Canada Mortgage and Housing Corporation [CMHC], old age security) or indirect (aid to blind and disabled persons, unemployment assistance, hospital insurance), influenced the development of modern social policy in Canada as a whole, including Quebec.

Social Policies of the Second Quebec Model

Compared with the social policies of the first, those of the second Quebec model were more distinct from those in the rest of Canada.

During the period of crisis and change in the 1980s and 1990s, all governments in Canada restructured their social programs and sought new ways of doing things. These attempts went hand-in-hand with efforts to redefine their vision of social and economic development, thus challenging the dominant Fordist-welfarist model. Some saw this challenge as leading inevitably to a worsening of the situation and therefore resisted, while others also questioned the Fordist-welfarist model but on the basis of very different, even contradictory, premises and objectives. These criticisms, in Quebec as elsewhere in America and the world, would translate into two distinct scenarios for the reconfiguration of social policies. The Right, representing the neoliberal perspective, advocated for the transfer of as many regulatory functions as possible to the market. The New Left advocated for a solidarity-based democratic reconfiguration dependent on a new sharing of responsibilities between the state and civil society.

Although Quebec is not the only province to experiment with new forms of institutionalization, it certainly has been an "incubator for novel ideas in the social field,"[12] as attested to by the emergence, over the past decade or so, of innovative social practices and policies suggesting a new model of solidarity-based democratic development. It should be pointed out that it is possible to discuss renewal of the Quebec model without necessarily suggesting naïvely that all economic and social policies of the past 15 years fit clearly and consistently within a single logic of development. Indeed, one must question the opinion that Quebec policies, particularly those under the three successive Parti Québécois governments since 1994, are either purely neoliberal or purely social democratic. The Quebec model draws on an array of often contradictory logics, which lead to tension, and this conflict emerges clearly in social and economic policies.[13] This is illustrated in table 1.[14]

To read this table correctly, one should keep in mind that the three logics or modes of regulation represent three ideal types, which interact. This sets the conditions for diverse correlations in which the three logics intermingle according to weightings that vary over time. (It should be kept in mind that this table was produced from the point of view of analyzing social policies in terms of services rather than cash or fiscal transfers.)

Two observations may serve to underline the analytical utility of this table. First, even though the current Quebec model does not correspond perfectly with any one type of regulation presented in the table but rather represents a combination of the three types, this does not mean that the place each occupies is identical. At this stage of the analysis I should state that I favour a Quebec model in which the dominant regulation is based on solidarity. This consolidation of solidarity-based regulation can be achieved only at the expense of social-statist regulation (as in Quebec's Quiet Revolution model) and neoliberal regulation (a strong current in North America and abroad). Based on studies of Quebec social policies over the the period 1995–2001, the characteristics of what can be called solidarity-based regulation have made advances at the expense of the two other types. This is not to say that solidarity-based regulation has been established irreversibly, or that it sets the tone for the entire configuration. The renewal of the

Views on	Solidarity- or partnership-based or renewed social democratic mode of regulation
1. Role of the state	State as partner and regulator
2. Crisis of the welfare state	Open to changes in the welfare state that give the third sector a larger role
3. Taxation	Strives for fiscal balance by changing organizational and operational methods
4. Market	Must be regulated
5. Centralization, decentralization or deconcentration	Decentralization
6. Public institutions and their accountability	Favours dual accountability of public institutions: bottom-up (i.e., public authorities that provide funding) and top-down (local communities to be served)
7. Participation of producers and users in the organization of services	Favours joint user/producer participation
8. Programming of services to individuals	Based on a "joint construction of supply and demand" (Jean-Louis Laville)
9. Social and solidarity-based economy (i.e., third-sector agencies)	Provides opportunities for reform of social policies if certain conditions of implementation are met
10. Relationships between the government and the third sector	Partnership-based relationship: reciprocity
Representative public figures (example)	Gérald Larose
Motto regarding services to individuals	Toward a new sharing of responsibility between the state, market, third sector and informal sector

Three Intersecting
Modes of
Regulation in
Social Policy
Reforms in Quebec
since the 1990s

Social-statist or neowelfarist or traditional social democratic mode of regulation	Neoliberal or neoconservative mode of regulation
Welfare state and entrepreneurial state	Minimal role for state; reliance on market forces
Defends welfare state and the social policy system of postwar years (1945–75)	Open to changes to the welfare state by increasing market role
Maintains high taxes to finance high-quality public services	Draconian decreases in taxes to encourage investment
Must be regulated	Must be self-regulated
Centralization	Deconcentration
Bottom-up accountability (i.e., public authorities and government that provides funding)	Reduce public institutions so as to increase role of market initiatives
Favours producer participation and wary of user participation	Favours user participation and wary of producer participation
Based on supply of public sector bodies (logic of producers of services)	Based on demand by private consumers who are seen as clients (consumerism)
Threatens to introduce neoliberal agenda while legitimizing the erosion of universal public services	A bargain that reduces costs of public services and creates unstable jobs
Tutelage or neowelfarist relationships	Subcontracting relationships
Buzz Hargrove	Claude Castonguay
Favours nationalization and defence of public services that are funded, regulated and provided through governmental bodies	Favours privatization and marketing of collective services

Quebec model is underway but it is still unclear what direction it will take, while public debate continues to be led by diametrically opposed proposals for renewal. For example, in the health and social services field, Claude Castonguay has often suggested that Quebec should adopt a neoliberal approach incorporating the private sector and market logic.[15] Others, such as Gérald Larose and Pierre Paquette, favour renewal based on local development, democratization, partnership, and recognition of the contribution of autonomous community organizations and the social economy.[16] Still others reject these two renewal strategies, falling back on an orthodox social-democratic position that is, to use Jean-Louis Laville's term, social-statist.[17]

The second observation is that 5 of the 10 parameters presented in the table can be used to analyze changes in social policy in many ways.

- ◆ They build on the contributions of actors who belong to the third sector of the social and solidarity-based economy and are developing a new relationship with the government (parameters 9 and 10); these third-sector actors can play a key role in services to individuals while taking into account a degree of government regulation and funding.

- ◆ They build on the democratization of the public-sector, which makes possible the development of relationships based on partnership rather than on power and control.

- ◆ They build on double empowerment — that is, the participation of user-citizens and workers; this feature relates to the social relations of production (the role of workers in the organization of work) and consumption (the role of citizens and users in planning the social policies that concern them — parameters 7 and 8).

- ◆ They build on the "double accountability" of public and third-sector organizations providing services or activities — that is, a bottom-up accountability to public authorities that fund these activities and a top-down accountability to the local and regional communities that are the targets of services and activities; this conception of accountability calls for a new form of governance and is different from the traditional understanding of accountability, which is bottom-up only.[18]

- ◆ They build on local development, decentralization and regionalization (in its fullest sense), which are the conditions for establishing a new relationship between the government and civil society (cf. parameter 5).

This suggests that parameters 9 and 10 are particularly useful when assessing the changes taking place in Quebec.[19] When these two elements are considered, in terms of both action and analysis, there are important spinoff effects on other parameters. For instance, a contribution to the reconfiguration of social policies by the third sector would quickly translate into renewed social practices that are highly compatible with the democratization of public institutions, local development, decentralization and regionalization.

It should be pointed out that this analysis uses the broad, inclusive definition of social economy[20] put forward by the *Chantier de l'économie sociale*, which assigns a large role to autonomous community organizations, cooperatives, advocacy groups and so on.[21] It adopts the concept of a "third sector of the social and solidarity-based economy" used by Alain Lipietz to distinguish the social economy from the solidarity-based economy in France, which corresponds with the new and former social economy in Quebec. This allows for the recognition of possible tensions between these two components without erecting a barrier between them.[22]

The contribution of the third sector of the social and solidarity-based economy to the reconfiguration of social policies in Quebec is not unique in North America, nor even new in Quebec. What *is* new, and what makes Quebec unique in North America, is that since 1996 the concept of the social economy has been officially recognized and supported by certain orders of government, particularly the provincial government[23]; it has entered into the public sphere and become a social and political actor in its own right, capable of making its mark on the institutional system. This has occurred not only because social movements asked and fought for it, but also because policy-makers were sensitive to these demands and able to respond to them, at least in part. Thus it may be concluded that a social and solidarity-based economy in Quebec is a matter of interest for both social movements and the government.[24]

In the rest of Canada the social economy exists but is not recognized as such by those involved or by observers. However, a sign that things are changing is the increasing interest on the part of organizations, socio-political actors and researchers in the concept of a third sector — the voluntary and private not-for-profit sector. For example, Keith Banting, Thomas Courchene and Susan Phillips have recently begun to write about the third sector.[25] Similarly, since 1999 the federal government has demonstrated an increasing interest in the third sector through its political and financial involvement in the Voluntary Sector Initiative, totalling $94 million in five years.[26] Surprisingly, the English-Canadian academe and government have remained practically silent on the potential for links with the concept of social economy as used in Quebec, despite the fact that the concepts of "voluntary sector" in English and "social economy" in French are clearly related.[27]

S e l e c t e d   C a s e s
o f   I n n o v a t i o n   i n
S o c i a l   P o l i c y

T HE SOCIAL POLICY REFORMS CARRIED OUT IN QUEBEC IN RECENT YEARS CANNOT BE explained solely by the emergence of a solidarity-based model of social development. But neither can they be examined without taking this emerging model into account. We will illustrate this by examining five cases: recognition of autonomous community organizations, social housing, early childhood centres (*Centres de la petite enfance* — CPEs), home care and programs for people with disabilities.

Recognition of Autonomous
Community Organizations

In the second Quebec model of social policy, the role of autonomous community organizations is innovative in both quantitative and qualitative terms.

In 2000–01, the Quebec government granted nearly $420 million in subsidies to approximately 5,000 autonomous community organizations through some 20 departments and government agencies, far more than the approximately $280 million granted in 1996–97. Thus, over a five-year period the government's financial support for autonomous community organizations increased by 10 percent per year, a significant amount given that the province was in the throes of budgetary cuts.[28]

The Quebec government's relationship with community organizations varies from sector to sector and department to department. Health and social service organizations (which are in fact involved much more in social services than in health) are ahead of other community organizations in this regard, because they have developed partnership-based relationships with the government — they have a say in the rules of the game. From 55 to 60 percent of the autonomous community organiza-

tions supported by the Quebec government are active in this field; they have succeeded in obtaining the lion's share of funding. Over the past 15 years they have
also succeeded in being increasingly recognized as partners by the government
(namely, the *ministère de la Santé et des Services sociaux* — MSSS) and, by extension,
public organizations in the administrative regions and local communities.[29] In other
sectors, relationships are based on subcontracting rather than partnership.[30] This is
true, for example, of autonomous community organizations that have had links in
the past with the *Ministère de l'Éducation* (popular education and advocacy groups)
or the *Ministère de la Sécurité du revenu*.[31]

Many have thus sought to extend the benefits obtained by the health organizations from the MSSS during the 1990s — such as funding for three-year periods — to all autonomous community organizations that interact with the Quebec
government. This process of recognition and support had been developing for
some years and intensified during the public hearings of summer and fall 2000.

This is basically what was proposed in the Larose report, released in
November 2000 following public hearings during which no fewer than 600 briefs
were presented.[32] The report proposed that the government recognize
autonomous community organizations not only for what they do but also for
what they are. It pointed out that partnerships between governments and community organizations are based on cooperation but do not exclude conflicts and
that "autonomous community organizations' function as critics contributes to
democratic life."[33] In September 2001 the government announced that it would
implement several of the report's recommendations. The reaction of the organizations concerned was, on the whole, positive.[34]

Quebec's expertise in this field goes beyond that of other Canadian
provinces and other North American jurisdictions; despite its limitations, it is
perfectly in line with the approach of the solidarity-based development model.
Surprisingly, this pivotal question of the relationships between governments and
community organizations rarely figures on the agenda at intergovernmental meetings, despite the fact that through it many other issues could be addressed. It consistently re-emerges when other social issues, notably housing, are examined.

Innovations in Social Housing

In Canada the greatest number of innovations in social housing over the past 10
years have occurred in Quebec and British Columbia, as a result of the ability of

those governments to respond somewhat to social pressure. It is paradoxical that new Quebec initiatives are springing up in the wake of the federal government's disengagement after 40 years of involvement in cost-shared programs for social housing across Canada. Although Ottawa continues to meet its previous commitments, since 1993–94 it has stopped participating in the development of new provincial programs through the CMHC while reserving the right to unilaterally embark on new targeted programs such as the homeless shelter program set up in 1999.

Three types of practices and policies attest to Quebec's innovations in social housing.[35]

First, social housing with community support allows socially vulnerable families and individuals (such as those with mental health problems) to remain in their own homes and to have an acceptable quality of life, rather than being institutionalized. The *Fédération des OSBL d'habitation de Montréal*, or FOHM (Montreal federation of not-for-profit housing organizations), experimented with this practice for some 12 years.[36] The experiment required unprecedented cooperation among actors in the public sector — in particular, managers of the *Offices municipaux d'habitation*, or OHM (municipal housing authority), and the *Société d'habitation du Québec*, or SHQ (Quebec housing corporation) — and actors in the third sector of the social economy, such as the FOHM, as well as human and material resources drawn from both the public and third sectors. This was a difficult convergence of intersectoral action and partnership-based work, giving rise to tensions among the various actors and cultures involved. Reaching agreements on sharing the costs of action between administrative units long accustomed to working on their own represented one of the most immediate challenges.

Second, the *Accès-Logis* social housing program was launched by the government in 1997 following the Summit on the Economy and Employment in the fall of 1996 and in response to demands for social housing channelled through the *Chantier de l'économie sociale*. Quebec spent $215 million, with no federal joint funding, on *Accès-Logis*, contributing to the creation of 1,200 new units per year over five years, for a total of 6,000. The units would be not-for-profit organizations (NPOs) or cooperatives — that is, belonging to the social economy. This government commitment, though modest relative to needs, was significant given the "zero deficit" goal pursued by the province from 1996 to 2000. Indeed, *Accès-Logis* was jeopardized repeatedly, but its goals were never abandoned. In 2001–02, the fifth and final year of the program, the target of 6,000 new units was nearly reached. This achievement owes much to the mobilization of actors in the community and within the cooperative movement, who continually urged provincial and municipal decision-makers to "deliver the goods." What will happen to the program at the end of its fifth year remains to be seen.

Third, the *Fonds québécois d'habitation communautaire*, or FQAC (Quebec community housing fund), was also created in 1997. Of the 19 members of the board of directors, 10 (i.e., the majority) come from the third sector of the social economy (communities, cooperatives and associations), the remaining nine coming from the public sector (7 members) or the private sector (2 members). Socially and politically, the FQAC is similar to a roundtable, a place of arbitration between the government and the third sector. This new governance authority has allowed actors in the social economy to continually press the authorities to meet their commitments with regard to *Accès-Logis* and other social housing needs. It is a roundtable that embodies and strongly symbolizes the search for the dual accountability (bottom-up and top-down) referred to above, although the FQAC's existence suffers from some legal ambiguity.

Social housing is an area of social policy about which SUFA has little to say. As a key element in an integrated social policy, it deserves greater attention from all orders of government in Canada. The innovations that have emerged in Quebec in recent years, although modest, have much to offer in terms of information and promise. They represent the potential contributions of actors in the social economy and the responsibilities of governments, and they remind us that social policies concern citizenship and empowerment as much as redistribution of wealth.

Early Childhood Centres (CPEs)

In the area of daycare services, Quebec's policy, like that of the other provinces, goes back some 30 years. In qualitative terms, however, it has made a quantum leap in the past four years. The history of daycare in Canada owes a great deal to the struggles of the New Democratic government in Manitoba, which led, in 1973, to greater flexibility in the interpretation of CAP rules, the program that allowed for federal joint funding of provincial daycare programs, under certain conditions. From 1973 to 1996, when it was dismantled and the Canada Health and Social Transfer (CHST) was introduced, CAP had considerable influence on social policies surrounding daycare. By prompting them to develop selective support programs for daycare, CAP slowed the momentum of the provinces, which at times was leading in the direction of developing daycare services for medium-income as well as poor or low-income families.

CAP also encouraged the provinces to rely on the third sector of the social and solidarity-based economy (i.e., not-for-profit daycare) rather than on commercial enterprises (i.e., for-profit daycare). In fact, under CAP the federal government shared the costs of provincial public assistance services as long as they were delivered either by public organizations or municipalities or by private, provincially accredited, not-for-profit organizations. This provision undoubtedly helped to slow down the privatization of daycare and fostered the development of the social economy in this sector.

Since 1997, Quebec's daycare policy has undergone major changes, including the establishment of early childhood centres (CPEs) and a wage increase for daycare workers in response to union demands. Paradoxically, it was the CAP's demise that gave rise to these innovations. The restructuring of federal transfer programs, announced in 1995 and carried out in 1996, dealt a financial blow to all provinces and territories, not least Quebec, imposing cutbacks in the order of 34 percent over two years. However, this restructuring gave Quebec the scope and political rationale it needed. It took a more universal and less selective approach, including the introduction of $5-a-day daycare services (replacing the previous rate of $25) for all children of pre-school age, regardless of socio-economic status. Moreover, it stipulated that daycare places be created in CPEs — private, not-for-profit organizations located not in the business sector but in the third sector.

The new family policy and wage agreement reflect recognition of the collective responsibility for early childhood services as well as the value of daycare work. The agreement, signed in May 1999 by the Confédération des syndicats nationaux (CSN) and the Quebec government, provided for a 35 percent average wage increase over four years, including 12 percent the first year, a forum to discuss the development of a retirement plan and the establishment of a committee on pay equity for all categories of daycare staff.

Despite the positive aspects of this reform, the implications of institutionalizing daycare and the consequences for democracy within CPEs warrant investigation. The new policy has increased red tape due to the necessarily rapid implementation of changes (the creation of places at the reduced rate, the establishment of an educational program for four-year-olds in CPEs and the creation of new places). The *ministère de la Famille et de l'Enfance*, or FCM (family and childhood ministry), was forced to review its objective — the creation of 200,000 places — and its schedule, which had been set for 2001, was extended to 2006. The number of daycare places has nevertheless increased, from 78,000 in 1998 to 114,000 in 2000 and 137,000 in 2001. However, 200,000 places are required to meet present needs, a frustrating situation for parents.[37] In brief, the current problems of the CPE policy are related to a growth crisis that has been generated partly by its popularity.

Despite ongoing questions about the gains and the future of daycare in Quebec, the approach since 1997 has helped to eliminate the negative influence of CAP — the propensity for selectivity — while retaining its positive influence — recourse to the contribution of the third sector for the provision of daycare. The next phase, consolidation, could stabilize the CPE network to an extent sufficient to meet what actors who have been interviewed qualify as its main challenge, remaining close to the community and the needs of parents, while also preserving its local flavour.

The Role of the Social Economy
in Home Care[38]

Quebec's interest in home-support services came late, indeed too late. The turning point in the structuring of the entire Quebec home-support system came in 1979 when the government adopted its first home-support policy. This policy accorded a key role to the public sector — the regional boards of health and social services (RRSSSs) at the regional level and the CLSCs at the local level — in the planning and delivery of home care. Although the policy has been amended and variously applied over the years, the fact remains that this initial stage of institutionalization has had an effect on the structure of the regime right up to the present, especially regarding the key role that the public sector plays in planning the supply of services and managing budget resources through the RRSSSs and CLSCs. However, an examination of changes in the supply of services over several years reveals regular fluctuations in the share of services delivered by the public sector, the market, the third sector of the social economy, and family and friends. The role of each party varies over time and in various components that make up the basket of home care.

In the area of domestic help — both light and heavy housekeeping — a sector that has been neglected or abandoned by the CLSCs since the mid-1980s, a network of social economy enterprises has emerged in the last 10 years. Three key periods can be distinguished in the history of the social economy enterprises in domestic help (EESADs).

The first phase, from 1990 to 1995, was an experimental one during which pilot projects by social economy enterprises appeared in some CLSC territories, initiated by local actors. These included the *Défi-Autonomie* (autonomy-challenge) Antoine Labelle project in the Mont-Laurier area and the *Aide communautaire Limoilou* (community assistance) project in the Quebec City area. The second phase (1995–96) represents the first attempt at institutionalization based on the Mont-Laurier model, with the goal of extending the *Défi-Autonomie* formula to some 20 territories. This formula was centred on users' cooperatives, into which employable income-security recipients could be integrated on a temporary basis, but it was soon abandoned in the wake of harsh criticism from social movements during the run-up to the two socio-economic summits of 1996. Starting with the 1997–98 fiscal year, the third phase (1997–2001) saw the implementation of the *Programme d'exonération financière pour les services d'aide domestique,* or PEFSAD (financial assistance for domestic services), which had been negotiated by social and government actors at the Summit on the Economy and Employment in fall 1996. Adjustments were made to the previous phase by opening the way for a form of institutionalization that was focused more on the quality of services than on integrating income-security recipients into the labour market.

The rules established under PEFSAD are financially constraining for enterprises and have frequently been criticized by the EESADs — as well as the *Chantier de l'économie sociale* — following budget speeches when they learned about the extent and the use of funds provided by Quebec. As a result of these criticisms, the government agreed to increase and stabilize its support for the EESADs after the 2001 budget speech. The PEFSAD's institutional rules, however, are less constraining in terms of democratic development within the enterprises than those of the 1995–96 *Défi-Autonomie* program. Local enterprises can thus opt for either not-for-profit status, users' cooperative status or solidarity-based cooperative status. In addition, EESADs have some leeway in their choice of personnel since they are not obliged, at least not formally, to hire income-security recipients. They also have leeway in their choice of clientele: they can provide services to regular households as well as to older or disabled persons with decreasing autonomy.

Since 1997 PEFSAD has been responsible for the creation of 4,000 jobs and a network of 103 accredited EESADs. This progress implies an increasing presence of the social economy in the delivery of home care, replacing services that were previously provided under the table by self-employed workers and not by CLSC nurses or visiting homemakers. In other words, EESADs' personnel are not intended to replace public-sector employees. However, there have been shifts in a small number of enterprises, and there is ambiguity and overlap in the programming of some CLSCs and EESADs.

The role of the social economy in the area of home care should be followed closely. Home support is now, more than ever before, the pivotal policy around which reforms in the vast field of health and welfare — taking into account relevant social determinants — should be structured. Vigilance is essential in this area, since economic imperatives could conflict with the social imperatives and the values of the social economy. The presence of the social economy in the area of home care can, nonetheless, be viewed as a means of curbing privatization. It also provides a greater diversity of services than if only the state or the market were the providers.

Policies for Persons with Disabilities[39]

In Canada, the bulk of direct interventions for persons with disabilities, except those relating to veterans and their families, is a provincial responsibility, albeit with some joint funding from the federal government. In Quebec, these include programs related to occupational health and safety, the Quebec Pension Plan, automobile insurance, income security, and health and social services.

Despite inadequacies and inconsistencies and despite criticisms by advocacy groups for the disabled, Quebec's policies in this area are often seen as progressive by experts in the field. This has been particularly true since the early 1980s when the *Office des personnes handicapées du Québec* (OPHQ) — which was established in 1978 spurred on by a vigilant community — put forward its philosophy advocating the full participation in society of persons with disabilities.[40] In 1984 this philosophy, which emphasizes handicapped persons' abilities instead of their disabilities, was articulated in *On Equal Terms*, a document that is still a source of inspiration today.[41] *On Equal Terms* has not yet resulted in the transformation of all policies and practices concerning persons with disabilities, but it is nevertheless a key reference, guiding numerous efforts to integrate persons with disabilities into society in terms of housing, transportation, leisure, education and labour market participation. It marks a break with the traditional approaches based on institutionalization, cure and compensation. *On Equal Terms* urges governments to assume their responsibilities while leaving room for the contributions of civil society and community actors — in short, it calls for reforms that fit perfectly with the second Quebec model.

The approach conveyed in documents such as *On Equal Terms* is fortunately not limited to Quebec. It is part of ongoing discussions in international fora, in particular the World Health Organization, due in part to the contributions of Patrick Fougeyrollas and the research teams he has led for 20 years. This approach has also been adopted in other Canadian regions, and even among federal authorities involved in examining Canada's social union. The employability assistance programs for people with disabilities are especially important in Ottawa's discourse on the social union. The document *In Unison*, produced in 1998 by experts for the federal government and the provincial and territorial governments (except Quebec), thus represents a milestone.[42]

In terms of its social vision, *In Unison* is very close to the principal elements of the second Quebec model identified here. It synthesizes the best of Canadian and international ideas concerning persons with disabilities. In planning social policies, it embraces principles calling for the democratization of what are called "consumer relationships," building on the empowerment of persons with disabilities and viewing them as capable of participating fully in society. The document even hints at the contribution of the social economy to the renewal of social policies:

> Opportunities for enhancing the integration and employment of persons with disabilities also could be explored through support for community economic development (CED) and self-employment. CED is an approach to local economic development that combines economic and social goals. It seeks to create employment opportunities through the development of locally-run and controlled businesses... Currently, there is a wide range of CED initiatives under way throughout the country.[43]

Though it is one component among many, community economic development (CED) is part and parcel of the social economy. By recognizing the contribution of CED to the renewal of social policies concerning persons with disabilities, *In Unison* takes an approach that is very similar to the key element of the second Quebec model. However, it remains tentative and rather intuitive and could be developed further.[44]

Though our examination of five social policy areas is sufficient to support the argument that a second Quebec model, distinct from the 1960s and 1970s model, has emerged in the last 10 years, it could well be supplemented by an examination of other social policies such as prescription drug insurance, income security and employability, loans, scholarships, work training, automobile insurance, occupational health and safety programs, and the Quebec Pension plan, as well as family policy components other than CPEs. The key to this new model is social innovation, even though these innovations have limits and remain fragile. In the context of the intergovernmental debate on Canada's social union, this puts Quebec in a quite different position from the one it occupied in the 1960s and 1970s vis-à-vis Ottawa and the other provinces and territories.

Interface with Canada's Social Union

IN THIS SECTION, IT IS ARGUED THAT THE FEDERAL GOVERNMENT'S DECISION TO HASTILY adopt the Social Union Framework Agreement without Quebec was a serious blunder, particularly in light of the wealth of expertise in social policy reform gained in Quebec over the last 10 years. The agreement was therefore condemned to remain an empty shell for three years, devoid of legitimacy, incapable of helping the governments involved to work together toward meeting the current needs of Canadians and Quebecers. In short, the agreement, because of the circumstances under which it was concluded and its terms and conditions, was destined to be stillborn, a meaningless three-year footnote. However, its demise is not a foregone conclusion: governments, including the government of Quebec, should reconsider the prospects for agreement on Canada's social union. As long as the strategies of all the parties can be renewed, including the highly defensive approach of the Quebec government, another social union agreement is still possible and indeed necessary.

Origins of Canada's Social Union

To understand today's debate on the social union, one must take into account several decades of federal-provincial meetings during which the social union and social policies were discussed. In fact, the debate is rooted in the Rowell-Sirois Commission of Inquiry in the late 1930s. While "social union" is defined as a set of principles and standards for intergovernmental relations in the area of social programs, its origins go back to the period when some governments in Canada became seriously interested in developing modern social policies. The exact timing is obviously different for each government, but the crisis of the 1930s was a turning point affecting all orders of government. Until then, it had not been difficult for the federal government to respect the distribution of powers as delineated in the Constitution. However, by the late 1930s Ottawa very much wanted to intervene in the social field following Keynes' thesis, and this political stridency was reinforced by the conclusions of the Rowell-Sirois report. The division of constitutional authority over social policies then became an issue and began to play a key role in federal-provincial meetings. The term social union was not yet in use, but the issues that it nurtured became important in intergovernmental relations. During the 1960s and 1970s social policy matters continued to be high on the agenda. The interface between the first Quebec model and the dynamics of intergovernmental relations in Canada, in particular the debates on Ottawa's spending power and the ability of the provinces to opt out, dates from this period.

The more immediate reasons for the debate on the social union are to be found, as Alain Noël pointed out,[45] in Paul Martin's February 1995 budget announcing the federal government's integrated action plan to fight the deficit, of which proposed measures to restructure its intervention in the social policy field were an integral part. In particular, Martin announced Ottawa's intention to reform the unemployment insurance program and transfer programs to the provinces. The two main transfer programs in effect at the time — CAP, related to social services and income security, and the Established Programs Financing (EPF), related to post-secondary education and health — were merged as of April 1, 1996, into the new CHST program. In announcing this program, Martin was able to anticipate 34 percent cutbacks in provincial transfers for 1996–97 and 1997–98. However, he was unable to reassure Canadians about the impact of the reform on "conditions" and "national standards." Indeed, with regard to health transfers, he could state that the five principles of the *Canada Health Act* would be respected but could not offer such guarantees for social services. Hence his request that the federal and provincial ministers responsible for welfare (and social services) come to an agreement on these principles. Although the term social union was not used in those days, the idea of a social union is evident in Martin's remarks: "The Minister of Human Resources Development will be inviting all provincial governments to work together on developing, through mutual consent, a set of shared principles and objectives that could underlie the new Canada Social Transfer."[46] In fact, federal-provincial talks were held in 1995–96, but they did not end in a "mutual agreement." In the meantime, in the February 1996 Speech from the Throne the federal government started to use the term social union to refer to the set of principles upon which the governments should agree to administer the CHST in the area of social services.

The Context of SUFA's Emergence

To understand the immediate context of SUFA's emergence, one must distinguish among four types of interventions by the federal government, taking into consideration the distribution of powers provided for in the Canadian constitution.[47]

1. Direct interventions to citizens in areas of federal jurisdiction in fields such as employment insurance, income redistribution programs for seniors, and programs related to Aboriginal peoples and veterans.

2. Indirect interventions via transfer payments to the provinces and territories for traditional cost-shared programs in areas of provincial jurisdiction. In this type of intervention, Ottawa usually shares the costs of provincial programs on a 50-50 basis, and provincial programs have to respect the guidelines set out in the federal legislation and the resulting bilateral federal-provincial agreements. These have included programs such as unemployment assistance in 1956, hospital insurance in 1957, health insurance in 1968 and CAP from 1966 to 1996.

3. Indirect interventions via transfer payments to the provinces and territories for block or per capita funding programs in areas of provincial jurisdiction. In this type of intervention, the amount transferred by Ottawa does not take into account the expenditures actually incurred by the provinces. Examples of such programs are the EPF, which appeared in 1977, and the CHST, which appeared in 1996.

4. Direct interventions to individuals and organizations in areas of provincial jurisdiction, sometimes publicized through an intermediary organization such as a foundation. Recent programs in this category are the Millennium Scholarships, the Health Transition Fund, the Youth Employment Strategy and social housing for the homeless.

Of these four types of intervention, the first is obviously the most advantageous for the federal government, which has used it as much as possible since the late 1930s. But direct intervention in areas of provincial jurisdiction (such as education, social assistance, and health and social services) has often been impossible for constitutional reasons. This is why, historically, Ottawa has made use of its spending power through the other three methods of intervention, changing its preferences for one method over another throughout the decades.

During the 1940s, 1950s and 1960s, the federal government showed a preference for traditional cost-shared programs. This formula had the advantage of allowing Ottawa to have a structuring influence on social programs by imposing conditions by which the provinces and territories would be eligible for federal funding. But the tactic also had disadvantages: the federal government got insufficient political visibility for its spending and could not predict the amount of its financial contribution to the provincial programs from year to year. In addition, the constitutionality of this method of intervention was criticized in Quebec, which, from the 1960s onwards, demanded the right to opt out of cost-shared programs.

In the 1970s, therefore, the federal government began to favour the third method of intervention (per capita transfer payments), as clearly reflected in the introduction of the EPF in 1977. This method was more compatible with Ottawa's will to control the costs of its participation in social programs. It thus had financial advantages, since Ottawa could unilaterally decide, from year to year, to alter the basis for assessing the amount of transfer payments. In this way, it could reduce its contribution to the provincial and territorial programs concerned without the respective governments being able to do anything about it. However, as with other methods of intervention, this method had social and political disadvantages. Among other things, the federal government was less able to implement and enforce national standards.

The fourth type of intervention, direct initiatives in areas of provincial jurisdiction, has emerged as a new course of federal action in the past few years. Prior to 1990, this would have been unthinkable for constitutional reasons. Ottawa has ventured onto shaky constitutional ground with this form of intervention because it represents a considerable broadening of the scope of its spending power. It therefore began to come under criticism by several provincial governments in the mid-1990s. Although the criticism has put the federal government on the defensive, it has not prevented the method from being used. The stakes are clear. By using this form of intervention, Ottawa has managed to get around the disadvantages related to the indirect formulas that it favoured earlier. One benefit is that it has regained the scope to control both its spending and national standards in the area of social policies, something it did not have with the other two methods.

The preceding comments offer a few clues to help interpret the meaning and impact on intergovernmental relations of the re-engineering of federal interventions in social policy since Paul Martin's 1995 budget. They also shed light on the context in which SUFA emerged.

The reconfiguration of federal transfer programs has been taking place since 1977. With the introduction of the EPF, the federal government was able to better control part of its transfer payments — those related to provincial programs for post-secondary education and health — while sheltering them from the financial contingencies of the shared-cost formula. From 1977 to 1996, Ottawa managed to effectively reduce its funding share in provincial programs in the areas concerned through repeated unilateral decisions to cap the transfer payments made to the provinces under the EPF. True, transfer payments made under CAP were still officially subject to the 50-50 rule during those years, but as of 1990 the federal government capped its transfer payments to the three richest provinces (Ontario, British Columbia and Alberta) under CAP. Thus from 1990 to 1996, even transfer payments made under CAP were a long way from the 50-50 rule.[48]

The restructuring sparked by the introduction of the CHST in 1996 confirmed and intensified this trend. The launching of the CHST marks the official withdrawal from the formula of traditional cost-shared programs and the victory of the per capita transfer formula. This formula, which had allowed Ottawa to gradually reduce its transfer payments for health and post-secondary education under the EPF, was from then on applied to transfer payments for social assistance. All transfer payments were now drawn from a single budget, calculated on the basis of population. In addition, the CHST's era began with the drastic cutbacks announced a year earlier in Martin's 1995 budget. In less than two years, from 1995 to 1997, cash transfer payments through the CHST were reduced by $7 billion, or 34 percent.[49]

The aggregate result of reductions in transfer payments since the introduction of the EPF in 1977 and the CHST in 1996 represents an enormous revenue shortfall for the provinces and territories, compared with the transfers they would have received had the 50-50 cost-sharing rule, which prevailed until 1977, been retained. This prompted Monique Jérôme-Forget to comment: "Following almost

15 years of freezes and caps in transfers to the provinces, Ottawa introduced further cutbacks when it rolled its funding for social programs into a single block fund,
the Canada Health and Social Transfer (CHST). As a result of these changes, the
provincial share of funding for health, post-secondary education and social assistance has increased significantly and is now close to 85 percent."[50] This estimate
dates from 1998. It was updated in August 2001 during the first ministers meeting
in Victoria, and showed that Ottawa's contribution to the costs of the programs concerned under the CHST was 14 percent, meaning that the provinces and territories
were assuming 86 percent of the costs.[51]

Although cutbacks and unilateral changes to transfer payments have been the
principal irritants to the provinces and to federal-provincial relations since 1995,
they are far from being the only ones. Three other factors have made the situation
even more explosive. First, by restructuring its unemployment insurance program,
which became "employment" insurance in the mid-1990s, the federal government
has transformed it into a cash cow, enlisted in the battle against the deficit. Thus this
program, which had an accumulated deficit of $6 billion in the early 1990s, has gen-
erated an accumulated surplus over the years, totalling $36 billion as of 31 March
2001.[52] These reductions in expenditures, combined with savings from cutbacks in
transfer payments, have helped Ottawa to achieve fiscal balance, and even a surplus
as of the 1997–98 fiscal year. Second, provincial governments, which were obliged
to look after the unemployed whose coverage was cancelled as a result of the restructuring, saw their expenditures on social policy rise considerably, contributing to the
debate on fiscal imbalance that has since emerged. Third, as a result of its budget surplus, Ottawa launched new direct initiatives in areas of provincial jurisdiction that
were then presented to the provinces as *faits accomplis*.

These are the main features of the context in which negotiations leading to
the signing of SUFA were held.

The Framework
Agreement without
Quebec: An Empty Shell

T HE PATH LEADING TO THE SIGNING OF SUFA HAS BEEN FAR FROM STRAIGHT. THERE
have been many twists and turns in the intergovernmental discussions along

the way. The strategic aims of the government actors were diverse and hard to reconcile, and in some cases changed en route.

Ottawa's goal was twofold: to legitimize increased use of the spending power (particularly with regard to the fourth method of intervention), and to reach an agreement on national standards that could be imposed on provincial social programs to replace those governing them during the CAP era.

The strategies of the provincial governments, excluding that of Quebec, though diverse and difficult to harmonize, have converged on one point — the need to force the federal government to increase social transfers to the provinces under the CHST. Moreover, the majority of provinces shared, albeit with varying degrees of enthusiasm, Ottawa's goal of reinforcing the national standards that had been weakened since the introduction of the CHST.

The main goal of the Quebec government was to oversee the federal government's use of its spending power (in particular with regard to the fourth method of intervention) while supporting the effort of the provinces to make Ottawa significantly increase the transfer payments made under the CHST. Quebec also supported the provinces' attempts to win long-term commitments in funding from the federal government, so that provincial public finance would not be continually taken by surprise.

From 1995 to 2001, Quebec remained defensive about the content of the discussions on the social union. This attitude can be seen in the evolution of its strategy at the annual first ministers' meetings from 1995 to 1998. At the August 1995 meeting in St. John's, the premier, Jacques Parizeau, had already left the premises when the issue of social policy came up for discussion. At the next three conferences, then-premier Lucien Bouchard abandoned the empty-chair strategy and endeavoured to participate in the discussions. Nevertheless, Quebec's strategy remained defensive. The province refused to join the federal-provincial process toward the social union. It was only at the first ministers' meeting of August 1998 that Quebec really embarked on the process, when it supported the provincial Saskatoon Consensus. During the Quebec election campaign of November 1998 the premier suddenly became the strongest advocate of Canada's social union. However, the social union sought by Bouchard was one that would prioritize curbing Ottawa's use of its spending power in areas of provincial jurisdiction. For the rest, in particular the content of social policies, Bouchard's discourse was minimalist and evasive.

The agreement signed in February 1999 by all the provinces except Quebec was, however, quite different from the one that Quebec had anticipated and wished for at the end of both the Saskatoon meeting in summer 1998 and the election campaign in November 1998. This agreement was much more in line with the Chrétien government's strategy. It was negotiated in parallel with another agreement specific to health funding, under which Ottawa would increase transfers to the provinces earmarked for health care. All the first ministers, including Quebec's, signed this agreement, which met their strategic goal of obtaining an increase in transfer payments. The effect of the health agreement was to make SUFA more attractive to the majority of premiers, but the provisions in section 5 of SUFA, on the federal spending power, were not worded to the satisfaction of Quebec and a number of other provinces. This section begins with lavish praise for the use of spending power in the history of social policies in Canada — not something that would win over Quebec. Subsequently, the only specifications about Ottawa's spending power were to oblige it to (1) consult with provincial and territorial governments "at least one year prior to renewal or significant funding changes in existing social transfers to provinces-territories" (i.e., the CHST), (2) "not introduce Canada-wide initiatives without the agreement of a majority of provincial governments," and (3) give at least three months' notice before using the spending power to "make transfers to individuals and to organizations."

The section on the spending power does little more than justify the methods of intervention in areas of provincial jurisdiction that Ottawa had in any case begun to use long before SUFA was signed. After all, the cutbacks in federal transfers in April 1996 had been clearly announced more than a year before, in Paul Martin's February 1995 budget. A few years later, SUFA merely suggested that this course of action was right. As André Burelle commented a few days after the adoption of SUFA: "To put it plainly, what the federal government is telling us in this agreement is that if it cannot go through the front door (transfers to the provinces and territories) to invade the areas of provincial jurisdiction, it will give three months' notice before breaking down the back door (transfers to individuals and organizations involved in the fields of health, education and social services)."[53]

On the other hand, the other sections of the agreement include several mostly relevant and well-intentioned assertions of principles and objectives: equal opportunity for all Canadians (section 1), mobility within Canada (section 2), public accountability and transparency (section 3), working in partnership (section 4) and dispute avoidance (section 6). But the means identified to oversee the implementation of these commitments remain vague.

To sum up, the 1999 agreement, because of the circumstances under which it was signed as well as the document itself, is an empty shell. In three years it has barely resulted in any concrete changes in terms of social policies. By acting hastily, without striving to include Quebec, the Chrétien government and the provincial governments that supported it during the last hours of negotiation did everything, when reaching the agreement, to discredit and trivialize it, making it unworkable. Those in government, academic, economic and social circles who have been closely following social policy issues in Canada are well aware that Quebec has developed, particularly in recent years, an expertise and a capacity for innovation in the area of social policy that should be part of an authentic intergovernmental process of social union.

Illegitimately born, SUFA was condemned to a troubled life and has proved "useless," as Michel Venne[54] astutely puts it. At the end of the third and final year of the agreement, it is hard to find ways in which it has changed the evolution of social policies and intergovernmental discussions in Canada. In fact, little has changed at all — it has neither helped much nor harmed much. It has in no way stopped Ottawa from using its spending power as it sees fit and has fostered the idea among some observers that Quebec was once again content to remain an observer in federal-provincial meetings on social policy issues. Moreover, it is impossible to know for sure whether Quebec, which did not sign the agreement, is concerned by its provisions.

It is tempting to conclude that Quebec and Canada would have been better served by having no agreement at all.

Conditions for a New and More Meaningful Agreement

Ultimately, the issue of Canada's social union must be reopened, and the sooner the better. Indeed, it will not be enough to simply touch up and extend the 1999 agreement, which would serve only to prolong the impasse. In order to get out of this mess, we need to start over on new basis, and the actors involved, including the Quebec government, have to adopt new strategies.

In this period of reconfiguration of social policies, which poses serious challenges to all orders of governments as well as to individuals and civil society organizations, it is in the interest of Quebec and the rest of Canada to find better ways of working together. Governments that deal with these issues by isolating themselves or by assuming a position of distrust and competition with other governments only end up weakening themselves. It can even be argued that the dissemination of information related to the second Quebec model is desirable and even necessary for both Quebec and the rest of Canada.

The advantage for Quebec should be examined first. As explained above, the solidarity-based model of social development that has emerged in Quebec in the last 10 years is both real and fragile. The model should become more firmly established and widely recognized. Quebec has little to gain from being isolated from Canada with its singular model, and has a real interest in having some of its innovations publicized, recognized, disseminated to other Canadian regions and taken up by other governments, including the federal government. Thus it is to Quebec's advantage when a province such as British Columbia expresses interest in its $5-a-day daycare program, or when a province such as Manitoba seeks information about its parental leave program, or when the federal government, through the Voluntary Sector Initiative, seeks information about its policy of recognizing and funding autonomous organizations. In brief, it is not true that the more the Quebec model differs from those in other regions of Canada and other countries the more interesting it becomes. The future of the Quebec model depends partly on Quebec's ability to have it recognized and discussed, and to export the most innovative principles and features elsewhere in Canada and abroad. If Quebec remains isolated, with its own unique model, it will quickly begin to stagnate and decline. The advantage for the other Canadian regions and governments is also clear. Several senior officials who follow social policy issues for the other provinces and the federal government have begun to say unofficially (and in private) that much would be lost in the intergovernmental discussions on social policy reforms if Quebec representatives were to stop participating. These people quickly realized that SUFA got off to a bad start because of Quebec's absence.

All of this points to the relevance, even the urgency, of maintaining a social union in Canada. It calls for the political actors involved and their advisers to agree to modify their strategies. In this regard, policy-makers must agree to ascribe more importance to the content of social issues in their discussions. A few words on the renewal of the Quebec strategy may serve to illustrate this argument.

It would be in Quebec's interest to abandon the defensive and mainly legal strategy to which it has confined itself since 1995. The Quebec government has weakened itself by using what could be called a "curbing strategy" to restrict Ottawa's spending power. It would benefit from the adoption of a more offensive strategy through which it could strongly express its desire to share information on its innovative experiments and learn from those of other governments.

This is not to suggest that all constitutional concerns should be abandoned, nor that oversight of the way in which Ottawa uses its spending power should be stopped. It is simply to suggest that more attention should be paid to the "social" component of the social union issue. The experience acquired by Quebec through the development of its second model puts it in a better position in 2002, relative to 1964 or 1974, to influence intergovernmental discussions on social policies. It should be confident enough to engage in discussions on the topics of accountability and transparency, as addressed in section 4 of SUFA. By adopting a position of transparency and assertiveness, Quebec will find more convincing arguments for diversity and, eventually, a more solid and incisive line of argument to reveal the limitations of the five principles of the *Canada Health Act* (public administration, comprehensiveness, universality, portability and accessibility). Indeed, although these five principles are asserted in section 1 of SUFA and are frequently praised by a section of the Canadian Left, the Liberal Party of Canada and the New Democratic Party, they nevertheless contain limitations and ambiguities. In particular, they have been used to develop and consolidate "hospital-centred" and "medical-centred" thinking, which often proves incapable of considering the nonmedical determinants (income, education, housing and employment) of the health and welfare of individuals. The somewhat formulaic reference to these five principles often has the effect of constraining us in simplistic binary reactions that place the state in opposition to the market. This theoretical analytical framework leaves little room for actors of the third sector of the social and solidarity-based economy, who have made a major contribution in the second Quebec model.

Conclusion

FOR THE LAST 10 YEARS, AS A MEMBER OF VARIOUS RESEARCH TEAMS,[55] I HAVE FOCUSED my writing on what is being recreated rather than what is being dismantled in ongoing transformations, including those related to social policies. In the context of the postwar social policy system, my interest is more focused on the transformations than on the crisis of the welfare state. To engage in such a discourse is to risk being perceived as having adopted the neoliberal agenda to dismantle the welfare state. Within the binary analytical framework (state/market) to which the traditional Left is still attached, the defence of the postwar social policy heritage is part and parcel of today's progressive agenda. Whereas in the 1970s criticism of these very social policies was an integral part of the rhetoric of the New Left, now it is inevitably perceived as a neoliberal position.

However, the innovations introduced in Quebec show the merit of examining other approaches to the current reconfigurations of social policy. Although the transformations of social policies can follow the neoliberal path, they can also follow a new, progressive path characterized as "solidarity based and democratic." The studies of social policies in which I have participated for the last 15 years have been based precisely on this approach. Their premise is that it is possible, even desirable, in Quebec as elsewhere, to move away from the Fordist-welfarist model of the 30-year postwar boom (1945–75) without adopting the neoliberal model. Hence my interest, in this paper, in the current debate on the Quebec model of development and the role attributed to it. As we have seen, this model emphasizes the contribution of the third sector of the social and solidarity-based economy and helps to renew social policies. It moves away from a centralizing and hierarchical conception of the state without opening the door to forms of privatization and deregulation championed by the neoliberal agenda.

The five policy sectors presented here (and to which others might be added) illustrate the type of practices that other governments, groups and individuals in the rest of Canada might learn about and discuss in developing their ideas and planning their reforms. In this sense, the exclusion, for all intents and purposes, of Quebec from SUFA was a serious error, causing the agreement to lose part of its meaning at the very outset and condemning it to having little impact on the evolution of social policies in Quebec and Canada.

The 1999 Social Union Framework Agreement cannot simply be touched up and extended. If it is to survive, the social union must be relaunched on new bases and be reopened by government actors who will agree to renew their strategy. With its second model, Quebec is in a good position to move from a defensive to a proactive strategy. It cannot function solely on the basis of a strategy of mistrust of the federal spending power. If it is to consolidate its model of social development, Quebec cannot remain isolated from the rest of Canada. Its model must become known, recognized and criticized, so that some of the innovations it has developed can be disseminated to other regions of Canada. It also needs to be questioned and enriched by social innovations developed in other regions of Canada, including by the federal government.

1   Bourque (2000).

2   Bourque (2000, pp. 183-190). It appears essential, because of the widespread perception that the Quebec state became neoliberal in 1986 and has remained so ever since (regardless of the government in power), to review the economic and social choices made by the Bourassa government between 1986 and 1993. One example of the statements often heard in progressive circles is that there was a neoliberal shift in Quebec around 1986 (Gill 1999, pp. 21-22).

3   This periodization of the history of Quebec social policies in the field of services to individuals (which goes beyond the field of health and social services) is further developed in Jetté, Lévesque, Mager and Vaillancourt (2000, pp. 27-28).

4   See Vaillancourt (1994); Lévesque, Bourque and Vaillancourt (1999); Vaillancourt, Aubry, D'Amours, Jetté, Thériault and Tremblay (2000).

5   The concept of a Fordist-welfarist model is explained in many of our writings. See, for example, Jetté, Lévesque, Mager and Vaillancourt (2000, pp. 23-24); Jetté, Lévesque and Vaillancourt (2001).

6   Comité d'étude sur l'assistance publique (1963).

7   For example, only the uninformed could think, in 1963, that "any individual in need has a right to assistance from the state, regardless of the immediate or remote cause of this need" (Recommendation 7) was a new idea or that it was unique to Quebec. Comité d'étude sur l'assistance publique (1963, p. 118). My translation.

8   Comité d'étude sur l'assistance publique (1963, p. 124). My translation.

9   On this subject, see Vaillancourt (1991, 1992a, 1992b, 1993, 1995, 1996b, 1997 [pp. 27-31], 1998).

10 In my writings on the relationship between Quebec and federal social policies, I always distinguish between the federal government's direct (e.g., employment insurance program and millennium scholarships) and indirect interventions (e.g., the Canada Health and Social Transfer). In its indirect interventions, it comes into contact with citizens not through its own social programs, but by participating in the joint funding of programs by others and, indeed, structuring such programs by establishing conditions for joint funding. See Vaillancourt (1996a).

11 Hence, the meaningful title of Alain Noël's analysis: "Collaborative Federalism with a Footnote" (2000).

12 Dion (1998).

13 The blend of logics of action that characterize the Quebec model can be seen in the current economic situation: the issue of the social economy from 1996 to 2000 was seen as important within the Executive Council Office (Ministère du Conseil exécutif) but occupied a rather marginal place in the budget speeches by the then finance minister, Bernard Landry, from 1997 to 2000. Pauline Marois did not break from this tradition in her March 2001 budget speech.

14 Similar attempts to develop such a typology can be found in Noël (1996, p. 21); Vaillancourt and Laville (1998, p. 131); Lévesque and Mendell (1999, p. 109); Taylor and Bassi (1998, pp. 122-123).

15 Castonguay (1997, 1999).

16 Larose (1999); Paquette (1999, 2000).

17 See, for example, Piotte (1998).

18 The traditional concept of accountability is still very strong in environments that are either closely related to or part of the government. For example, it is prominent in the Clair report. On this subject, see the critique by Vaillancourt (2000).

19 In this paper, the term "third sector" is not used in opposition to "social and solidarity-based economy," nor is social economy used in opposition to solidarity-based economy. The terms social economy and solidarity-based economy are employed in the sense used in "Appel pour une économie sociale et solidaire rendu public," an article that appeared in Le Devoir in April 1998, repro-

duced in Arteau (1998). On the concept of the third sector, see Vaillancourt (1998, 1998/99). See also Lorendahl (1998).

20   This definition was first proposed in *Osons la solidarité* (Chantier de l'économie sociale, 1996) and was taken up in another strategic document produced by the Chantier de l'économie sociale (2001). The first document had been presented at the Summit on the Economy and Employment in October 1996 and was ratified by all the social partners present and the Quebec government. It was subsequently adopted by the government as well as many policy-makers and actors within the social movement. However, when implemented, it is occasionally reduced to its entrepreneurial dimension, a tendency that has been criticized by the women's movement.

21   Certain researchers such as Deena White prefer to place community organizations outside the social economy; see White (2001).

22   Lipietz (2000, pp. 58-60; 2001). The latter report was published in France following an inquiry by Lipietz into the social and solidarity-based economy for the minister of employment and solidarity, Martine Aubry, in September 1998. On the question of the relationship between the social and solidarity-based economy, see Laville (1994, pp. 9-89) for the French historical context and Vaillancourt and Favreau (2001, pp. 69-83) for the Quebec context.

23   The Quebec government's recognition of the social economy becomes clear when the Quebec situation is compared to that of Ontario, New Brunswick or Saskatchewan. On this topic, see Vaillancourt and Tremblay (2001).

24   Vaillancourt and Favreau (2001, pp. 74-78).

25   Banting (2000, pp. 1-28); Brock and Banting (2001); Courchene (2001, pp. 111-119); see also Susan Phillips in this book. It should be noted that by referring to the contribution of community action, the final report of the National Forum on

Health (February 1997) implicitly includes the issue of the third sector and the social economy in its analysis. However, the treatment of this topic remained superficial and inconsistent. See National Forum on Health (1997, pp. 26-27).

26   For information on the Voluntary Sector Initiative (VSI), see its Website: http://www.vsi-isbc.ca. Also see Phillips (2001a); Brock and Banting (2001, pp. 8-14).

27   However, two chapters in Brock and Banting's most recent book promote the concept of the social economy (Brock and Banting, 2001, ch. 3 and 7).

28   Secrétariat à l'action communautaire autonome du Québec (SACA) (2000, pp. 28-29).

29   This assessment of the relationship between community organizations and the Quebec government in the field of health and social services seems to be shared by White (2001). Phillips (2001a) presents the Quebec experience of community organizations, along with that of Newfoundland, as something that might prompt the federal government to act (pp. 12-27).

30   Basing the relationship between the government and the community organizations on partnership means that the community organizations have a say in the rules of the game — for example, in the area of evaluation. When relationships are based on tutelage, in accordance with state regulation, the government and public organizations treat community organizations as instruments or mere appendages. When relationships are based on subcontracting, in accordance with market regulation, this suggests that the community organizations are seen as financial instruments. See Vaillancourt and Laville (1998, pp. 119-135); Lewis (1999).

31   See Vaillancourt and Tremblay (2001, pp. 27-31).

32   Larose (2000, pp. 2-34).

33   Larose (2000, p. 9). My translation.

34 Gouvernement du Québec (2001). For the initial reactions of community organizations, see the article by Dutrisac (2001).

35 For a synthesis of our studies on social housing, see Vaillancourt and Ducharme (2000). See also Vaillancourt and Tremblay (2001, pp. 47-53).

36 See Thériault, Jetté, Mathieu and Vaillancourt (2000). Similar types of experiment have taken place in Montreal and in the regions.

37 On the problem of lack of CPE places, see Léger (2001a, 2001b).

38 See Vaillancourt and Tremblay (2001, pp. 39-47).

39 Since summer 2000, the Laboratoire de recherche sur les pratiques et les politiques sociales (LAREPPS) has, owing to a substantial HRDC grant, drawn up an inventory and an assessment of over 2,000 programs and measures intended for persons with disabilities in Quebec, taking into account contributions of actors in the social and solidarity-based economy as well as actors in the public sector. More exhaustive results in this field were expected in summer 2002.

40 For a retrospective, documented, informed and critical history of programs intended for persons with disabilities in Quebec, see the recently defended thesis by Boucher (2001).

41 Office des personnes handicapées du Québec (1984). The 1984 document *On Equal Terms* and similar government documents produced and disseminated subsequently owe much to the work of the research teams led by the internationally renowned thinker Patrick Fougeyrollas.

42 Federal, Provincial and Territorial Ministers Responsible for Social Services (1998).

43 Federal, Provincial and Territorial Ministers Responsible for Social Services (1998, p. 28).

44 See Prince in this book for more information on the federal policy.

45 Noël (1998).

46 Martin (1995, p. 21).

47 The analysis that follows includes a reformulation and an update of arguments developed in other writings, including Vaillancourt (1996a, 1997).

48 See Courchene (2001, pp. 68-70).

49 See calculations done in Vaillancourt (1996a, pp. 83-85).

50 Jérôme-Forget (1998, p. 5).

51 Gagnon (2001, p. A1). The figures made public at the first ministers' meeting in Victoria in August 2001 had first been announced in the press release at the end the Provincial-Territorial Finance Ministers Meeting held on June 13 and 14, 2001, in Montreal. See http//www.scics.gc.ca

52 Calculations based on HRDC figures reported in Zehler (2001).

53 Burelle (1999) [translation].

54 Venne (2000).

55 I am referring to the following: the Économie sociale, santé et bien-être (ESSBE) research team; Laboratoire de recherche sur les pratiques et les politiques sociales (LAREPPS) (http//www.unites.uqam.ca/essbe/); Centre de recherche sur les innovations sociales dans l'économie sociale, les entreprises et les syndicats (CRISES) (http//www.unites.uqam.ca/crises/); and Alliance de recherche université communauté (ARUC) sur l'économie sociale (www.aruc-es.uqam.ca).

Arteau, M. "Appel en faveur d'une économie sociale et solidaire." *Nouvelles pratiques sociales*, Vol. 11, no. 1 (spring 1998): 1-8.

Banting, K., ed. *The Nonprofit Sector in Canada: Roles and Relationships.* Kingston: Queen's University School of Policy Studies, 2000.

Boucher, N. *Mise en jeu de la différence corporelle au Québec: Pour une sociologie du handicap.* Thesis, Faculté des études supérieures, Université Laval, Quebec, 2001.

Bourque, G.L. *Le modèle québécois de développement: De l'émergence au renouvellement.* Sainte-Foy, Quebec: Presses de l'Université du Québec, 2000.

Brock, K.L., and K.G. Banting, eds. *The Nonprofit Sector and Government in a New Century.* Montreal and Kingston: McGill-Queen's University Press, 2001.

Burelle, A. "Mise en tutelle des provinces." *Le Devoir*, February 15, 1999: A7.

Castonguay, C. "Nos élus devront faire preuve de courage: La révision du modèle québécois doit aussi mener à mettre davantage l'accent sur une plus grande liberté de choix personnels." *La Presse*, November 17, 1999: B3.

———. "Un large débat s'impose en décembre: La question de la place du secteur privé dans la santé doit être abordée." *La Presse*, November 6, 1997: B3.

Chantier de l'économie sociale. *De nouveau, nous osons... Document de positionnement stratégique.* Montreal, 2001.

———. *Osons la solidarité.* Montreal, 1996.

Comité d'études sur l'assistance publique. *Rapport du comité d'étude sur l'assistance publique* (Boucher report). Quebec: Gouvernement du Québec, 1963.

Courchene, T.J. *A State of Minds: Toward a Human Capital Future for Canadians.* Montreal: Institute for Research on Public Policy, 2001.

Dion, S. "Union sociale veut dire entraide canadienne." *Le Devoir*, December 12-13, 1998: A11.

Dutrisac, R. "Québec donne de l'oxygène au milieu." *Le Devoir*, September 6, 2001: A4.

Federal/Provincial/Territorial Ministers Responsible for Social Services. *UNISON: A Canadian Approach to Disability Issues* (Policy Document). Ottawa: 1998.

Gagnon, K. "Consensus à Victoria." *La Presse*, August 3, 2001: A1.

Gill, L. *Le néolibéralisme.* Montreal: Chaire d'études socio-économiques de UQAM, 1999.

Gouvernement du Québec. *Politique gouvernementale: L'action communautaire une contribution essentielle à l'exercice de la citoyenneté et au développement social du Québec.* Quebec: Gouvernement du Québec, 2001.

Jérôme-Forget, M. "Canada's Social Union: Staking Out the Future of Federalism." *Policy Options*, Vol. 19, no. 9 (November 1998): 4-5.

Jetté, C., B. Lévesque, L. Mager and Y. Vaillancourt. *Économie sociale et transformation de l'État-providence dans le domaine de la santé et du bien-être: Une recension des écrits (1990–2000).* Sainte-Foy, Quebec: Presses de l'Université du Québec, 2000.

Jetté, C., B. Lévesque and Y. Vaillancourt. *The Social Economy and the Future of Health and Welfare in Quebec and Canada* (Cahiers du LAREPPS, no. 01-04). Montreal: Université du Québec à Montréal, 2001.

Larose, G. *Proposition de politique de soutien et de reconnaissance de l'action communautaire: Le milieu communautaire: un acteur essentiel au développement du Québec* (Larose report). Montreal: Ministère de la Solidarité sociale, 2000.

———. "Un modèle à réinventer: Certains aspects du modèle québécois ont fait leur temps." *La Presse*, June 8, 1999: B3.

Laville, J.-L., ed. *L'économie solidaire: Une perspective internationale,* 2nd ed. Paris: Desclée de Brouwer, 1994.

Léger, M.-F. "Dans la jungle des garderies à 5$..." *La Presse*, August 31, 2001a: A4.

———. "Le manque de places irrite de plus en plus." *La Presse*, August 22, 2001b: A3.

Lévesque, B., G.L. Bourque and Y. Vaillancourt. "Trois positions dans le débat sur le modèle québécois." *Nouvelles pratiques sociales*, Vol. 12, no. 2 (autumn 1999): 1-10.

Lévesque, B., and M. Mendell. "L'économie sociale au Québec: Éléments théoriques et empiriques pour le débat et la recherche." *Lien social et politiques*, no. 41 (spring 1999).

Lewis, J. "Reviewing the Relationship between the Voluntary Sector and the State in Britain in the 1990s." *VOLUNTAS: International Journal of Voluntary and Nonprofit Organizations*, Vol. 10, no. 2 (September 1999): 255-270.

Lipietz, A. *Rapport sur l'économie sociale et Solidaire* (Cahiers du LAREPPS, no. 01-01). Montreal: Université du Québec à Montréal, 2001.

——. "L'économie solidaire: 'réminiscence' de l'économie sociale?" *Économie et humanisme*, no. 354 (October 2000).

Lorendahl, B. "L'intégration de l'économie publique et de l'économie sociale et coopérative: Vers un nouveau modèle suédois?" *Nouvelles pratiques sociales*, Vol. 11, no. 2 (autumn 1998): 41-61.

Martin, P. *Budget Speech*. Ottawa: Department of Finance, 1995.

National Forum on Health. *Canada Health Action: Building on the Legacy*. Final Report. Ottawa: 1997.

Noël, A. "Without Quebec: Collaborative Federalism with a Footnote?" *Policy Matters*, Vol. 1, no. 2 (March 2000).

——. "Les trois unions sociales." *Policy Options*, Vol. 19, no. 9 (November 1998): 26-29.

——. "Vers un nouvel État-providence? Enjeux démocratiques." *Politique et Sociétés*, no. 30 (autumn 1996) (15th year).

Office des personnes handicapées du Québec. *On Equal Terms: The Social Integration of Handicapped Persons: A Challenge for Everyone*. Quebec: Gouvernement du Québec, 1984.

Paquette, P. "La démocratisation: Un enjeu majeur pour le modèle québécois." *La Presse*, June 23, 2000: B3.

——. "Le modèle québécois ne sert pas qu'en temps de crise." *Le Devoir*, February 1, 1999: A7.

Phillips, S.D., with Havi Echenberg and Rachel Laforest. *A Federal Government-Voluntary Sector Accord: Implications for Canada's Voluntary Sector*. Ottawa: Voluntary Sector Initiative Secretariat, 2001a.

Piotte, J.-M. *Du combat au partenariat: Interventions critiques sur le syndicalisme québécois*. Montreal: Éditions Nota Bene, 1998.

Secrétariat à l'action communautaire autonome du Québec (SACA). *Proposition de politique: Le milieu communautaire: Un acteur essentiel au développement du Québec*. Quebec: SACA, 2000.

Taylor, M., and A. Bassi. "Unpacking the State: The Implications for the Third Sector of Changing Relationships between National and Local Government." *VOLUNTAS: International Journal of Voluntary and Nonprofit Organizations*, Vol. 9, no. 2 (June 1998).

Thériault, L., C. Jetté, R. Mathieu and Y. Vaillancourt. *Social Housing with Community Support: An Examination of the FOHM Experience*. Ottawa: Caledon Institute of Social Policy, 2000.

Vaillancourt, Y. "Le rapport Clair et la mondialisation." *Nouvelles pratiques sociales*, Vol. 13, no. 2 (December 2000): 1-12.

——. "Tiers secteur et reconfiguration des politiques sociales." *Nouvelles pratiques sociales*, Vol. 11, no. 2 (autumn 1998) and Vol. 12, no. 1 (spring 1999).

——. *De l'oubli d'encadrer le pouvoir de dépenser*. Brief presented to the Parliamentary Commission on the Calgary Declaration, Québec, June 8, 1998.

—— with Luc Thériault. *Transfert canadien en matière de santé et de programmes sociaux: Enjeux pour le Québec* (Cahiers du LAREPPS, no. 97-07). Montreal: Université du Québec à Montréal, 1997.

——. "Remaking Canadian Social Policy: A Québec Viewpoint." In *Remaking Canadian Social Policy: Staking Claims and Forging Change*, ed. J. Pulkingham and G. Ternowetsky. Halifax: Fernwood Books, 1996a.

——. "Les origines du Régime de l'assistance publique du Canada: Une lecture québécoise (1960–1966)." *Canadian Review of Social Policy*, no. 37 (spring 1996b): 21-50.

———. "Les origines du RAPC: Une lecture québécoise (1960–1966): Le rôle du ministère des Finances." *Canadian Reviews of Social Policy*, no. 36 (December 1995): 27-38.

———. "Éléments de problématique concernant l'arrimage entre le communautaire et le public dans le domaine de la santé et des services sociaux." *Nouvelles pratiques sociales*, Vol. 7, no. 2 (autumn 1994): 227-248.

———. "Quebec and the Federal Government: The Struggle Over Opting Out." In *Canadian Society: Understanding and Surviving in the 1990s*, ed. D. Glenday. Toronto: McClelland & Stewart, 1993.

———. "Les origines du RAPC examinées en mettant l'accent sur le rôle du ministère de la Santé nationale et du Bien-être social: Une lecture québécoise (1960–1966)." *Canadian Review of Social Policy*, no. 29-30 (November 1992a): 25-51.

———. "Un bilan de l'opting out des programmes fédéraux à frais partagés dans le domaine social (1964–1992)." In *Bilan québécois du fédéralisme canadien*, ed. F. Rocher. Montreal: VLB, 1992b.

———. "Un bilan québécois des quinze premières années du Régime d'assistance publique du Canada (1966–1981)." *Nouvelles pratiques sociales*, Vol. 4, no. 2 (autumn, 1991): 115-146.

Vaillancourt, Y., F. Aubry, M. D'Amours, C. Jetté, L. Thériault and L. Tremblay. *Économie sociale, santé et bien-être: La spécificité du modèle québécois au Canada* (Cahiers du LAREPPS, no. 00-01). Montreal: Université du Québec à Montréal, 2000.

Vaillancourt, Y., and M.-N. Ducharme, with R. Cohen, C. Roy and C. Jetté. *Le logement social, une composante importante des politiques sociales en reconfiguration: État de la situation au Québec* (Cahiers du LAREPPS, no. 00-08). Montreal: Université du Québec à Montréal, 2000.

Vaillancourt, Y., and L. Favreau. "Le modèle québécois d'économie sociale et solidaire." *Revue internationale de l'économie sociale: RECMA*, no. 281 (July 2001).

Vaillancourt, Y., and J.-L. Laville. "Les rapports entre associations et État: Un enjeu politique." *Une seule solution, l'association? Socio-économie du fait associatif*, revue du MAUSS, no. 11 (1st semester) (1998).

Vaillancourt, Y., and L. Tremblay, eds. *L'économie sociale dans le domaine de la santé et du bien-être au Canada: Une perspective interprovinciale*. Montreal: LAREPPS, 2001.

Venne, M. "Inutile union sociale." *Le Devoir*, June 9, 2000: A8.

White, D. "Maîtriser un mouvement, dompter une idéologie — l'État et le secteur communautaire au Québec." *ISUMA: Canadian Journal of Policy Research*, Vol. 2, no. 2 (2001).

Zehler, E. "Assurance-emploi: Un dossier à suivre." *Le Devoir*, April 28-29, 2001: E8.

Canada's Social
Union in
Perspective:
Looking into the
European Mirror

Introduction

C ANADA AND QUEBEC HAVE TWO VERY DIFFERENT, INDEED OPPOSING, PERSPECTIVES
on the European Union (EU). In Canada the focus is on the close relationship that the European Community (EC) has established between economic integration and political integration. From this perspective, complete economic and
monetary integration is impossible in the absence of a confederal or federal power
that is hierarchically superior to the entities to be integrated.[1] In Quebec, on the
other hand, the focus is on the political aspect of European institutions, particularly the importance accorded sovereignty, which is seen as institutionally innovative and a source of inspiration. Indeed, in Quebec any problems associated with
the economic dimension of the union tend to be disregarded.[2]

Canada's interest lies in the level of economic integration of EU member
states as compared with the level of economic integration that exists in Canada.
Nevertheless, some authors express reservations, believing that if Canadians were
more familiar with the institutional characteristics of the EU — limited democracy, lack of a means to redistribute the gains achieved through economic integration, inability of member states to defend their political interests internationally
— "it is unlikely that the EC would be regarded as a 'political model' superior to
the form of federalism that Canada has developed."[3] Applied to Canada, "whole-
sale decentralization [which characterizes the EU] would render the government
system ineffectual in meeting the essential needs or goals of Canadians."[4]

The situation is quite different in Quebec, where the current form of
Canadian federalism is seen as untenable because it ignores the national aspirations of Quebecers.[5] It is also believed, since NAFTA came into effect, that eco-

nomic integration should not necessarily be limited to Canadian borders.[6] The EU model thus offers the kind of partnership that would be an ideal trade-off "between integration and national autonomy for both Canada and Quebec."[7] Indeed, during the 1995 referendum campaign Quebec sovereignists advocated a Canada-Quebec economic union and political institutions resembling those of the EU — a council, a parliamentary assembly and a dispute resolution tribunal similar to the European Court of Justice.[8] But in Quebec there are dissenting authors as well, with some arguing that the European model is no "blueprint"[9] and that "the optimal solution does not lie in the creation of joint political institutions, whether inspired by the experience of the European Union or by the tripartite agreement reached on the eve of the 1995 Quebec referendum."[10]

In this paper I suggest a different approach, one that could break the impasse between these two positions. One of the main weaknesses of these perspectives is that they focus on specific, though opposite, institutional aspects of the European construction — integration for one, autonomy for the other — and do not take into account the continuing development of European institutions. They disregard the overall coherence of the institutions as well as their historical dynamics, without which the European experience cannot be fully understood.

When considering Canada in light of the EU, it is a mistake to think that institutions can simply be copied without taking into account their historical and cultural context. We will not find in the European experiment a simple remedy to deal with Canada's institutional crisis — the inability to formally recognize the asymmetry and multinational character of the federation — because there are crises on both sides of the Atlantic, and crisis, in any case, is the driving force behind both evolutionary processes. The comparison will be useful only if it helps to reveal significant similarities in the *dynamics* of political innovation. When we consider these dynamics, what appears to be taking shape is a "post-Westphalian"[11] response to the search, on both sides of the Atlantic, for a form of political unity that also respects the diversity of the various parts and addresses the need to recognize the national dimension. The institutional dynamics in both Europe and Canada reflect an opposition to and questioning of the political order. Since both situations involve several levels of government, they both require a new form of cooperation and collective management of intergovernmental conflict.

The features of the Canadian political landscape that I will be examining here are not particular institutions or laws, but rather *processes* of institutionalization and socio-political *dynamics*, with their specific forms of innovation and possible scenarios of evolution. That is why, with regard to the Canadian social union, I am less interested in the Social Union Framework Agreement (SUFA) itself than in the dynamic behind it. I will argue that this dynamic can be considered a "functional equivalent" of the process in which the EU has increasingly been involved since the signing of the Treaty of Maastricht, despite the principle of subsidiarity that it also incorporates.

From this perspective it can be observed that although the trajectory of the EU is opposite to that of the Canadian confederation (i.e., the emergence of a federal political order based on pre-existing sovereign states, in the case of the EU, versus the construction of a nation-state and recognition of the Aboriginal and Quebec nations within the existing federal system, in the case of Canada) the EU is inventing institutional forms similar to those that have been established, though often more informally, in Canada. Viewed from this broader perspective, the institutional innovations engendered by the Canadian political system — at the cost of an apparent instability due to intergovernmental rivalry — may be seen more positively. In brief, the European experience can be used to counter Canadians' and Quebecers' negative view of their political system. This is the main lesson of the European experience for Canada.

Canada and the EU can thus be seen as political arenas in which a new form of government and international society is being invented.[12] Emerging within them are similar forms of multinational, asymmetrical federalism, blending supranationalism with intergovernmentalism. This federalism is based not on a hierarchy of powers between the federal government and federated entities, but on a hierarchy of values between equal orders of government that compete for the allegiance of citizens.[13]

What Canada and Quebec stand to gain from Europe's ongoing experiment is an appreciation for the way in which they solve their jurisdictional conflicts on a day-to-day basis. Thus they may come to appreciate the mechanisms they have developed to deal with conflicts as the expression of a "well-understood federal principle,"[14] rather than mere stopgaps in the absence of the ideal: the all-powerful sovereign state that some would like Canada to be and others would like Quebec to be.

For example, an institutional innovation such as the "right to opt out" — which was somewhat disparaged in English Canada because of its implied asymmetry — when given the more palatable label of *enhanced cooperation*, as it is in the treaties of Amsterdam and Nice, gains pertinence[15] and legitimacy. The political dynamics of the social union thus echo the type of asymmetrical, multinational federalism that is emerging in Europe. What is even more interesting is that these institutions have the potential to help deal with other situations where territorial recomposition is taking place due to globalization.

I will develop my argument in two stages. I will first attempt to show that the EU and Canada are mirror images of each other. The two political entities are challenged to invent a new form of multilevel socio-political organization whose cohesion is not national.[16] I will then show how the dynamic of the social union process in Canada, in terms of both intergovernmental relations and resourcing of the welfare state, is reflected in social developments in Europe after the signing of the Treaty of Maastricht. Indeed, despite all the political difficulties, the innovations brought about by the social union process and the right to opt out, on the one hand, and *the open method of coordination* and *enhanced cooperation*, on the other, attest to a real and positive evolution toward the development of a new multinational federalism.

Canada and the European Union: Mirror Images of the Federalization Process

T HERE ARE TWO REASONS WHY IT IS RELEVANT TO COMPARE THE EU AND CANADA. One relates to *intergovernmental federalism*, the particular form of federalism that prevails in both political arenas. The other relates to the *agenda building* style that governs public policy-making in both the EU and Canada, a style characterized by the need for permanent political innovations.

The Multinationalization of Canada and the Federalization of Europe

Canada and the EU are two economic and political entities that, like other states in the developed world, participate actively in globalization. What sets them apart from most of the other states is the fact that they do not have the bases to form nation-states, since distinct national communities coexist within them.[17]

In Canada, Quebec is struggling to achieve recognition as a nation-state. (Another struggle for nation-state status is arguably in the making, as Aboriginal peoples are demanding institutional recognition.) Quebec's emergence as a nation-state poses a challenge to the federal political order, which was originally constituted as a centralized system. As a result, the question of recognizing the multinational character of the federation is being raised more and more often.[18] In the EU, where the nation-state is the starting point, the reverse is true. The constantly evolving federal level is trying to establish a place for itself by reorganizing the regional political order, without, however, being able to get beyond its multinational character.

Thus it is reasonable to conclude that, barring a chance mishap, the EU and Canada are heading toward a similar reformulation of the principles of federalism. Indeed, it is through this reformulation that a compromise will be found between supranationalism and intergovernmentalism.

Figure 1 shows that the absence of a true federal state in Europe and the absence of a true nation-state in Canada do not prevent the European and Canadian trajectories from converging toward a new type of federal pact.[19] However, this paper will dwell less on finding similarities in the two entities with regard to particular terms and institutional forms than on comparing their dynamics.

However, although the EU and Canada are likely to arrive at the same destination, they are taking opposite, not parallel, routes to get there. That is why I have chosen to use the metaphor of a mirror: a mirror reverses the direction in which the reflected image is read, thus the process of federalization that prevails in Europe reflects the process of multinationalization that can be observed in Canada.

Figure 2 depicts the duality of the processes of nationalization (or, more precisely, *nationification*) and federalization. In fact, in Canada, although Quebec's national claim is clear and explicit, that of the Rest of Canada (or ROC) is not — indeed, it is even denied, having been subsumed within the vision of a Canada-wide nationality.

Thus, while Alan Cairns considers that "the overall description of Canada as a multinational country, while not yet commonplace, has clearly become frequent enough to suggest that we are entering a new era," he nevertheless wonders how many nations the country will ultimately comprise. Not only is there uncertainty about the number of Aboriginal nations seeking recognition, but "ROC, or English Canada, or Anglophone Canada has almost no desire to wear new institutional clothing as a national partner to Quebec and Aboriginal nations.

Figure 1 202

Historical
Dynamics of the
Establishment of a
New Type of
Federal Pact in
Canada and Europe

Sovereign nation-states

EUROPE

Pooling of competences with
development of an interstate
executive federalism

Competitive state building
through the construction of the
EU as a federal state

New federal
pact

CANADA

Competitive state building with
construction of the Quebec
provincial state

Unseating of the federal state
with development of an
interstate executive federalism

Centralized federation

Figure 2

The Federalization
of Europe as a
Reflection of the
Multinationalization
of Canada

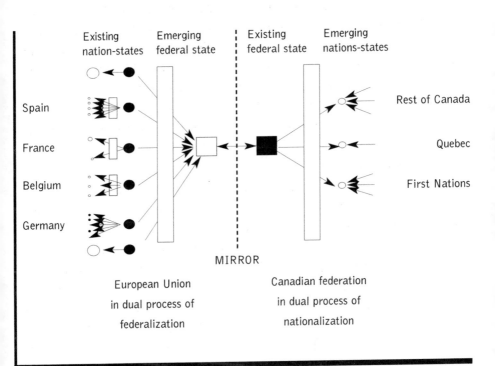

Existing nation-states   Emerging federal state   Existing federal state   Emerging nations-states

Spain

France

Belgium

Germany

Rest of Canada

Quebec

First Nations

MIRROR

European Union
in dual process of
federalization

Canadian federation
in dual process of
nationalization

It lacks nationalist self-consciousness. It is headless, voiceless, institutionless (on the whole), and has negligible ambition to constitute itself as a nation."[20]

Hence, the multinationalization of the Canadian federation has two facets, not one — as the Quebec vision seems to presume — since it implies not only the denationalization of federal institutions but also the constitution of anglophone provinces into one or several national entities with representative political institutions.[21] In fact, the new social policies advocated by Ottawa as well as the social union process appear to presage the development of a vision of federalism and the emergence of "national" forms of solidarity that are specific to the ROC.

When the anglophone provinces first met to discuss the social union, they considered three possible types of program — federal, provincial and national. In addition to those programs administered and implemented by Ottawa and the provinces, there were those that were identified as national, administered jointly and implemented by one of the two levels of government.[22] Thus there emerged in ROC a specific conception of what is "national," a conception that did not involve being exclusively represented by the federal government; the de facto exclusion of Quebec from SUFA appears to attest to this.

The situation in Canada illustrates that multinational federalism can involve not only two but three levels of government, which is also true of the EU, where a dual process of federalization can be observed. The supranational construction of the EU has gone hand-in-hand with the federalization of a large number of its member states. While Belgium and Spain are the most obvious examples, the process can also be observed in Italy, the United Kingdom[23] and even France (with the current discussion on the special status of Corsica). If we consider, moreover, the already federal character of Germany and Austria, it becomes clear that Europe is moving toward a complex multinational polity with three levels of government (the EU, member states and nationality-based regions) that can claim to have equal status as federal entities.

The fact that the multinationalization of Canada mirrors the federalization of the EU shows that it is not the centralizing features of the European institutional dynamic that prevent it from serving "as a model for those who favour a decentralization of the Canadian federation."[24] Rather, it is because the exercise is self-referential for Canada, which ultimately can only see its own image in the EU. Nevertheless, such an exercise is useful since the distance created by reflection leads us to value the innovations adopted in the process of multinationalization in Canada, in much the way we value the innovations associated with the process of "communitarization" in Europe.

The Same Intergovernmental Federalism
Governed by a Similar Policy Pattern

From a theoretical standpoint, it is legitimate to compare recent Canadian and European institutional dynamics only because of the structural similarities, both logical and historical, between the Canadian federation and the EU. Two concepts help to illustrate these similarities: "interstate" or "intergovernmental" federalism, and an "agenda-building policy pattern."

Interstate federalism, unlike the intrastate form, ascribes an important role to intergovernmentalism. Diplomatic relations between the federal government and the federated entities, in the form of intergovernmental meetings that bring together the first ministers or the federal and provincial ministers,[25] coexist with specifically federal — or supranational — institutions.

In instrastate federalism, in contrast, intergovernmentalism is weak. The federated entities participate directly in the federal government through a second chamber of Parliament (the Senate). Interstate federalism is much rarer than intrastate federalism. Canada[26] and the EU[27] are typical examples of the former — which is not surprising since this form of intergovernmental federalism is more likely to be found where territorial entities are culturally heterogeneous (for example, as a result of linguistic diversity) and inclined to demand a greater share of sovereignty by presenting themselves as nations.

Despite the longer Canadian experience, the EU reflects a more highly institutionalized form of intergovernmental federalism. The right of federated entities to opt out emerged in Canada (for example, in the areas of taxation and government pension plans) long before it emerged as a possible solution to the problems encountered during European integration. In fact, the institutionalization in Europe of innovations first developed in Canada might bring Canadians to change their perception of their own processes of accommodation. The European experience demonstrates that intergovernmental federalism is not merely a response to a temporary inability to achieve the ideal of the founding fathers of American federalism. On the contrary, the intergovernmental federalism common to the EU, and Canada can and should be seen as an adaptable, stable, even ideal form of regulation in the context of multinational society.[28]

In interstate federalism, unlike in the intrastate form, the federal government does not benefit from the legitimacy associated with shared decision-making powers between the House of Commons and the Senate. Its legitimacy, therefore, must be founded on socio-economic interests and its ability to maintain a mutually beneficial federation. In order to do so, it must use specific procedures to develop its policies, a policy pattern that has been termed "agenda building." This form of federalism leads to the constitutional rigidity that results from the presence of multiple veto points.[29] This is why sectoral public policies, which can be used to circumvent these veto points, are important for the construction and maintenance of the federation.

Examining policy patterns means focusing on the comparative dynamics of innovation in public policy. Within a federation, these dynamics depend largely on the way competitive state building is regulated. Thus, the policy pattern is the customary way the federal or supranational government develops its capacity for initiative and institutional change through public policies. The concept thus refers to policy innovation schemes and to the ways in which policies are carried out. Conceptualization in terms of patterns means that these schemes are recurrent and affect a range of public policies.

Analyses of social policies show that Canada's policy pattern can be categorized as one of agenda building and staging.[30] This stands in contrast to the American pattern of empire building and targeting, which is not highly conducive to innovation because it results from a static balance of powers between Congress and the presidency, which only authorizes change by leaps and bounds during serious crises.[31]

Canada's federal government must ensure that its power relationships with the provinces strengthen its legitimacy vis-à-vis all citizens (nation building). It therefore must continually include in its policy agenda social innovations beyond its established fields of jurisdiction.[32] In the general interest of the country, it uses its spending power to enter the provinces' constitutional fields of jurisdiction.[33] This "spillover" may occur with or without the consent of the provinces, which are not all concerned to the same degree with preserving their exclusive jurisdictions and are not dependent to the same extent on federal resources to implement their own social policies.[34] Also, depending on the political, economic and financial contexts, the federal government may or may not be open to negotiation and may attempt to make unilateral decisions.

In any event, the policy pattern specific to the Canadian federation, whether it takes the form of conflict or cooperation, is conducive to innovation. When a co-operative pattern is adopted (regulation of competitive state building through collective negotiation between governments), the federal government is induced to financially support the adoption of provincial "good practices" at the national level. For example, Ottawa supports the diffusion of programs such as health insurance and the Canada Assistance Plan (CAP), which are implemented by the provinces. When Ottawa adopts a unilateral approach, as it did in 1995, the provinces are induced to set their own agendas in their fields of jurisdiction by using the resources of intergovernmentalism. As a result they may claim a greater share of the federation's tax resources, which is the main obstacle to Ottawa's effective use of its spending power.[35]

The policy pattern of *agenda building* (and the related pattern of *staging*) is also characteristic of what has been labelled the "Monnet method," which has allowed the supranational process of European integration to progress by stages.

According to neofunctionalist theorists, this method has two variants.[36] The first is based on the success achieved in a given area of integration, which may result in a search for similar success in related areas.[37] The second is based on spillover effects — that is, the introduction of a minor institutional innovation in a secondary sector of integration that is likely to spill over into an adjacent sector. A functional deficit is thus created, which in turn requires a new intervention at the EC level, which, while reducing the EC's deficit, spills over into a third sector, and so on.[38] Since these spillovers can be foreseen at least in the medium term, the Commission of the European Communities (CEC), the main architect of the integration process, may establish a forward-looking agenda for the gradual construction of supranational domains.

Obviously, since in the last instance the council (intergovernmental) is the community's decision-making power, the Monnet method presumes that member states are ready or constrained to cooperate. The commission, which acts as the executive for the EC, does not have a spending power (which Canada does have) to force such cooperation, but it does have the functional equivalent — a regulatory instrument based on the *conditional agenda-setting power*.[39] This power facilitates the adoption of legislation in the form proposed by the commission, because the rule on which it is based stipulates that for any legislation submitted to a vote by the council only a majority is required to adopt it, but unanimity is required to amend it.[40] According to George Tsebelis, this asymmetry is key to the Monnet method and the spillover effects, and results in the gradual construction by the commission of the EU's supranational domains.

As has been the case with Canada's cooperative executive federalism, the Monnet method is likely to come up against the resistance of certain member states that are reluctant to relinquish their powers. Thus, although the conditional agenda-setting power was introduced at the very beginning in the 1957 Treaty of Rome, it has long been blocked by French opposition, initiated by de Gaulle, to qualified majority voting (QMV). This opposition led to the 1966 Luxembourg compromise, which granted the right of veto to each of the council's member states. It was not until 1986, with the *Single European Act*, that QMV was restored in a number of fields and the CEC could effectively exercise its power. As we shall see, this revived and accelerated the pace of European construction.

In the meantime, from 1957 to 1985 European construction progressed slowly and in limited fields. In order to break the impasses created by uncooperative intergovernmentalism, the commission had to use subterfuge and sectoral strategies to circumvent veto points.[41] Therefore, not only did the federation develop slowly, but the process of integration was fragmented. In fact, "the outcome was a mass of detailed regulations and directives, emerging out of a disjointed Brussels process that appeared to outsiders to pursue petty harmonization with enthusiasm while failing (because it lacked the capacity and authority) to tackle broader issues."[42] Thus, low politics won out over high politics[43] and integration had little legitimacy.[44]

However, this institutional stagnation does not invalidate the idea that, from the outset, there has been a process of agenda building based on the Monnet method. In a context of conflict-ridden relationships hampering intergovernmental cooperation, the similarity between the Canadian and European policy patterns lies in how they construct their public policies by circumventing the obstacles created by opposition to the way official institutions operate (e.g., through constitutions and treaties). Of course, since the trajectories of federalization in the two regions run in opposite directions, the actors seeking such loopholes are not the same.

In the Canadian case, the provinces use diverse strategies to evade the unilateralism of the federal government or the veto of certain provinces on constitutional changes. One strategy — the equivalent of European "commitology" — consists in using interprovincial ministerial conferences and meetings, though they have no constitutional bases, to develop common fronts. Another involves the adoption of policies that are then presented as a *fait accompli* and promoted as exemplary, thus paving the way for direct funding from federal tax resources, as in the case of health insurance in the 1960s. A third strategy involves the negotiation of bilateral agreements with Ottawa in particular sectors.

On the whole, the Canadian policy pattern resembles that of the EU except on two counts. First, in Europe the *informal* political agenda is developed principally at the initiative of (quasi) federal authorities, while in Canada it is developed principally by the federated entities. This reflects the fact that the *official* agenda is dominated by member states in Europe and by the federal government in Canada. Second, European intergovernmental federalism is founded on an essentially legislative power, while the Canadian variant is based on a power that is first and foremost financial. Ottawa has spending power but limited regulatory power in the provinces' fields of jurisdiction. The supranational authorities of the EU have few financial resources and little spending power, but they do have strong regulatory power through the conditional agenda-setting power and the jurisprudence of the European Court of Justice.

Thus we can draw the first general lesson. The weakening of federal power, inevitable if the multinationalization of the Canadian federation continues, must not be allowed to undermine interprovincial redistributive programs such as equalization. Rather, it must lead to a negotiated reduction in arbitrary measures by the federal government in the management of these programs. Otherwise, Ottawa will intervene arbitrarily through small, nitpicking sectoral regulations, driven by the requirements of the common market and the economic and monetary union, which will be much more insidious and damaging for the diversity and political unity of the federation.

Canadian Social Union and European Social Policies: Toward a Renewal of Cooperative Executive Federalism

IN ORDER TO DRAW ADDITIONAL LESSONS FROM THE COMPARISON OF CANADIAN SOCIAL union and current EU social policies, we now return to our starting point — a focus on dynamics rather than on static institutional forms. First I will show that the dynamics of SUFA led to the reinstitution of cooperative federalism through the collective action of the provinces. Then I will argue that the extension of the EU's social powers reflects a renewed form of cooperative intergovernmental dynamics that is the result of the EC's initiative.

In the context of this renewal of cooperative intergovernmental federalism, we will examine the hypothesis of a crossing point in the trajectories of multinationalization in Canada and federalization in the EU. This crossing point would define an institutional balance that, because it is common to both experiments, could be considered a characteristic specific to multinational federalism.

I will first attempt to determine the political and social impact of the social union process on the evolution of intergovernmental relations in Canada. I will then show how, since implementation of the social programs resulting from the Treaty of Maastricht, the emerging institutional forms of European social welfare can be seen as reflections of those that emerged through the dynamics of SUFA.

Political and Social Dynamics of SUFA in
Canada and Quebec

At their annual meeting in 1995, the premiers reacted to Ottawa's drastic unilateral cuts in provincial transfers and brutal neoliberal social policy reform by forming a new common front, at first without Quebec. In response to federal unilateralism and in order to produce their own solutions to the social and political problems facing the federation, the premiers resolved to "reform and renew social welfare in Canada." They drew up a program to negotiate a new "social union" with Ottawa and to outline "the contours of a renewed federalism."[45]

However, the provincial governments were divided over what place federal programs should occupy in the social welfare system. The Conservative governments of Ontario and Alberta proposed an interprovincial, confederal, minimalist structure in which the federal level would be done away with entirely[46] and in which the imposition of federal standards would be countered by the consensus-based adoption of national standards by the provinces.

The other anglophone provinces, in particular the Atlantic provinces, were opposed to Ottawa's withdrawing totally, seeing it as a threat to the redistribution of tax resources and therefore to their own ability to fulfill their social mission. Some provinces, mainly those in the West, also feared that interprovincialism would lead the larger provinces to impose their own policies; they favoured involving the federal government in the social field while leaving the provinces to play the most active role. This position finally won the support of all anglophone premiers during their 1996 annual meeting and led to the creation of the Provincial/Territorial Council on Social Policy Renewal.

The position of the anglophone provinces was not to reject a permanent role for the federal government in their areas of jurisdiction, but to negotiate, in return for funds, the new division of responsibilities sought by Ottawa in addition to the formal distribution of powers. It was out of the question for the Quebec government to participate in these negotiations, since at that time it was striving to recover all of its constitutional prerogatives on social matters. Quebec did not join the interprovincial discussions until the end of 1997, finally signing the Saskatoon Consensus with the other provinces in August 1998. This agreement recognized the provinces' rights to develop their own policy in their areas of exclusive jurisdiction by opting out of any Canada-wide program, with full compensation. In return for this right to opt out, Quebec recognized Ottawa's role in the social field and the principle of Canada-wide programs.[47]

Threatened by Ontario and Alberta's confederal interprovincialism and undoubtedly concerned about Quebec joining the interprovincial process, Ottawa began to negotiate in December 1997, even though there was a risk that its hands would be tied by the institutionalization of new federal-provincial relations. These talks led to the signing of the Social Union Framework Agreement on February 4, 1999.

SUFA strengthened the federal government's position, since it represented a serious compromise of the position the provinces had jointly developed with Quebec. Nevertheless, the agreement was ambivalent, because it also changed the political relationships established by the 1995 neoliberal reform between Ottawa and the provinces. Although the provinces agreed to give the federal government far more control over social matters than they ever had before, they demanded and got a federal commitment to boost the financial resources going into the health system and improve the new National Child Benefit (NCB) in exchange.[48]

This deal did not stop the agreement from being viewed as seriously flawed by observers in Quebec and the other provinces.[49] In fact, it did not resolve the issue of overlapping responsibilities and was insufficient to restrain the federal spending power in areas of provincial jurisdiction. It was highly centralizing, since joint decisions now required the approval of only six provinces — which could entail as little as 15 percent of Canada's population. The agreement's major flaw, however, was that it did not recognize the right to opt out, which was why Quebec refused to sign. That said, SUFA also marked the defeat of the interprovincial confederal position and represented a readjustment of Ottawa's priorities, favouring internal political and social dynamics over external economic constraints.

Beyond SUFA's immediate implications, the neoliberal shock of 1994–95 and the political process that it initiated altered the Canadian political landscape by opening the door to a range of scenarios (see table 1). In addition to the recurring scenario that reflects Quebec's stance in which "two opposing types of state logic" coexist within the framework of "classic federalism" (in which powers are clearly separated), Gérard Boismenu and Jane Jenson identify three others: the interprovincial and confederal one discussed above; that outlined by the federal government, described as "flexible decentralization with central normalization"; and the scenario of a united front of anglophone provinces advancing their own vision of what is "national," in particular what the provinces and Ottawa share.[50]

SUFA established a kind of compromise among these scenarios. First, as we have seen, it marked the withdrawal of the confederal vision. It also bridged the gap between the federal "central normalization" and the provincial common front, while reinforcing the divergence between the latter and the "classic federalism" defended by Quebec.

However, it is an irony of history that this situation in fact reinforces the asymmetry of the federation and the distinctiveness of Quebec, because that province is not party to SUFA.[51] And yet, because the social policies advocated by the various protagonists are in fact closer in terms of content than in terms of the institutional framework necessary for their implementation, Quebec's position is compatible with SUFA through bilateral negotiations with Ottawa.[52] Thus bilateral agreements between Quebec and Ottawa, like those in the employment sector, could certainly be envisaged and would help to avoid the institutional impasse on the right to opt out.[53]

The dynamics created by the unilateralism of the 1995 federal reforms could therefore speed up the development of an asymmetrical and binational federal system — possibly multinational, provided that the rightful place of the First Nations is recognized.[54]

The concept of nation espoused by SUFA is specific to English Canada, in that the provinces agree to an intrastate type of federalism with the federal government at the centre.[55] This concept clashes with Quebec's vision, in which

Table 1

Four Scenarios for the Development of the Canadian Federation

Political Model ⇒ / Social solidarity space ⇓	Interstate		Intrastate	
	Principle of mutual recognition	Maintenance of provincial characteristics	Federal harmonization	Principle of convergence
	Scenario *a*		**Scenario *b***	
Provincial funding	Primacy of interprovincialism *Confederal model*	Absolute: "The Conservative Canada of the wealthiest provinces"	Through the market: "Canada of the federal Liberal government"	Strong and centralized union through legal means: *American model*
	Scenario *d*		**Scenario *c***	
Federal equalization	Intergovernmental/ federal balance *Canadian model*	Relative: "Multinational asymmetrical Canada"	Through politics: "Canada of the social union"	Strong and centralized union through social welfare: *German model*

nationhood develops at the provincial level and federalism is a partnership among several national entities that share some of their domains under intergovernmental federalism. Although these two understandings are built on different territorial and linguistic foundations, they have a common history and social values and thus may be linked through multinational federalism, a type of federalism that would satisfy both Quebec's vision and the anglophone provinces' pragmatism, into a union dominated by Ottawa. The political dynamics of SUFA thus represent the potential for compromise between the three federalist scenarios, leading to a new multinational, partnership-based form of intergovernmental federalism.[56]

However, such a compromise is certainly not inevitable. Another possible outcome is "residual federalism,"[57] a resurgence of confederalism among the wealthiest provinces whereby, for lack of a political agreement, any political conflict would be settled by the market.[58] This possibility is reinforced by the situation in Alberta and the election of the Liberals in British Columbia in 2001.[59] Nevertheless, such a situation would be intrinsically unstable, because any economic and financial imbalance directly affecting the social and political structure would eventually lead to the break-up of the country.[60]

One must also consider the possibility that the political dynamics underlying SUFA could serve to renew social policies and, indirectly, the federal link. In this regard, SUFA's greatest achievement, apart from its indirect role in boosting funding of various social policies,[61] is the introduction of the NCB in 1998. Three aspects of this program show that the Canadian welfare state is embarking on a new course that, while renewing its postwar roots,[62] could revive the federal link.

The NCB is an instrument for reducing social inequalities. Its basic benefit is very broad vertical redistribution in addition to horizontal redistribution among families, both with and without children. Though it has neoliberal features, the NCB represents a significant social innovation, in line with the universalist, redistributive tradition of the Canadian welfare state. Moreover, by setting limits on the harmonization of Canadian social policies with the American model, the NCB strengthens the link among the Canadian provinces.

The NCB's status as a national program (as defined by the anglophone provinces) in the tradition of Canadian welfarist values brings it closer to the social programs established in the 1960s. As its "integrating" spirit is shared by Quebec, which in 1997 implemented a similar family policy, the NCB is essentially a synthesis of federal, provincial and Quebec aims.

This situation of "co-management more or less under federal tutelage for provinces other than Quebec" and of "Quebec autonomy in the sector concerned, with the assurance of a degree of compatibility with the arbitration reached in Canada" is similar to the situation that prevailed in 1965 when the public pension plan was introduced, linking the Canada Pension Plan and the Quebec Pension Plan.[63] Until now, this arrangement has remained exceptional, as Ottawa subsequently successfully trivialized the Quebec position. The fact that the NCB has, de facto, renewed this mechanism suggests that Canadian intergovernmental federalism is developing pragmatically into an asymmetrical multinational model.

Nonetheless, the new political compromise reached by SUFA has created a much more contentious situation than the previous executive, cooperative federalism. Whereas in the 1960s the provinces played a dominant role in building the Canadian welfare state, they remain (except for Quebec) in the background under SUFA. In fact, the NCB is an adaptation of a federal program aimed at leaving some room for provincial initiatives. In the cases of the pension plan and CAP, where federal-provincial cooperation was pushed the furthest, Ottawa participated in programs that were first defined by the provinces. Therefore SUFA is indicative less of a return to the cooperative federalism of the 1960s and 1970s than of its re-appearance in a new, highly centralized and contentious form, described by Ken Battle as "collaborative federalism."[64]

Since the agreement does not formally recognize the specificity of Quebec, it is seen in that province as containing serious limitations, as described by Alain Noël.[65] However, these limitations do not preclude the future development of asymmetrical multinational federalism in Canada. They mean only that, in order to have its asymmetrical position in the federation recognized, Quebec must continue to use the second and third types of subterfuge noted above — that is, social policies that could be used as a model for all of Canada and bilateral negotiation. This is no doubt frustrating for Quebec, but it does not mean that the Canadian federal system is leaving its multinationalization trajectory.

The Rising Power of Social Europe:
Canadian-Style Development?

To understand the origins of European social policies, one must distinguish among three periods.

Before 1985, EC action was limited to the field of industrial relations and was subject to the unanimity rule. The 1985–92 period was a transitional one during which the commission regained its conditional agenda-setting power and the principle of enhanced cooperation began to emerge. The period from 1993 to the present saw a renewed, innovative and broadened policy through which a variant of the Monnet method, the open method of coordination, was implemented.

From 1957 to 1984 the Treaty of Rome offered a limited basis for EC action. In the social field it provided only for a delegation of powers to the commission concerning the free movement of workers, the creation of the European Social Fund (ESF), and equal pay for women and men. These provisions gave rise to only a few achievements related to the rights of workers migrating between member states, gender equality, labour rights and the establishment of structural funds limited in their mission. This period was characterized by a "growing number of social proposals 'pending' before the Council" and the inability to implement them successfully.[66]

The 1985–92 period heralded an extension of EC powers and social policies. European institutions adopted a series of new instruments. The restoration of QMV in the *Single European Act* of 1987 was the greatest achievement of this era. Moreover, the budget allowance for the structural funds — the favoured instruments of "economic and social cohesion" within the EC — was doubled in 1988. The dialogue between employers and unions — the "European social partners" — resumed, and the Community Charter of the Fundamental Social Rights of Workers, the Social Charter, was adopted in December 1989 concurrently with a social program aimed at establishing a "core of minimum provisions" common to all member states (workplace health and safety, protection of workers' rights).

What is striking here is that, although one member state — the United Kingdom — refused to sign the Social Charter, the others nonetheless chose to refer to it in a protocol appended to the Treaty of Maastricht in 1992. While recording the British decision to opt out, this protocol instituted the Social Policy Agreement, which extended the EC's powers, introduced QMV in several areas and recognized the role of social partners in EC social regulation.[67]

The Treaty of Maastricht thus instituted a right to opt out similar to that recognized in Canada in 1965 when Quebec implemented its own pension plan, parallel to the Canada Pension Plan, the same right Quebec had sought during the negotiations that led to the signature of SUFA.[68] In fact, the European

Protocol — signed by 12 member states to allow the Social Policy Agreement, signed by only 11 member states, to be incorporated into the treaty — stipulated that the 11 member states could use the EU's institutions to pursue the objectives of the agreement, but that the United Kingdom did not have to bear expenses other than the operating costs of EC institutions.

The notion of a *right to opt out* was, however, struck from European official language and replaced by that of *enhanced cooperation* — a term that promotes supranational integration and the EU's viewpoint, rather than the autonomy and particular viewpoint of any member state. The Canadian right to opt out is thus reversed in the European context, which shows the difference between the two trajectories of multinationalization and federalization. In Canada, the right to opt out is promoted primarily by the evolving Quebec nation-state, based on its own conception of the Canadian federation. In Europe, it is promoted by the EC's institutions, which view it as a means of continuing the march toward political integration despite the opposition of some member states.

Two factors played a key role in the decision to adopt this wording. The first was the implementation of the euro. Some member states were given the option of declining to participate in the monetary union, while others had to meet the convergence criteria in order to join the monetary union. The second factor was the Schengen Agreement on the opening of borders and free movement of persons, which applied only to some member states (this agreement was originally not part of the Treaty of Maastricht but was subsequently incorporated into the Treaty of Amsterdam).

The post-Maastricht period, which began in 1993, saw the proliferation of EU initiatives based on these innovations. With new institutional resources allowing it to change its integration method in favour of incentives and cooperation, the EU extended its domain in matters of social welfare well beyond the boundaries of business and labour. The convergence method, which had allowed for the creation of the Economic and Monetary Union (EMU), spilled over, first into employment policy then into the field of social welfare and the fight against exclusion and poverty. In addition to the consolidation of minimum social standards through several directives and the conclusion of the first European agreements through social dialogue,[69] the employment policy was presented as a priority of the EU and the debate on broadening its powers regarding social welfare was launched in 1994.[70]

All of these developments were amplified by the 1997 Treaty of Amsterdam. An entire section (coming right after the section on the EMU) was devoted to employment, which then became part of the EU's domain even though the member states remain primarily responsible for policy implementation.[71] With the end of the British withdrawal, the Social Policy Agreement was incorporated into the treaty and included in the "Community *acquis*," the rights and obligations that all applicant countries must agree to respect before joining the EU. Lastly, the mechanism of enhanced cooperation proposed by France and Germany was codified for the first time, despite the "distrust of many member states." In return, the other member states later obtained the proviso that "recourse to the mechanism be limited by numerous conditions."[72]

The recognition of employment as an EC domain was immediately translated into the implementation of a "convergence procedure" using what would later be described as the open method of coordination. The aim of this procedure, which is similar to the one instituted in the Treaty of Maastricht for transition to the euro,[73] was to guide national policies toward common European objectives. Thus the commission's employment guidelines are adopted every year by the European Council through majority voting. Member states must incorporate them into their employment policies by establishing a National Employment Action Plan (NEAP), whose implementation is examined annually at the EC level.[74]

In 1999 this employment policy was transformed into a "strategy *for* employment" involving all EC policies and actions and acting retroactively on the EU's macro-economic policy. The "Cologne process" thus provided for the establishment by the commission of a macro-economic dialogue with the European Council, the European Central Bank and the social partners.[75]

Finally, in 2000 Europe's welfarist dimension was given a powerful impetus[76] when the open method of coordination, previously tested in the area of employment, was applied to social welfare — though unanimity was still required in this domain. Social welfare, including the priority issues of "promoting social inclusion" and "eradicating poverty," was incorporated into the European social program appended to the Treaty of Nice in December 2000. The Employment Committee and the Social Protection Committee (created by the Treaty of Nice to administer the convergence policies) would both be called on to develop the *Broad Economic Policy Guidelines* (BEPG).[77]

Considering that henceforth the return to sustained economic growth and full employment would not lead to a spontaneous decrease in poverty and exclusion within the EU, but would, on the contrary, make "their persistence more unacceptable," the European Council meeting in Nice required that each member state implement "from now until June 2001, the open method of coordination...a National Action Plan to combat poverty and social exclusion over a two-year period, based on jointly set goals. This plan specifies the objectives of national policies and the indicators used to evaluate the results."[78]

It is still too early to assess the real impact of these new strategies for employment and social welfare. Even with the benefit of hindsight and information on European employment policy, all that can be said is that it is now common practice to refer to "the promotion of employment as a universal solution to all social problems."[79] In fact, the decrease in unemployment in Europe at the turn of the new millennium is probably due more to a "return to growth rather than a significant change in the methods of labour-market regulation."[80]

Moreover, even if the European employment strategy has had an effect, it is difficult to determine how much of this is due to its method and how much to its policy. Although the process created an "unquestionable obligation to act," "the guidelines under the title 'Employment' in the Treaty are indicative only, and the examination of National Plans by the Commission does not include any sanction."[81] The limitations of the open method of coordination are thus similar to those of any incentive-based policy. They were recognized by the EC authorities, which, in the case of economic convergence, imposed obligations and sanctions.

Lastly, EC employment policies "mobilize only very limited funds," hence the lack of financial incentives, which might be the reason why member states merely present pre-established national policies within the framework of the EU's priority guidelines. The guidelines adopted at the European level are in fact quite flexible for member states.[82]

Some actors and observers nevertheless believe that this process has great potential and that "the political pressure on member states should not be underestimated. The process of multilateral surveillance takes shape gradually and the examination of implemented policies by peers is conducted without leniency...The media and political impact of critical recommendations on such a sensitive subject as employment is obvious and need not be backed up by legal or financial sanctions."[83] Furthermore, the NEAPs can have a political impact within member states by altering the balance of power and arbitration between the employment and finance administrations while fostering "the involvement of national actors in Community projects."[84]

Lastly, the open method of coordination in the area of employment policy has created a powerful dynamic, among European bureaucratic and political elites, in favour of full employment. It has also reduced the influence of supporters of a restrictive policy who are concerned more with monetary stability than economic growth.[85]

This makes one wonder if the rather mixed results of the European employment strategy are not due to the economic orientation and the very content of the policies advocated. During the 1990s, the European Commission adjusted its ideology away from reinforcing workers' rights in favour of a neoliberal social program of wage restraint and labour market flexibility.[86] Within the Labour/Social Affairs Council "the lack of consensus on content and the clash of positions among member states, which are sometimes in direct opposition and tend to cancel each other out, give a clear advantage to the initial authority, in this case the Commission."[87] Clearly, the results of the strategy adopted depend largely on the commission's ideological position.

Given this situation, observers believe there was a structural change in the "European social model" put forward by European institutions whereby the redistributive model of solidarity gave way to a model of competitive and productivist solidarity.[88]

But the year 2000 might have been a turning point for this neoliberal conception of social Europe. The application of the open method of coordination to social welfare was accompanied by a reorientation in the European social program at the Summit of Lisbon and in the European Social Agenda appended to the Treaty of Nice.[89] In the agenda, four themes that had been taboo in the 1990s[90] re-emerged: the "return to full employment," the "reduction of inequalities," an "affirmation that social matters cannot be reduced to economics even though they should contribute to economic development," and the rejection of a "simple dichotomy between the state and the market with a place for social economy and civil society."[91]

This reorientation, which is not merely rhetorical and could signal a new course of action, is reminiscent of that observed in Canada between 1995 and 1999. It reflects the same contradiction between a neoliberal program and the need to rectify social and regional inequalities, in order to ensure social cohesion and maintain a territorial link in the context of an intergovernmental federalism subject to centrifugal forces.[92] Yet the open method of coordination is insufficient to resolve a problem of such magnitude. In order to have all member states follow the same "benchmarking" (which requires additional expenses) — for example, fight exclusion and eradicate poverty — the EU cannot avoid engaging in considerable financial redistribution.[93]

In view of "the necessity to fully take into account the principle of subsidiarity and the differences in traditions and situations, on social and employment matters, between the member states,"[94] the open method of coordination is a means of bypassing the principle of subsidiarity, which, in the area of social welfare, leads to the veto.[95] However, this method is justified only if the goal is to reduce the disparity among member states in terms of resources, and it therefore cannot only take the form of "soft law." The development of social Europe thus depends on the EU increasing its budget,[96] given the limits imposed on its spending power by Agenda 2000, signed in 1999 in Cologne. The open method of coordination can help foster awareness of the need to extend the EU's taxing power, but it cannot replace a truly democratic European government,[97] the starting point for a federal government with sufficient taxing power to administer equalization.[98]

Thus, despite — or because of — its recent institutional innovations, Europe is, like Canada, at a crossroads: the financial program established at Cologne is as great an obstacle to the EU as SUFA is to the Canadian federation. Of course, in Europe the impasse is financial, whereas in Canada it is regulatory and even constitutional. This is another reflection of the the EU's and Canada's opposite trajectories along the axis of multinational federalization.

The political process of constructing social Europe raises the issue of the possible political configurations in the EU itself. As in the case of Canada, this issue can be understood in light of four scenarios (see table 2) constructed by cross-tabulating two variables. One, which reflects the degree of political sovereignty — strong or weak — that member states would preserve, is correlated with the interstate or intrastate configuration that the EU would take. The other, which is specific to the social dimension and solidarity, corresponds to the presence or absence of EC funding in addition to national funding.[99]

Scenario *a*, called "Confederalism" and "Europe at a standstill," is espoused mainly by the United Kingdom but also by Denmark and Sweden, which reject monetary integration. In this scenario, member states jealously guard the maximum powers. Scenario *b*, named "American-style federalism" and "Liberal Europe," is the hegemony of the supranational, which moves ahead while hiding behind the "laws of the market," with the rules of competition and respect for the "four freedoms" assured by the European Court of Justice. This is the scenario favoured by the neoliberal eurocracy, those who hold positions mainly in the European Commission's most influential directorates of economic affairs, finance and competition.

The current political debate in Europe is polarized between these two scenarios, an indication of how difficult it is for the actors and public opinion to understand the issues involved in European construction and the consequences of the financial impasse. In both scenarios the political and social choices are in fact disposed of: in one there is a struggle to maintain the status quo, while in the other social choices are left to the market. While these scenarios do not offer solutions to the socio-economic and socio-political problems posed by the transition to the euro, they are relevant as "nondecision" or "go-with-the-flow" scenarios. On the other hand, scenario *c*, "social integration Europe," and scenario *d*, "Europe of equality in respect of differences," leave much room for politics.

Scenario *c*, illustrated by the creation of the Common Agricultural Policy on the inception of the EC, is espoused by a number of member states — France (under François Mitterrand and Jacques Delors when he was president of the European Commission), Italy and Belgium, as well as Germany. It corresponds to a high degree of political and social integration, with institutional harmonization and a hierarchical configuration of powers between the EU and member states. As with scenario *b*, this is an intrastate-type of federalism, as illustrated by the organization of the European Central Bank.

Scenario *d*, which builds on the current European institutional arrangements characterized by the absence of a clear hierarchy, a blend of the supranational and the intergovernmental, and the potential for enhanced cooperation and open coordination, leaves room for EC funding and a single currency. In this scenario, affirmation of the need for a democratic European government is coupled with a will to limit the EU's role to "high politics" (common defence, maintaining peace among member states, management of common public goods such as currency, coordination of national policies with potential cross-border impact, common welfare standards, etc.). Currently this scenario is espoused by disparate forces in the intellectual community,

Table 2

Four Scenarios for the Development of European Integration

Political Model ⇒ / Social solidarity space ⬇	Interstate		Intrastate	
	Principle of mutual recognition	Maintenance of national characteristics	Supranational harmonization	Principle of convergence
	Scenario a		*Scenario b*	
Maintaining national space	Primacy of intergovernmental *Confederalism*	Absolute: "Europe at a standstill"	Through the market: "liberal Europe"	Strong and centralized union based in law: *American-style federalism*
	Scenario d		*Scenario c*	
Development of EC funding	Balance between intergovernmental and supranational *Canadian-style federalism*	Relative: "Europe of equality in respect of differences"	Through politics: "Social integration Europe"	Strong and centralized union based on currency: *German-style federalism*

Source: Théret (2001a, p. 21).

rather than by the political and bureaucratic communities.[100] Nevertheless, given the fact that, since Maastricht, European institutions have attempted to reconcile the principle of subsidiarity with development of the EU's social powers; intergovernmentalism with supranationalism; and recognition of member states' historical, cultural and social characteristics with economic, monetary and political integration scenario *d* increasingly makes more sense.

In addition to the consensus-based promotion of the open method of coordination almost as a standard in view of social integration, two factors make scenario *d* the most likely trajectory toward political integration. It entails less financial interference by the EU in national affairs, and it is open to compromise with supporters of the other scenarios. Faced with political and social problems resulting from the construction of a "liberal Europe," the supporters of scenario *b* should retreat to the "social integration Europe" camp (scenario *c*), opting for a reorientation of supranationalism toward intrastate federalism, as did the European Council at the end of the 1990s. However, given the difficulties in achieving social harmonization and the resistance of supporters of intergovernmentalism, supporters of a "Europe of equality in respect of differences" (an official objective of benchmarking and open coordination) should attract their attention. Inasmuch as they are aware of the importance, from the sovereignist viewpoint, of defining a clearer division of powers between the EU and member states, supporters of "Europe at a standstill" (scenario *a*) should come closer to this scenario as well.

The possible adoption of the "Canadian model" by an EU that is faced with the social policy issue and must therefore mobilize a cooperative executive federalism (open method of coordination) open to asymmetry (enhanced cooperation) shows that Europe and Canada are on similar trajectories toward intergovernmental multinational federalism.[101] However, this is only one possibility. Although it is certainly in line with the structural trend toward institutional and historical configuration, it is not the inevitable outcome. History has taught us not to rely too heavily on the "wisdom of nations." Other models of a divided Europe, or a Europe of "varying geometry" (*Europe à géométrie variable*), can also be envisaged.[102]

The fact remains that the EU's federalization challenge — to simultaneously broaden its democratic foundations (and thus become more heterogeneous) and also deepen them — echoes Canada's multinationalization challenge. The fact that Europe and Canada have experimented with similar instruments in taking up this challenge indicates that they are on promising trajectories. If the right to opt out in Canada is reflected in the EU's enhanced cooperation, and if collaborative federalism is reflected in the open method of coordination, it is because the scope of these institutional innovations extends beyond the particular contexts that gave rise to them.

Conclusion

I N THE CONTEXT OF GLOBALIZATION AND POLITICAL POLYCENTRISM, "THE EU STANDS apart, because it has given rise to a proliferation of powers, concurrent or shared by member states and even regions and firms. Therefore the EU is a true laboratory, perhaps the most advanced experiment in a federalism involving several levels of government."[103]

On the other side of the Atlantic, despite existing tensions,

> the Canadian experiment [also] appears to be an avant-garde experiment in the peaceful, democratic search for a federal system that, without being highly centralized, is strong enough to counterbalance a periphery filled with differentiated statuses. Current debates about the EU, arguments about the "stable core," multi-speed Europe, and concentric circles reflect a degree of Canadianization of ongoing processes... The Canadian Confederation and the European Union have, depending on traditions, undertaken different steps and processes in their difficult quest for a new political legitimacy. In democracies, this search...calls into question the traditional concepts of sovereignty, federation and confederation, as well as the barriers separating domestic from international law, and thus traditional ways of thinking.[104]

These views appear to be supported by the recent histories of the social union in Canada and of social Europe. We have seen that the scenarios of the American model of the United States of Europe and that of legal and market attempts to harmonize the political and social institutions of the various member states are both shaky. The idea that Europe ultimately will become a truly multinational federation is gaining ground. Europe will have to recognize, indeed build on, its differences and deal with asymmetries in the context of an intergovernmental cooperative federalism (and thus abandon German-style federalism) in which federal authorities will not have the legitimacy, at the national level, to reduce member states to mere decentralized, territorial collectivities.

In Canada as well, the time has come for multinational federalism and official recognition of existing asymmetries. What we have seen in the social union process is a redeployment of the institutional innovations that were at the root of a Canada-wide welfare state developed along European rather than American lines. These innovations have helped maintain the constitutional prerogatives of the provinces in the social field. SUFA appears to have put a temporary halt to this dynamic. The recent pragmatic evolution of European institutions is mobilizing these same institutional formulas, which is proof that they can contribute to resolving the problems presented by intergovernmental federalism in the context of the multinationalization of large political entities. This should provide Canada with a reason to update the formulas and institutionalize them.

The Canadian and European experiences legitimize and thus reinforce each other. At a time when the United Nations' international Westphalian system is in crisis, there is a pressing need for a new political order. This cross-sectional analysis of experiences on both sides of the Atlantic is intended to contribute to a discussion of the institutional mechanisms that might help us to build and understand federal pacts that are better suited to the current context of globalization.

The social and interregional equalization carried out by the Canadian federal government mirrors one of the main challenges to the multinational political and social construction of Europe. By the same token, the institutionalization of enhanced cooperation within the EU and the development of a new, open method of coordinating national policies show that the main stumbling block to multinationalism in Canada is the federal government's failure to institutionally recognize Quebec's national specificity and to truly regulate federal spending power through the use of the opting-out formula.

1   Leslie (1991, 1996).

2   Turp (2000); Rocher (1998).

3   Leslie (1991, p. viii).

4   Leslie (1991, p. ix).

5   Rocher (1998, p. 111); Norrie and Percy (1998, p. 83).

6   Rocher (1994); Martin (1995).

7   Norrie and Percy (1998, p. 83).

8   Parizeau, Bouchard and Dumont (1995).

9   Rocher (1998, p. 121).

10   Rocher (1998, p. 124).

11   On the question of the United Nations' Westphalian system, see Caporaso (1996) and Dehove (1997).

12   Dehove (1997).

13   Van Kersbergen (1997).

14   Noël (1998, p. 242).

15   Vaillancourt (1992).

16   Leibfried and Pierson (1995).

17   Beer (1995).

18   Resnick (1994); Cairns (1995, 2000); Laforest and Gibbins (1998); Poirier (1999).

19   In this figure Canada is described as a centralized federation because, constitutionally, Ottawa has residual powers (for jurisdictions not explicitly assigned to either level of government) and the right to disallow provincial laws; it also has de facto — if not always de jure — spending power in fields of provincial jurisdiction. The federal government's power is, ultimately, always superior to that of the federated entities.

20   Cairns (2000, pp. 8, 11, 12).

21   The question of the constitution of federations of Aboriginal groups also comes up in discussions about how many may claim to be nations (Cairns 2000, pp. 9, 11).

22   Boismenu and Jenson (1997).

23   Croisat and Quermonne (1999).

24   Doern (1992).

25   Simeon (1972) [translation].

26   Simeon (1972); Smiley (1977); Courchene (1986); Smiley and Watts (1986).

27   Sbragia (1993); Croisat and Quermonne (1999); Dehove and Théret (2000).

28   Théret (2000).

29   Banting (1985); Scharpf (1988); Héritier (1999).

30   Leman (1977); Maioni (1992).

31   Empire building corresponds to the construction of institutional fortresses (such as the Social Security Administration in the United States after the New Deal) in which innovators from the last great open crisis of the established political system are entrenched. In the United States, it is associated with targeting because the compromises between Washington and the federated states, which, under the permanent regime, the American political system imposes on all other institutional fields, drive the residual and targeted policies. See Leman (1977) and Maioni (1992).

32   Théret (1997, pp. 122-124, 148-154).

33   Poirier (1999, pp. 53-55).

34   The provinces can also try to maintain or recover their constitutional powers by exercising them in an innovative way (province building).

35   Nevertheless, spending power can also be subject to legal challenges (Poirier, 1999). In the case of a successful challenge, the federal government must use constitutional amendments to intervene (this was true of the unemployment insurance program, for example).

36   For a descriptive synthesis of various theories used to explain the methods of European construction, see Tsebelis and Kreppel (1998).

37   Haas (1958).

38   Nye (1971).

39   "The term 'agenda setting' refers to who introduces the specific wording of legislation, and has to be differentiated from the initiation of legislation. We focus on the specific wording and not on the mere general idea of it, because of the obvious regulatory consequences of the wording: changing the date of enforcement of a rule, or the limit amount of a substance, has significant redistributive consequences among countries as well as among companies and individuals.

The qualifier 'conditional' refers to the fact that the Council can ultimately decide to modify the Commission's proposal, but such a modification requires a unanimous decision" (Tsebelis and Kreppel, 1998, pp. 41-42). The European Parliament also has this power, though to a lesser degree.

. 40 As Johanne Poirier has pointed out to me, it is also easier for a Canadian province to accept this spending power when it is used than to contest it by trying to recover corresponding federal resources for itself by invoking the opting-out formula.

41 Héritier (1999); Dehove and Théret (2000). These strategies obviously continue to be used in the many fields that still require a unanimous vote.

42 Wallace (1994, p. 75).

43 Wallace (1994, pp. 67, 80).

44 It is therefore not surprising to find that for nearly 30 years the original treaties were not amended and that many of their articles fell into disuse.

45 Boismenu and Jenson (1997, p. 131) [translation].

46 Boismenu and Jenson (1997).

47 Noël (2000a).

48 The agreement emerged out of an alliance between the federal government and the small provinces that are most dependent on federal transfers. It was ratified by Ontario and Alberta in exchange for a substantial increase in transfer payments under the Canada Health and Social Transfer (CHST) and the indexing of transfers on the basis of population.

49 Robson and Schwanen (1999); Gagnon and Segal (2000).

50 Boismenu and Jenson (1997).

51 Noël (2000a).

52 See Yves Vaillancourt's chapter in this volume.

53 The solution adopted for the National Child Benefit may be seen as foreshadowing such an agreement since the federal government pays Quebec families even though the Quebec government has not made a commitment based on its own family policy.

54 Kymlicka (1998).

55 This concept is expressed from a leftist perspective by the Canadian Policy Research Networks, for whom the goal of the social union is to support a political approach that limits the social and political risks to Canada of the federal globalization strategy. For this group, the social union is all the rights and obligations of Canadian citizens and governments that confer significance and act on the sense of collective destiny. The social union embodies the sense of collective responsibility among citizens, the federal pact (between and among the regions) and the contract (between citizens and governments) relative to the management of public affairs. It can be perceived as a factor of integration of values and behaviours in three broad areas: policies and social programs, federalism and intergovernmental relations, and democratic commitment and public responsibility (O'Hara, 1998, p. 5). To sum up, the social union helps to articulate the three dimensions — social, territorial and democratic — of Canadian citizenship.

56 Noël (1998).

57 Robinson (1995).

58 Jenson (1998).

59 See Roger Gibbins' chapter in this volume.

60 Bourne (1995).

61 See Michael Prince's chapter in this volume.

62 Battle (1997).

63 Boismenu and Jenson (1997).

64 Battle (1997, p. 115).

65 Noël (2000b).

66 Venturini (1998).

67 Rhodes (1995, p. 112).

68 The similarity is even more striking if one recalls that Quebec, while considerably influencing the organization of this plan, which it continued to help administer, withdrew from it and implemented its own plan (Banting, 1985). In fact, in 1989, when the European Protocol was presented, "the British managed to dilute the substance and alter the spirit of a document to

which it finally did not subscribe," as the Social Charter referred no longer to the social rights of citizens but rather to those of workers, thus reducing it to an instrument subordinate to the achievement of a single market (Rhodes, 1995, pp. 96-97). This no doubt helped Tony Blair in 1997, when the Treaty of Amsterdam was signed.

69 Rhodes (1995).

70 Venturini (1998).

71 Aubin (1999, p. 113).

72 Quermonne (1999, p. 73) [translation]. In the report on the reform of European institutions, produced by the French Commissariat général du plan, chaired by Jean-Louis Quermonne — who is in favour of the political integration of Europe — this codification is deemed "too constraining," "too limited" and "legally vague." Enhanced cooperation "must involve a majority of member states, must be a decision of the Council with a qualified majority, but can be appealed before the European Council, which has to agree unanimously, and…can intervene only 'as a last resort, when the objectives of the treaties cannot be achieved by applying the relevant procedures that were provided for'; moreover, it excludes 'the entire foreign and common security policy'; lastly, it is not known whether new forms of enhanced cooperation 'outside the Treaty' are still possible since the Treaty of Amsterdam came into force" (p. 73). Moreover, it should be noted that the definition of enhanced cooperation was again specified in the Treaty of Nice (cf. European Council 2000, pp. 12-20).

73 Atkinson (2000, p. 57).

74 Aubin (1999, p. 114). For details of these guidelines and a definition of the four pillars under which they are grouped, see Barbier (1998, pp. 366-367) and Aubin (1999, pp. 117-118).

75 Barbier (2000).

76 Atkinson (2000, p. 57).

77 Council (Employment and Social Policy), (2000).

78 Conseil Européen 2000, appendix I to "conclusions de la présidence," "Agenda social européen," p. 14 [translation]. The open method of coordination also calls for the exchange of experiences and the generalization of best practices from state to state, which resembles the Canadian method of building the welfare state on the basis of provincial innovations (Théret, 1997). Moreover, it can be observed that, as in the case of the NCB in Canada, the European "social union" was formed by making poverty a priority issue.

79 Barbier (2001) [translation].

80 Chassard (2001, p. 23) [translation].

81 Barbier (1999) [translation].

82 Barbier (2000).

83 Aubin (1999, p. 121). Thus, as governments are obliged to justify their actions according to a common framework of different realities and assess them in light of results achieved elsewhere, "soft convergence" establishes ideas and categories that "provide a cognitive matrix, already widely accepted and internalized, which structures national public actions well beyond their incentive aspect" (Rouault 2000, pp. 16-17) [translation].

84 Aubin (1999, p. 120).

85 Chassard (2001, p. 23).

86 Chassard (2001, p. 23).

87 Aubin (1999, p. 116) [translation].

88 Streeck (1999, p. 4).

89 Conseil Européen (2000).

90 Math (2000); Chambaz (2000).

91 Conseil Européen (2000, pp. 4, 5) [translation].

92 Théret (1999, 2001b).

93 On the subject of eradicating poverty, the Belgian government proposed that all member states match the average performance of the three member states that are most effective in this area; according to some estimates, this would have meant reducing the average European poverty rate from 18 to 12 percent and increasing social transfers by 2 percent of GNP (Atkinson, 2000).

94   Conseil Européen (2000, p. 8).

95   This is no doubt why it has become a kind
      of general standard for EC intervention,
      including in the field of education
      (Ministère de l'Éducation nationale, 2001).
      On the need for legitimity, which pushes
      the EU and the Canadian government to
      "invest" in social welfare, see Poirier (2001)
      and Théret (2001a).

96   Chassard (2001, p. 25).

97   Boyer and Dehove (2001, pp. 188-189).

98   The paucity of structural funds is not the
      only problem. Their operating logic is also
      inadequate since it is based not on equal-
      ization but on non-recurring, targeted and
      conditional distribution, which is closer to
      the logic of American grants-in-aid than to
      that of Canadian transfer programs. On this
      point, see Anderson (1995), Smith (1997)
      and Rouault (2000).

99   Maurice (1999, p. 101) presents four other
      scenarios. They are similar to those presented
      here but do not include the problem of sover-
      eignty, no doubt for political reasons (this is
      an official report commissioned by the French
      government). Moreover, the "sovereignty"
      variable may be seen as concealing a variable
      that is more economic in nature and linked to
      interstate labour mobility as an adjusted vari-
      able (Théret, 2001a, p. 23).

100   It is referred to in a series of texts, includ-
      ing official reports. See Leibfried (1994);
      Wallace (1994); Leibfried and Pierson
      (1995); Croisat (1996); Dehove (1997);
      Théret (1997); Maurice (1999);
      Quermonne (1999); Croisat and
      Quermonne (1999); Dehove and Théret
      (2000); Théret (2001a); Boyer and Dehove
      (2001). Most striking politically is Jacques
      Delors's recent conversion to the idea of a
      federation of nation-states.

101   This similarity can be extended to the other
      scenarios, as may be seen when one com-
      pares tables 1 and 2.

102   Leifried (1994); Dehove (1997).

103   Croisat and Quermonne (1999, p. 60)
      [translation].

104   Croisat (1996, p. 258) [translation].

Anderson, J. J. "Structural Funds and the Social Dimension of EU Policy: Springboard or Stumbling Block?" In *European Social Policy: Between Fragmentation and Integration*, ed. S. Leibfried and P. Pierson. Washington, DC: Brookings Institution, 1995.

Atkinson, T. "Agenda social européen: comparaison des pauvretés et transferts sociaux." In *Questions européennes: Conseil d'analyse économique*. Paris: La documentation française, 2000.

Aubin, C. "Comment Bruxelles traite du social: l'exemple de la stratégie européenne pour l'emploi." *Revue française des affaires sociales*, Vol. 53, no. 3-4 (December 1999): 107-124.

Banting, K.G. "Federalism and Income Security: Themes and Variations." In *Ottawa and the Provinces: The Distribution of Money and Power*, Vol. 1, ed. T. J. Courchene, D. W. Conklin and G. A. Cook. Toronto: Ontario Economic Council, 1985.

Barbier, J.-C. "Europe sociale: l'emploi d'abord." *Centre d'Études de l'Emploi*, no. 44 (March 2001).

———. "La Stratégie européenne pour l'emploi, deux ans après." *Centre d'Études de l'Emploi*, no. 37 (January 2000).

———. "La stratégie européenne pour l'emploi: limites et potentialités." *Centre d'Études de l'Emploi*, no. 31 (January 1999).

———. "À la recherche de la politique européenne de l'emploi." In *Les politiques de l'emploi en Europe et aux États-Unis*, ed. J. Barbier and J. Gauthié. Paris: PUF, 1998.

Battle, K. "The 1997 Budget and the Child Benefits Package." In *The 1997 Federal Budget: Retrospect and Prospect*, ed. T.J. Courchene and T.A. Wilson. Kingston and Toronto: John Deutsch Institute for the Study of Economic Policy, Queen's University, Institute for Policy Analysis, University of Toronto, 1997.

Beer, S. H. "Federalism and the Nation State: What Can Be Learned from the American Experience?" In *Rethinking Federalism: Citizens, Markets, and Governments in a Changing World*, ed. K. Knop, S. Ostry, R. Simeon and K. Swinton. Vancouver: University of British Columbia Press, 1995.

Boismenu, G., and J. Jenson. "La dislocation du régime de citoyenneté canadien et l'évolution du régime fédératif." *Cahiers d'Histoire*, Vol. 17, no. 1-2 (1997): 126-146.

———. "A Social Union or a Federal State? Competing Visions of Intergovernmental Relations in the New Liberal Era." In *How Ottawa Spends, 1998–99: Balancing Act*, ed. Leslie A. Pal. Toronto: Lorimer, 1990.

Bourne, L.S. "Living on the Periphery: Regional Science and the Future of the Canadian Experiment." *Canadian Journal of Regional Science*. Vol. XVIII, no. 1 (spring 1995): 21-37.

Boyer, R., and M. Dehove. "Du 'gouvernement économique' au gouvernement tout court: Vers un fédéralisme à l'européenne." *Critique internationale*, no. 11 (2001): 179-195.

Cairns, A.C. "Searching for Multinational Canada: The Rhetoric of Confusion." *Center for Constitutional Studies*, April 13, 2000 (mimeo).

———. "Constitutional Government and the Two Faces of Ethnicity: Federalism Is Not Enough." In *Rethinking Federalism: Citizens, Markets, and Governments in a Changing World*, ed. K. Knop, S. Ostry, R. Simeon and K. Swinton. Vancouver: University of British Columbia Press, 1995.

Caporaso, J.A. "The European Union and Forms of the State: Wesphalian, Regulatory or Post-Modern?" *Journal of Common Market Studies*, Vol. 34, no. 1 (March 1996): 29-52.

Chambaz, C. "Inégalités et discriminations: indicateurs statistiques et débats européens." In *Réduire les inégalités: quel rôle pour la protection sociale?*, ed. C. Daniel and C. Le Clainche. Paris: DREES-MIRE, 2000.

Chassard, Y. "European Integration and Social Protection: From the Spaak Report to the Open Method of Cooperation." In *Social Exclusion and Social Protection: The Future Role for the European Union*, ed. I. Begg and D. Mayes. London: Edward Elgar, 2001.

Conseil européen. Agenda social européen, Annexe I aux conclusions de la présidence, Nice, 7-9 December, 2000.

Council (Employment and Social Policy). *Outcomes of Proceedings: Follow-up of the Lisbon European Council — Conclusions of the Council (Employment and Social Policy) of 6 June 2000.* Brussels: CCE, 2000.

Courchene, T.J. *La gestion économique et le partage des pouvoirs.* Ottawa: Supply and Services Canada, 1986.

Croisat, M. "Le fédéralisme dans l'Union Européenne au regard de l'expérience canadienne." In *De la cinquième République à l'Europe: Hommage à Jean-Louis Quermonne,* ed. F. d'Arcy and L. Rouban. Paris: Presses de la Fondation nationale de sciences politiques, 1996.

Croisat, M., and J. Quermonne. *L'Europe et le fédéralisme.* Paris: Montchrestien, 1999.

Dehove, M. "L'Union européenne inaugure-t-elle un nouveau grand régime d'organisation des pouvoirs publics et de la société internationale ?" *L'Année de la régulation,* Vol. 1 (1997).

Dehove, M., and B. Théret. "L'Union européenne comme innovation institutionnelle." In *Innovations institutionnelles et territoires,* ed. M. Tallard, B. Théret and D. Uri. Paris: L'Harmattan, 2000.

Doern, G.B. *Europe Uniting: The EC Model and Canada's Constitutional Debate.* Toronto: C.D. Howe Institute, 1992.

European Council. *Treaty of Nice: Provisional text Approved by the Intergovernmental Conference on Institutional Reform,* 7–9 December 2000. Brussels: Conference of the Representatives of the Governments of the Member States.

Gagnon, A.-G., and Hugh Segal, eds. *The Canadian Social Union without Quebec: 8 Critical Analyses.* Montreal: Institute for Research on Public Policy and Quebec Studies Program of McGill University, 2000.

Haas, E. *The Uniting of Europe.* London: Stevens Press, 1958.

Héritier, A. *Policy Making and Diversity in Europe — Escaping the Deadlocks.* Cambridge: Cambridge University Press, 1999.

Jenson, J. "Recognising Difference: Distinct Societies, Citizenship Regimes and Partnership." In *Beyond the Impasse: Towards Reconciliation,* ed. Guy Laforest and Roger Gibbins. Montreal: Institute for Research on Public Policy, 1998.

Kymlicka, W. "Multinational Federalism in Canada: Rethinking the Partnership." In *Beyond the Impasse: Towards Reconciliation,* ed. Guy Laforest and Roger Gibbins. Montreal: Institute for Research on Public Policy, 1998.

Laforest, Guy, and Roger Gibbins, eds. *Beyond the Impasse: Towards Reconciliation.* Montreal: IRPP, 1998.

Leibfried, S. "The Social Dimension of the European Union: En Route to Positively Joint Sovereignty." *Journal of European Social Policy,* Vol. 4, no. 4 (November 1994): 239-262.

Leibfried, S., and P. Pierson, eds. *European Social Policy: Between Fragmentation and Integration.* Washington: Brookings Institution, 1995.

Leman, C. "Patterns of Policy Development: Social Security in the United States and Canada." *Public Policy,* Vol. 25, no. 2 (1977): 261-280.

Leslie, P.M. *Le modèle de Maastricht: Point de vue canadien sur l'Union européenne.* Kingston: Institute for Intergovernmental Relations, Queen's University, 1996.

——. *La communauté européenne: Un modèle politique pour le Canada.* Ottawa: Supply and Services Canada, 1991.

Maioni, A. *Explaining Differences in Welfare State Development: A Comparative Study of Health Insurance in Canada and the United States.* Doctoral dissertation. Evanston, IL: Northwestern University, 1992.

Martin, P. "Le nationalisme québécois et le choix du libre-échange continental." In *L'espace québécois,* ed. A. Gagnon and A. Noël. Montreal: Éditions Québec/Amérique, 1995.

Math, A. "Protection sociale et inégalités: les débats européens." In *Réduire les inégalités:*

quel rôle pour la protection sociale?, ed.
C. Daniel and C. Le Clainche. Paris:
DREES-MIRE, 2000.

Maurice, J., ed. *Emploi, négociations collectives,
protection sociale: vers quelle Europe sociale?*
Paris: La documentation française —
Commissariat Général du Plan, 1999.

Ministère de l'éducation nationale. "Sommet
européen des chefs d'État et de gouvernement de Nice: principales conclusions de la
Présidence française dans le domaine de
l'éducation." *La lettre Flash*. Paris: Ministère
de l'éducation nationale, 2001.

Noël, A. "General Study of the Framework
Agreement." In *The Canadian Social Union
without Quebec: 8 Critical Analyses*, ed.
Alain-G. Gagnon and Hugh Segal.
Montreal: Institute for Research on Public
Policy and Quebec Studies Program of
McGill University, 2000*a*.

———. "Without Quebec: Collaborative
Federalism with a Footnote?" *Policy Matters*,
Vol. 1, no. 2 (March 2000*b*).

———. "The Federal Principle, Solidarity and
Partnership." In *Beyond the Impasse: Towards
Reconciliation*, ed. Guy Laforest and Roger
Gibbins. Montreal: Institute for Research on
Public Policy, 1998.

Norrie, K., and M. Percy. "A Canada-Quebec
Partnership: The Economic Dimensions." In
Beyond the Impasse: Towards Reconciliation,
ed. Guy Laforest and Roger Gibbins.
Montreal: Institute for Research on Public
Policy, 1998.

Nye, J. "Comparing common markets: A Revised
Neofunctional Model." In *Regional Integration*,
ed. L. Lindberg and S. Scheingold. Cambridge,
MA: Harvard University Press, 1971.

O'Hara, K. "Renforcer l'Union sociale: les
prochaines étapes." *Réflexion*, no. 2
(November 1998).

Parizeau, Jacques, Lucien Bouchard and Mario
Dumont. *Texte de l'entente de principe entre le
Parti québécois, le Bloc québécois et l'Action démoc-
ratique du Québec*. Montreal: June 9, 1995.

Poirier, J. "Le défi de la cohésion sociale dans les
espaces politiques multinationaux: La

décentralisation du pouvoir normatif dans
le domaine social en Europe et au Canada."
Communication au Colloque sur la cohésion sociale, Université du Québec à
Montréal, January 2001.

———. "The Social Union: Solution or Challenge
for Canadian Federalism?" In *Sociaal Beleid
en Federalisme*, ed. S. Vansteenkiste and
M. Taeymans. Brussels: Larcier, 1999.

Quermonne, J., ed. *L'Union européenne en quête
d'institutions légitimes et efficaces*. Paris : La
documentation française, Commissariat
Général du Plan, 1999.

Resnick, P. "Toward a Multinational
Federalism: Asymetrical and Confederal
Alternatives." In *Seeking a New Canadian
Partnership: Asymetrical and Confederal
Options*, ed. F. Leslie Seidle. Montreal:
Institute for Research on Public Policy,
1994.

Rhodes, M. "A Regulatory Conundrum:
Industrial Relations and the Social
Dimension." In *European Social Policy:
Between Fragmentation and Integration*, ed. S.
Leibfried and P. Pierson. Washington DC:
Brookings Institution, 1995.

Robinson, I. "Trade Policy, Globalization, and the
Future of Canadian Federalism." In *New
Trends in Canadian Federalism*, ed. F. Rocher
and M. Smith. Peterborough: Broadview
Press, 1995.

Robson, W.B.P., and D. Schwanen. "The Social
Union Agreement: Too Flawed to Last."
Backgrounder. Toronto: C.D. Howe
Institute, 1999.

Rocher, F. "Economic Partnership and Political
Integration: Recasting Quebec-Canada's
Economic Union." In *Beyond the Impasse:
Towards Reconciliation*, ed. Guy Laforest and
Roger Gibbins. Montreal: Institute for
Research on Public Policy, 1998.

———. "Le Québec en Amérique du Nord: la
stratégie continentale." In *Québec: État et
société*, ed. Alain-G. Gagnon. Montreal:
Éditions Québec/Amérique, 1994.

Rouault, S. "De l'insertion professionnelle à la
valorisation du capital humain: un change-

ment de paradigme accompagné par l'Union européenne?" *Politique européenne*, L'Europe sociale, no. 2 (2000).

Sbragia, A.M. "The European Community: A Balancing Act." *Publius: The Journal of Federalism*, Vol. 23, no. 3 (Summer 1993): 23-38.

Scharpf, F. W. "The Joint-Decision Trap: Lessons from German Federalism and European Integration." *Public Administration*, Vol. 66 (1998): 239-278.

Simeon, R. *Federal-Provincial Diplomacy: The Making of Recent Policy in Canada*. Toronto: University of Toronto Press, 1972.

Smiley, D.V. "Federal-Provincial Conflict in Canada." In *Canadian Federalism: Myth or Reality?*, ed. J.P. Meekison. Toronto: Methuen, 1977.

Smiley, D.V., and R.L. Watts. *Le fédéralisme intra-étatique au Canada*. Ottawa: Supply and Services Canada, 1986.

Smith, A. "La subsidiarité, la cohésion et la Communauté européenne." In *Territoires et subsidiarité: L'action publique locale à la lumière d'un principe controversé*, ed. A. Faure. Paris: L'Harmattan, 1997.

Streeck, W. "Competitive Solidarity: Rethinking the 'European Social Model'." Max Planck Institute für Gesellschaftsforschung Working Paper, Vol. 99, no. 8 (1999).

Théret, B. "L'Europe sociale, condition de l'Europe politique." In *L'Europe sociale: le défi*, dir. G. Schumacher. Nancy-Nürtingen: FUEVOCOPLU, 2001*a*.

——. "La protection sociale dans le pacte fédéral canadien: Histoire d'une crise et de son dénouement." *Critique internationale*, no. 11 (2001*b*): 145-160.

—— "Régionalisme et fédéralisme: Une analyse comparative de la régulation des tensions économiques entre régions par les programmes de transferts intergouvernementaux fédéraux canadien et américain." *Revista Mexicana de Estudios Canadienses*, Vol. 1, no. 2 (2000): 25-82.

——. *Du fédéralisme et de la protection sociale en Amérique et en particulier au Canada: L'État-providence canadien en perspective historique et comparée avec le système américain de politiques sociales en vue d'en tirer quelques enseignements pour la consolidation sociale de l'Union européenne*. Paris: Commissariat Général du Plan, 1997.

Tsebelis, G., and A. Kreppel. "The History of Conditional Agenda-Setting in European Institutions." *European Journal of Political Research*, Vol. 33, no. 1 (January1998): 41-71.

Turp, D. "États-nations, multinations et organisations supranationales." Intervention aux Treizièmes Entretiens du Centre Jacques Cartier, Université de Montréal, October 4, 2000.

Vaillancourt, Yves. "Un bilan de l'opting out du Québec des programmes fédéraux à frais partagés dans le domaine social (1964-1992)." In *Bilan québécois du fédéralisme canadien*, ed. F. Rocher. Montreal: VLB Éditeur, 1992.

Van Kersbergen, K. "Double Allegiance in European Integration: Publics, Nation-states, and Social Policy." *European University Institute*, Working Paper RSC, Vol. 97, no. 15 (1997).

Venturini, P. "Les perspectives de la politique sociale européenne: quelques réflexions." In *Les enjeux sociaux de l'union économique et monétaire*. Brussels: Observatoire social européen, 1998.

Wallace, W. *Regional Integration: The West European Experience*. Washington: Brookings Institution, 1994.

A F r a m e w o r k t o
I m p r o v e t h e S o c i a l
U n i o n f o r C a n a d i a n s
(t h e S o c i a l U n i o n
F r a m e w o r k
A g r e e m e n t)

T HE FOLLOWING AGREEMENT IS BASED UPON A MUTUAL RESPECT BETWEEN ORDERS OF GOVERN-
   ment and a willingness to work more closely together to meet the needs of Canadians.

1 . P r i n c i p l e s

C ANADA'S SOCIAL UNION SHOULD REFLECT AND GIVE EXPRESSION TO THE FUNDAMEN-
   tal values of Canadians — equality, respect for diversity, fairness, individual
dignity and responsibility, and mutual aid and our responsibilities for one another.

Within their respective constitutional jurisdictions and powers, governments commit to the following principles:

All Canadians Are Equal
◆ Treat all Canadians with fairness and equity
◆ Promote equality of opportunity for all Canadians
◆ Respect the equality, rights and dignity of all Canadian women and
  men and their diverse needs

Meeting the Needs of Canadians
◆ Ensure access for all Canadians, wherever they live or move in Canada, to
  essential social programs and services of reasonably comparable quality
◆ Provide appropriate assistance to those in need
◆ Respect the principles of medicare: comprehensiveness, universality,
  portability, public administration and accessibility
◆ Promote the full and active participation of all Canadians in
  Canada's social and economic life
◆ Work in partnership with individuals, families, communities, volun-
  tary organizations, business and labour, and ensure appropriate
  opportunities for Canadians to have meaningful input into social
  policies and programs

Sustaining Social Programs and Services
◆ Ensure adequate, affordable, stable and sustainable funding for social programs

Aboriginal Peoples of Canada
◆ For greater certainty, nothing in this agreement abrogates or derogates from any Aboriginal, treaty or other rights of Aboriginal peoples including self-government.

2. Mobility within Canada

ALL GOVERNMENTS BELIEVE THAT THE FREEDOM OF MOVEMENT OF CANADIANS TO pursue opportunities anywhere in Canada is an essential element of Canadian citizenship.

Governments will ensure that no new barriers to mobility are created in new social policy initiatives.

Governments will eliminate, within three years, any residency-based policies or practices which constrain access to post-secondary education, training, health and social services and social assistance unless they can be demonstrated to be reasonable and consistent with the principles of the Social Union Framework.

Accordingly, sector Ministers will submit annual reports to the Ministerial Council identifying residency-based barriers to access and providing action plans to eliminate them.

Governments are also committed to ensure, by July 1, 2001, full compliance with the mobility provisions of the *Agreement on Internal Trade* by all entities subject to those provisions, including the requirements for mutual recognition of occupational qualifications and for eliminating residency requirements for access to employment opportunities

3. Informing Canadians — Public Accountability and Transparency

CANADA'S SOCIAL UNION CAN BE STRENGTHENED BY ENHANCING EACH GOVERNMENT'S transparency and accountability to its constituents. Each government therefore agrees to:

Achieving and Measuring Results

◆ Monitor and measure outcomes of its social programs and report regularly to its constituents on the performance of these programs

◆ Share information and best practices to support the development of outcome measures, and work with other governments to develop, over time, comparable indicators to measure progress on agreed objectives

◆ Publicly recognize and explain the respective roles and contributions of governments

◆ Use funds transferred from another order of government for the purposes agreed and pass on increases to its residents

◆ Use third parties, as appropriate, to assist in assessing progress on social priorities

Involvement of Canadians

◆ Ensure effective mechanisms for Canadians to participate in developing social priorities and reviewing outcomes

Ensuring Fair and Transparent Practices

◆ Make eligibility criteria and service commitments for social programs publicly available

◆ Have in place appropriate mechanisms for citizens to appeal unfair administrative practices and bring complaints about access and service

◆ Report publicly on citizens' appeals and complaints, ensuring that confidentiality requirements are met

4. Working in Partnership for Canadians

Joint Planning and Collaboration

THE MINISTERIAL COUNCIL HAS DEMONSTRATED THE BENEFITS OF JOINT PLANNING and mutual help through which governments share knowledge and learn from each other.

Governments therefore agree to

◆ Undertake joint planning to share information on social trends, problems and priorities and to work together to identify priorities for collaborative action

◆ Collaborate on implementation of joint priorities when this would result in more effective and efficient service to Canadians, including as appropriate joint development of objectives and principles, clarification of roles and responsibilities, and flexible implementation to respect diverse needs and circumstances, complement existing measures and avoid duplication

Reciprocal Notice and Consultation

The actions of one government or order of government often have significant effects on other governments. In a manner consistent with the principles of our system of parliamentary government and the budget-making process, governments therefore agree to:

♦ Give one another advance notice prior to implementation of a major change in a social policy or program which will likely substantially affect another government
♦ Offer to consult prior to implementing new social policies and programs that are likely to substantially affect other governments or the social union more generally. Governments participating in these consultations will have the opportunity to identify potential duplication and to propose alternative approaches to achieve flexible and effective implementation

Equitable Treatment

For any new Canada-wide social initiatives, arrangements made with one province/territory will be made available to all provinces/territories in a manner consistent with their diverse circumstances.

Aboriginal Peoples

Governments will work with the Aboriginal peoples of Canada to find practical solutions to address their pressing needs.

5. The Federal Spending Power — Improving Social Programs for Canadians

Social Transfers to Provinces and Territories

THE USE OF THE FEDERAL SPENDING POWER UNDER THE CONSTITUTION HAS BEEN essential to the development of Canada's social union. An important use of the spending power by the Government of Canada has been to transfer money to the provincial and territorial governments. These transfers support the delivery of social programs and services by provinces and territories in order to promote equality of opportunity and mobility for all Canadians and to pursue Canada-wide objectives.

Conditional social transfers have enabled governments to introduce new and innovative social programs, such as Medicare, and to ensure that they are available to all Canadians. When the federal government uses such conditional transfers, whether cost-shared or block-funded, it should proceed in a cooperative manner that is respectful of the provincial and territorial governments and their priorities.

Funding Predictability

The Government of Canada will consult with provincial and territorial governments at least one year prior to renewal or significant funding changes in existing social transfers to provinces/territories, unless otherwise agreed, and will build due notice provisions into any new social transfers to provincial/territorial governments.

New Canada-Wide Initiatives Supported
by Transfers to Provinces and Territories

With respect to any new Canada-wide initiatives in health care, post-secondary education, social assistance and social services that are funded through intergovernmental transfers, whether block-funded or cost-shared, the Government of Canada will:

- ◆ Work collaboratively with all provincial and territorial governments to identify Canada-wide priorities and objectives
- ◆ Not introduce such new initiatives without the agreement of a majority of provincial governments

Each provincial and territorial government will determine the detailed program design and mix best suited to its own needs and circumstances to meet the agreed objectives.

A provincial/territorial government which, because of its existing programming, does not require the total transfer to fulfill the agreed objectives would be able to reinvest any funds not required for those objectives in the same or a related priority area.

The Government of Canada and the provincial/territorial governments will agree on an accountability framework for such new social initiatives and investments.

All provincial and territorial governments that meet or commit to meet the agreed Canada-wide objectives and agree to respect the accountability framework will receive their share of available funding.

Direct Federal Spending

Another use of the federal spending power is making transfers to individuals and to organizations in order to promote equality of opportunity, mobility, and other Canada-wide objectives.

When the federal government introduces new Canada-wide initiatives funded through direct transfers to individuals or organizations for health care, post-secondary education, social assistance and social services, it will, prior to implementation, give at least three months' notice and offer to consult. Governments participating in these consultations will have the opportunity to identify potential duplication and to propose alternative approaches to achieve flexible and effective implementation.

6. Dispute Avoidance and Resolution

G OVERNMENTS ARE COMMITTED TO WORKING COLLABORATIVELY TO AVOID AND resolve intergovernmental disputes. Respecting existing legislative provisions, mechanisms to avoid and resolve disputes should:

- ◆ Be simple, timely, efficient, effective and transparent
- ◆ Allow maximum flexibility for governments to resolve disputes in a non-adversarial way
- ◆ Ensure that sectors design processes appropriate to their needs
- ◆ Provide for appropriate use of third parties for expert assistance and advice while ensuring democratic accountability by elected officials

Dispute avoidance and resolution will apply to commitments on mobility, intergovernmental transfers, interpretation of the *Canada Health Act* principles, and, as appropriate, on any new joint initiative.

Sector Ministers should be guided by the following process, as appropriate:

Dispute Avoidance
- ◆ Governments are committed to working together and avoiding disputes through information-sharing, joint planning, collaboration, advance notice and early consultation, and flexibility in implementation

Sector Negotiations
- ◆ Sector negotiations to resolve disputes will be based on joint fact-finding
- ◆ A written joint fact-finding report will be submitted to governments involved, who will have the opportunity to comment on the report before its completion
- ◆ Governments involved may seek assistance of a third party for fact-finding, advice, or mediation
- ◆ At the request of either party in a dispute, fact-finding or mediation reports will be made public

Review Provisions
- ◆ Any government can require a review of a decision or action one year after it enters into effect or when changing circumstances justify

Each government involved in a dispute may consult and seek advice from third parties, including interested or knowledgeable persons or groups, at all stages of the process.

Governments will report publicly on an annual basis on the nature of intergovernmental disputes and their resolution.

Role of the Ministerial Council

The Ministerial Council will support sector Ministers by collecting information on effective ways of implementing the agreement and avoiding disputes and receiving reports from jurisdictions on progress on commitments under the Social Union Framework Agreement.

7. Review of the Social Union Framework Agreement

BY THE END OF THE THIRD YEAR OF THE FRAMEWORK AGREEMENT, GOVERNMENTS will jointly undertake a full review of the Agreement and its implementation and make appropriate adjustments to the Framework as required. This review will ensure significant opportunities for input and feed-back from Canadians and all interested parties, including social policy experts, private sector and voluntary organizations.

Christian Dufour conducts research and teaches at the École nationale d'administration publique in Montreal. From 1975 to 1987 he worked for the Quebec public service in the field of federal-provincial relations and immigration. From 1987 to 1992 he taught in the Political Science Department at Université Laval. He is the author of *Lettre aux souverainistes québécois et aux fédéralistes canadiens qui sont restés fidèles au Québec* (2000), *La rupture tranquille* (1992) and *A Canadian Challenge: Le défi québécois* (1990). He has also contributed to several edited works and is the author of many articles in academic journals and newspapers.

Sarah Fortin has been with the Institute for Research on Public Policy since September 1997. She has been Research Director for Social Policy since October 2001 and assistant editor of the Institute's magazine, *Policy Options*, since September 2002. She co-directed the project *As I Recall Si je me souviens: Historical Perspectives* (1999) and coordinated the publication of *The Canadian Social Union Without Quebec: Eight Critical Analyses* (2000).

Roger Gibbins has been with the Department of Political Science at the University of Calgary since 1973. In 1998 he became President and CEO of the Canada West Foundation and was elected a Fellow of the Royal Society of Canada. In 1999-2000 he served as President of the Canadian Political Science Association. He has published numerous books, articles and book chapters, most dealing with Western Canadian themes and issues. His most recent publications include *Beyond the Impasse: Towards Reconciliation* (with Guy Laforest, 1998) and *A Better Alberta Advantage: A Proposal to Eliminate Alberta Provincial Personal Income Tax* (2000).

Alain Noël is Professor in the Department of Political Science at Université de Montréal, and director of the Centre de recherche sur les politiques et le développement social at the same institution. He is the author of several studies on federalism and social policy. His most recent publications include *L'aide au conditionnel* (with P. Dufour and G. Boismenu, 2003) and *Labour Market Policy and Federalism: Comparing the Employment Strategies of Federations* (2003). In recent years, he has also acted as an expert consultant for the Quebec government (Secrétariat aux affaires intergouvernementales canadiennes; Ministère de l'Emploi et de la Solidarité). In 2001-2002 he served as a member of Quebec's Commission on Fiscal Imbalance.

Susan D. Phillips is Professor in the School of Public Policy and Administration at Carleton University and Senior Research Associate of the Centre for Voluntary Sector Research and Development, also located at Carleton. Her research focuses on civil society-state relationships in comparative perspective. Her work has been published in numerous academic journals. Her most recent publications include *Urban Affairs: Back on the Policy Agenda* (with Caroline Andrew and Katherine A. Graham, 2002) and *Mapping the Links: Citizen involvement in Policy* Processes with Michael Orsini, 2002).

Michael J. Prince is Lansdowne Professor of Social Policy in the Faculty of Human and Social Development and Acting Dean of Human and Social Development at the University of Victoria. He has been a consultant or adviser to several departments and agencies of the federal government as well as to provincial, territorial, First Nations and local governments, including four Royal commissions. His most recent publications include *Changing the Rules: Canadian Regulatory Regimes and Institutions* (1999) and *Changing Politics of Canadian Social Policy* (with James J. Rice, 2000).

France St-Hilaire is Vice-President, Research, at the Institute for Research on Public Policy. She currently oversees the Institute's research agenda and coordinates ongoing projects on the linkages between economic and social policy. She is the author of a number of monographs and articles in the areas of public finance, social policy and fiscal federalism. Her most recent publications include *Towards a Social Understanding of Productivity* (co-edited with Keith Banting and Andrew Sharpe, 2002) and *Money, Politics, and Health Care: Reconstructing the Federal-Provincial Partnership* (co-authored and co-edited with Harvey Lazar, 2003).

Bruno Théret is Research Director at the Centre National de la Recherche Scientifique at the Institut de Recherche Interdisciplinaire en Socio-économie, Université Paris Dauphine. His research areas are the analysis of public finance, relations between the state and the economy, systems of social protection and the theory of institutions. He is the author of several studies, including *Protection sociale et fédéralisme: l'Europe dans le miroir de l'Amérique du Nord* (2002) and *Innovations institutionnelles et territoires* (co-edited with M. Tallard and D. Uri, 2000).

Yves Vaillancourt is Professor in the School of Social Work at the Université du Québec à Montréal. He is also director of the Laboratoire de recherche sur les pratiques et les politiques sociales, and director of the Économie sociale, santé et bien-être research team. He is also active within the Centre de recherche sur les innovations sociales dans l'économie sociale, l'entreprise et les syndicats and the Community-University Research Alliance in social economy. In recent years he has published numerous works on social policy reforms in Quebec and Canada that take into account the dynamics of federal-provincial relations. He has been editor of the journal *Nouvelles pratiques sociales* since its founding in 1988. He is co-editor (with François Aubry and Christian Jetté) of *L'économie sociale dans les services à domicile*, to be published in fall 2003.

AGMV Marquis

MEMBRE DE SCABRINI MEDIA

Quebec, Canada
2003

5120055